Bending Toward Justice

Bending Toward Justice

Sr. Kate Kuenstler and the Struggle for Parish Rights

Christine Schenk, CSJ

A SHEED & WARD BOOK

ROWMAN & LITTLEFIELD

Lanham • Boulder • New York • London

Published by Rowman & Littlefield
An imprint of The Rowman & Littlefield Publishing Group, Inc.
4501 Forbes Boulevard, Suite 200, Lanham, Maryland 20706
www.rowman.com

86-90 Paul Street, London EC2A 4NE

British Library Cataloguing in Publication Information available

Library of Congress Cataloging-in-Publication Data available

ISBN 9798881800475 (cloth : alk. paper) | ISBN 9798881800482 (ebook)

♾TM The paper used in this publication meets the minimum requirements of American
National Standard for Information Sciences—Permanence of Paper for Printed Library
Materials, ANSI/NISO Z39.48-1992.

To Catholics everywhere—but especially those in the dioceses of Camden, Syracuse, Cleveland, and the Archdiocese of New York— who, in the face of injustice, fought to save their parish homes.

To the Poor Handmaids of Jesus Christ who supported Sr. Kate Kuenstler in good times and in hard times.

To the staff, trustees, and members of FutureChurch: We seek changes that will provide all Roman Catholics the opportunity to participate fully in Church life and leadership.

Contents

Acknowledgments   ix

1   Context—A Church in Crisis   1

2   Seeds of a Prophetic Life   9

3   Canon Law Studies in Rome   15

4   Catholics Discover They Have Rights: Belleville Debacles and Discoveries   29

5   Advocate for the Laity—St. Mary Parish, Jamesville, New York   45

6   Making a Way Where There was No Way   65

7   In the Diocese of Cleveland, Catholics Rise Up   95

8   Parishioners Persevere   119

9   A Landmark Ruling—Rome Upholds Cleveland Appeals   137

10   Bringing Forth a Harvest   153

11   "Making All Things Revenue"—Archdiocese of New York   165

12   Perseverance, Pain, and the Will of God   185

Epilogue: A Change in Diocesan Reconfiguration Practices   203

Notes	209
Bibliography	245
Index	247
About the Author	257

Acknowledgments

This book was supposed to have been jointly authored with my friend and colleague, Sr. Kate Kuenstler, PHJC. But God had other plans and called Kate home in October 2019.

In my capacity as the founding director of FutureChurch, I worked with Kate for over twelve years as she created, and FutureChurch distributed, canonical resources for hundreds of Catholics who were struggling to preserve their parish homes.

This is as much their story as it is hers.

Kate was determined to tell the story of her advocacy on behalf of brave Catholics before she died. During her final illness we were able to audiotape hours of priceless interviews.

I am grateful to the Poor Handmaids of Jesus Christ who gave me access to all of Kate's professional files. These were invaluable in documenting how it is that one gutsy canon lawyer, and many hundreds of determined Catholics, were able to change the trajectory of canon law in the Catholic Church.

I am also grateful for the following Catholic leaders in the dioceses of Syracuse (Colleen Kenney LaTray), Camden (Msgr. Lou Marrucci), Cleveland (the late Rev. Bob Begin, Len Calabrese, Phillip and Phillis Clipps, Mike Griffin, Bob Kloos, Rick Krivanka, Sr. Sheila Marie Tobbe, Ildiko Peller), and the Archdiocese of New York (Kalman Chany) who graciously agreed to hours of interviews and supplied detailed canonical documentation for this project. Joe Young supplied important background about recent reconfigurations in the Archdiocese of St. Louis. Canon lawyer Robert Flummerfelt, who continued Kate's work after her death, provided helpful documentation about recent recourses in a number of dioceses.

No book ever comes into being solely because of its author. This one is no exception. I am grateful to the Congregation of the Sisters of St. Joseph who allowed me the time and space to work on a project dear to my heart. I also thank Russ Petrus and Deb Rose at FutureChurch for their staunch support and for continuing to provide Kate's canonical resources via the FutureChurch website. I am especially grateful to Dr. Carole Sargent, director of scholarly publications at Georgetown University, whose belief in this book kept my hope alive and led me to Sheed & Ward. I know Kate is doing a happy dance—and so am I.

Unless otherwise indicated, all quotations from Sr. Kate Kuenstler in the chapters that follow are from a series of audiotaped interviews conducted by the author in July, August, and October 2019. Transcripts of these interviews, as well as those of other subjects interviewed, and all relevant emails and canonical files cited in this book, have been given to the Poor Handmaids of Jesus Christ to be housed in their archives at the University of Notre Dame, Kuenstler Collection. FutureChurch archival documents are housed at Loyola University, Chicago.

Chapter 1

Context—A Church in Crisis

This is the story of a brave and brilliant woman whose pastoral skill and pioneering expertise in canon law helped ordinary Catholics save their beloved church homes. Sister Kate Kuenstler's tireless defense of the canonical rights of parishes and lay people in the Church changed Vatican policy from automatically accepting US bishops' decisions to close their parishes and sell vibrant churches to one that preserves them as worship sites instead. Because of her innovative work, hundreds of Catholic laity (and a few good priests) successfully opposed their bishops' callous decisions to close their cherished parishes and sell its churches. Sister Kate's profound love for the Catholic Church and her belief in its people opened a way—for the first time—for ordinary Catholics to exercise substantial leverage in Church decision-making. Her canonical work can be seen as both a precursor to and prerequisite for Pope Francis's desire to create synodal structures in the Church as modeled by the 2021–2024 Synod on Synodality.

Although the 1983 *Code of Canon Law* acknowledges that—as the People of God—Catholic laity have rights and obligations in the Church, very few Catholics ever exercise those rights. This is because in most disputes the Vatican usually sides with the local bishop. The massive legal and financial fallout from failure to address clergy sex abuse and an ever-worsening priest shortage led too many US bishops to regard parish property as so much disposable income. Substantial numbers chose to shrink the number of parishes to fit the shrinking number of priests in their dioceses. Between 2000 and 2022 US bishops closed 2,897 parishes for a 15.1 percent decline overall.[1] During the same time period, the number of US priests decreased by 11,355 for a 24.9 percent decline.[2] Meanwhile, the number of Catholics has increased by 6.6 million over the past decade, going from 59.9 million in 2000 to 66.5 million in 2022.[3]

As these historic changes unfolded, the People of God watched helplessly as their bishops treated beloved parish communities as so many Starbucks franchises to be disposed of rather than reverencing them for what they are—the Body of Christ. In the summer of 2004, the Archdiocese of Boston announced it would close eighty-three parishes. This led to massive resistance, with Catholics in nine parishes choosing to occupy their churches for twenty-four hours a day rather than allow the Archdiocese to close and sell them. Despite assurances that money from the sale of churches would not be used to pay attorney fees for Boston's clergy sex abuse scandal, a Vatican high court later affirmed that pending financial ruin necessitated the sale of Boston churches because the Archdiocese was on the verge of bankruptcy.[4] The Boston debacle shone light on the reality that the most staunchly faithful of Catholics felt completely powerless in Church decision-making even though it was their own considerable time, talent, and treasure that had built their church communities.

Enter Sister Kate Kuenstler and her religious congregation—the Poor Handmaids of Jesus Christ—who in 1988 had asked her to study canon law. In 1995 Sister Kate received her doctor of jurisprudence in canon law from the Pontifical University of St. Thomas Aquinas in Rome, Italy. In the course of her studies, she became passionate about justice and the rights of Catholic laity in the Church. She also encountered firsthand the murky ways of clericalism and the slippery slope of Vatican politics. Before studying canon law, Kate had received a master's degree in theology. For eight years she educated adult catechists in parishes in the Midwest. These experiences left her uniquely positioned to pioneer groundbreaking jurisprudence that gave Catholics greatly needed tools to defend their own rights and those of their parish homes.

Between 2006 and 2011 Sister Kate assisted hundreds of parishioners from Buffalo, Camden, Syracuse, New York City, and many other dioceses as they lodged at least seventy-five canonical appeals opposing the closures of their vibrant, solvent parishes. Every single recourse was denied, first by the diocesan bishop and later by the Vatican's Congregation for the Clergy.[5] Kate would not give up. In 2011, her persistence paid off. Against all odds the appeals of parishioners at St. Vincent Pallotti Parish in the Camden Diocese and St. Mary Jamesville Parish in the diocese of Syracuse reached the Vatican's highest court, the Apostolic Signatura. Bishop Joseph Galante reversed himself and named St. Vincent Pallotti as the parish seat while Bishop Robert J. Cunningham was required to keep St. Mary Church open for regular worship. The tide had turned. Catholics in other dioceses, including Allentown, Springfield, Cleveland, the Archdiocese of New York, Indianapolis, Houston, and others soon won their appeals, saving scores of parishes and churches.

Sister Kate's pioneering canonical jurisprudence was subsequently validated by Vatican guidelines issued in April 2013 and again in August 2020.[6] Although she forged a new pathway in canon law, her role in defending and claiming parishioner rights is known to only a few. Hence the need for this book. In it I will tell the story of a remarkable woman whose rootedness in a God of love—and of justice—helped her overcome seemingly insurmountable odds. Equally important to this story is the witness of many thousands of parishioners—and some good priests—who bravely stood in the breach and fought for their church communities. Sister Kate's untimely death in October 2019 left many Catholic activists feeling bereft. Yet she herself was at peace. She did not fear death although she fought hard to live. "Perhaps my role was to begin this work on behalf of the laity," she told me, expressing the conviction that it was now far enough along for others to follow.

Kate Kuenstler's unwavering love for parish communities paved the way for lay Catholics to—for the first time—exercise leverage in Church decisions that affected them directly. Her passion for empowering the laity helped prepare the way for synodality to become a Catholic reality at the 2021–2024 Synod on Synodality. Because of her faith in the People of God, the arc of Catholic history may at last be bending toward justice.

***

The story begins in January 2002 when the *Boston Globe*'s Spotlight team uncovered widespread clergy sex abuse of minors that Bernard Cardinal Law had successfully hidden for decades. Horrified Bostonians learned that over five hundred victims had been abused by an estimated 7 percent of archdiocesan priests.[7] The Archdiocese soon paid out $85 million in sex abuse settlements, a figure that did not include private funds paid out over the years.[8] By 2007 that number would reach $615 million.[9] After receiving a vote of no confidence, first from the archdiocesan finance council and then from his own priests, Cardinal Law resigned in disgrace.[10] He quickly received a golden parachute from the Vatican and was appointed archpriest at the prestigious Santa Maria Maggiore basilica. Until his retirement in 2011, Law continued to serve on eight powerful Vatican congregations including the Congregation of Bishops, where he would shape the US hierarchy for a generation.[11]

In addition to the Congregation of Bishops, Law served on virtually every powerful Congregation at the Vatican, including Oriental Churches, Clergy, Divine Worship and Discipline of the Sacraments, Evangelization of Peoples, Institutes of Consecrated Life and Societies of Apostolic Life, Catholic Education, and the Pontifical Councils for the Family and for Culture. He also served on the Congregation for the Clergy, the dicastery that routinely rubber-stamped any given bishop's decision to close a parish and sell its church, no matter how vibrant and solvent it was.[12] Until late 2010, not one parish appeal from US Catholics was ever granted.[13] That would change, thanks to Sister Kate Kuenstler's pioneering canonical acumen and the courage of Catholic laity, priests, and high-profile activists such as Peter Borré, the passionate leader of Boston's Council of Parishes.

After their dishonored cardinal moved to Rome, Boston Catholics were left reeling, and not only from the clergy abuse scandal. Law had left the Archdiocese over $30 million in debt. Worse, the clergy pension fund was $60.3 million in arrears, even though Catholics had faithfully contributed for this purpose every Christmas and Easter. Between 1986 and 2002 Law had inexplicably authorized the diocese to make no contributions to the priest retirement fund but diverted the pension contributions for other purposes.[14] In 2004, to staunch the flow of red ink, auxiliary bishop Richard Lennon sent canonical decrees to eighty-three Boston parishes informing them that they would be suppressed.[15] Parish assets, including the sale of the church and its property, would revert to the Archdiocese. As Law's protégé, Lennon had been appointed acting administrator of the Boston Archdiocese until Archbishop (and soon to be Cardinal) Sean O'Malley was installed in July 2003. A proudly self-taught canon lawyer, Richard Lennon was the architect of Boston's disastrous parish reconfiguration plan.[16] He would later bring his dubious canonical expertise to Cleveland. In 2009, following his Boston playbook, he likewise sent decrees merging or closing fifty-two Cleveland-area parishes. All were in economically challenged inner-city Cleveland neighborhoods, poorer sections of the inner-ring suburbs of Cleveland, Akron, and Lorain.[17] In 2012, Sister Kate exposed Lennon's faulty understanding of canon law. For the first time, the Vatican overrode a bishop's decree to suppress a parish—in this case, eleven of them in the Cleveland diocese—and Richard Lennon would be ordered to reopen every parish that had appealed.

But we're ahead of our story. After receiving the decrees that suppressed their parishes, Boston Catholics courageously fought to preserve their church homes even as these vital, wealthy parishes were summarily put on the chopping block. St. James in Wellesley was located on eight acres of property worth $14 million.[18] Infant Jesus Parish in Brookline had $4 million in savings. In Concord, Our Lady Help of Christians Parish had $800,000 in the bank and had recently opened a $1.3 million parish center.[19] Located on thirty acres of prime real estate near the Atlantic Ocean, St. Frances Xavier Cabrini Parish had extraordinarily committed parishioners who would occupy their church for twelve years before being ejected by Cardinal O'Malley in 2016.[20] The pastor of St. Susanna Parish in Dedham, Father Stephen Josoma, could see no reason his parish should be suppressed except that it sat on eight shaded acres of valuable real estate. One of fifty-eight priests who had signed the letter demanding that Cardinal Law resign, Josoma met with Cardinal O'Malley to plead his case, even going so far as to offer a check for $600,000 for parish land assessed at $320,000. The cardinal refused. The actual value of the property was a great deal more than $600,000, and he knew it.[21]

Boston's Catholics pushed back hard. As John Seitz shows, at the beginning of summer 2005, fifteen parishes appealed to the Vatican. Nine of them began round-the-clock vigils. Others sued the Archdiocese in civil court, while still more considered occupying the properties.[22] Catholics from sixteen parishes on the closure list soon formed a coalition called the Council of Parishes. The organization's skilled leadership quickly cultivated relationships with the media. Seitz shows how they became the key figures in a PR conflict between Catholics and their archdiocese.[23] In succeeding years, Council of Parishes cofounder, Peter Borré, assisted similar coalitions of resisting Catholics by offering media connections, encouraging church vigils, and providing consultation and translation services as they pursued canonical appeals to Rome.

Boston's Catholic resistance initially produced positive results. Closure decisions were reversed for four occupied parishes as well as several others that held regular prayer vigils. Other endangered parishes had their closing dates put off indefinitely or delayed.[24] By early 2008, seventy-five Boston parishes had been closed or merged. Five churches were still being occupied around the clock by Catholics who loved their churches too much to let them go without a fight.[25] Ironically, although the Archdiocese had projected it would receive $200 million from the sale of church property, by 2008—after closing or merging seventy-five parishes—it had netted only $62.7 million.[26] Yet every one of Boston's fifteen appeals would eventually be rejected by the Congregation for the Clergy, the last in 2014.[27] Although the Archdiocese had repeatedly promised that no money from church sales would be used to pay clergy sex abuse settlements, in 2008 the Vatican cited financial fallout from the sex abuse crisis as a reason for rejecting an appeal from Catholics at St. Jeanne D'Arc Parish.[28]

Cardinal O'Malley had listed reasons why the draconian reconfigurations were needed, including a decline in Mass attendance, demographic shifts of Catholics moving to the suburbs, financial problems, and a declining number of priests.[29] As the clergy sex abuse crisis exploded in dioceses across the country, other US bishops quickly followed Boston's lead by merging vibrant, viable parishes and trying to sell their churches. It solved two looming problems, because there was a desperate need to raise money for burgeoning attorney fees and settlements resulting from clergy sex abuse, and bishops had too few priests to staff their parishes because of the ever-deepening priest shortage. Both crises continue into the present day.

SHRINKING PARISHES TO FIT THE NUMBER OF PRIESTS

Between 2000 and 2022, the number of US priests decreased by 24.9 percent, from 45,699 in the year 2000 to 34,344 in 2022.[30] The diocesan priesthood is also aging. Just 66 percent of diocesan priests were actively engaged in ministry in 2022 compared to 75 percent in 2000.[31] The number of graduate-level seminarians has also decreased significantly with 3,483 in 2000-01 and just 2,759 in 2022-23.[32] Ordinations increased very slightly with 442 in 2000 compared to 451 in 2022.[33] Still, neither seminarian numbers nor ordinations are sufficient to offset priests who are retiring. Mary Gautier, a senior research associate at the Center for Applied Research in the Apostolate at Georgetown University, found that US churches need "two to three times" the annual number of diocesan ordinations to keep up with parish demand.[34]

The unrelenting shortage of priests continues to put great pressure on US bishops who believe they must have a priest in each parish church to adequately minister to the Catholic people. For far too many bishops, an easy solution has been to shrink the number of parishes to fit the number of priests available. The trend is to herd Catholics into ever larger churches. To do this, bishops are merging financially viable and ministerially effective parish communities and then hoping to sell their churches. Often the preponderance of closures affected small, socially conscious parish communities that served low-income neighborhoods. In the Archdiocese of Boston, an informal statistical study found that 60 percent of suppressed parishes were located in towns with low or modest income. As previously noted, in the Diocese of Cleveland, all 2009 closures involved inner-city parishes or inner-ring suburb parishes, the majority of which were solvent even if burdened with aging buildings.[35] These parishes provided important ministries in poorer areas in which the church served as a trusted anchor in troubled neighborhoods.[36]

CLERGY SEX ABUSE PAYOUTS

Ever-present attorney fees and large financial settlements arising from covering up clergy sex abuse also contributed to parish downsizing. From 1950 until 2017 there were 19,361 allegations of clergy sex abuse in the Catholic Church. Most alleged abusers were born between 1930 and 1950, with the most common decade of ordination being the 1960s.[37] Hence, the majority of allegations that finally came to light were decades old. They were also soul-killing for victim/survivors for as many years.[38] A 2020 audit of two hundred US dioceses reported a fourfold increase in allegations—4,434 compared to 1,451 reported in 2018.[39] The increase was thought to be due to the recent lifting of the statutes of limitations in fifteen states, and recent compensation programs that the Church ran for victims and survivors.[40] Half (2,237) of the allegations listed in 2019 were deemed credible, with 57 percent occurring before 1975, 41 percent between 1975 and 1999, and 2 percent since 2000.[41] The smaller number of recent claims encouraged church officials, who believed it showed their efforts were working.[42] As of August 2023 a total of thirty-two dioceses and three religious orders had filed for bankruptcy protection as a direct result of lawsuits.[43] The marked increase in bankruptcy filings was due to lifting the statutes of limitations in many states. Since the issue first came to light in the 1980s, total settlements for US Catholic clergy sex abuse had reached $3 billion by late 2023 and are projected to reach $4 billion.[44]

CATHOLICS STOP ATTENDING MASS—EVEN BEFORE THE PANDEMIC

Between the sex abuse scandal and resulting parish closures, large numbers of Catholics felt alienated and no longer attended Mass. Predictably, Sunday collections also declined.[45] In the year 2000, before the scandal became widely publicized, surveys indicated that 30.8 percent of Catholics attended Mass weekly. In 2022 the percentage of weekly Mass-goers had declined to just 17.3 percent.[46] Lest we think this decline was owing only to the pandemic, the percentage was 23.4 percent in 2015 compared with 30.8 in 2000. Perhaps most concerning is the steep decline in infant baptisms from 996,199 in 2000 to only 437,942 in 2022.[47]

This suggests that younger families are distancing themselves from the Church. Another grave concern is the number of those raised Catholic who no longer self-identify as such. A 2018 Pew research study found that Catholicism has experienced a greater net loss due to religious switching than has any other religious tradition in the United States. The Catholic Church in the United States is facing huge challenges.

This array of factors—clergy sex abuse, the priest shortage, and Catholics distancing themselves from the institutional Church—provide important context for Sr. Kate Kuenstler's canonical advocacy on behalf of ordinary Catholics.

Chapter 2

Seeds of a Prophetic Life

Mary Kathleen Kuenstler grew up on a family farm near a tiny town in southern Illinois called Wendelin (population roughly one thousand). Her parents, Lorraine Buerster Kuenstler and Lawrence Kuenstler, adopted her at four months of age. Born on January 21, 1949, in St. Mary's Hospital in East St. Louis, Illinois, she was the first of three children her parents would adopt.

The Sunday after adopting her, Kate's proud father carried his baby daughter to the Holy Cross Parish convent in Wendelin and introduced her to the four sisters of the Congregation of the Poor Handmaids of Jesus Christ (PHJC) living there. No one could have known that Kuenstler herself would eventually join their community. In coming years, she relished telling people that this indeed made her "a lifer."

Like all farming children, Kate was assigned chores at an early age. At six her job was to milk the cow before supper so the family would have cream for after-dinner coffee, and milk for breakfast. In later years she watered the hogs, tended the garden, canned or froze "all of our food," and became a skilled seamstress. Kate deeply valued her rootedness in her large extended family and in the close-knit Catholic community that made up life in Wendelin. Both parents were leaders in her parish. She sums up her relationally rich childhood: "Although, I couldn't name it at the time, looking back, that whole community atmosphere was what I was experiencing as a child. We saw each other at church and then we would come together as a family on Sunday afternoon."[1] It is perhaps unsurprising, then, that Kate would spend much of her professional life defending the rights of small Catholic parishes like the one she grew up in.

Kate's earliest explicit memories of God are interwoven with the beauty of her family's farm. Around the age of six, after both siblings refused to play with her, she remembers walking alone in the eighty acres of forest adjacent

9

Figure 2.1   Kate with her family (l-r): Lorraine Buerster Keunstler, Kate, Lawrence Kuenstler, and siblings Matthew and Agnes. Courtesy of Poor Handmaids of Jesus Christ

to the family home. As she trudged through the trees, she sensed a deep sacredness within the leafy splendor surrounding her. Another time, as she sat on the back of her dad's pickup truck, she noticed "all the green around . . . the soybeans and corn . . . by then I had learned about the story of creation. And I knew God had created all of this. It became like a three-dimensional reality—that God was real—that this was a part of God's plan. And I was part of it too. It made me happy."

Another early vivid learning about God came from her father. "When Dad ended planting season, he would go out and he'd pray over the crops in the cool of the evening," Kate recalled. She joined him one evening and—apparently puzzling over something she had picked up in school—asked if God loved Protestants and Catholics the same way. Her father gently replied, "See that tree line over there that divides the property that we own from the Hintershers property, and the one on the other side that belongs to the Denzmores?" Both families were Protestant. "Now you know," her father continued, "when God sends the rain, the rain does not shut off at the edge of [anyone's] property. So God loves everybody because the rain comes, and it does not discriminate between anybody's religion." This experience permanently shaped Kate's outlook: "So I mean those are the attitudes and the beliefs and the value system that influenced me the rest of my life."

Figure 2.2 Kate Kuenstler at Ancilla Domini High School. Courtesy of Poor Handmaids of Jesus Christ

While Kate herself is a bit vague about when the idea to be a sister entered her mind, her sister Agnes well remembers that Kate had always wanted to be a nun. Kate once asked Agnes, "Was there anything special that happened that I made the decision to become a sister?" Agnes replied, "Oh God, no, Kate, you wanted to be a sister from the day you were born." A treasured family photograph pictures five-year-old Kate clad in white sandals, a ruffled summer dress, and one of her mother's white dish towels draped veil-like over her head.

After completing eighth grade at the small Wendelin school taught by the PHJC sisters, Kate moved 250 miles away to attend the community's Ancilla Domini High School. Located at the PHJC motherhouse at the tiny Indiana crossroad known as Donaldson, the campus also included a junior college established in 1937. Both schools were designed to educate young women planning to enter the order. Kate was very shy in high school owing, she believes, to low self-esteem: "I had this false attitude that because I came from the farm and so many of those girls came from the city, they knew more than I did."

Donaldson high school students (aspirants) went home over the summer. Although Kate didn't particularly relish returning to farm chores because she never planned on being a farmer's wife, she loved immersing herself again in her cherished rural landscape. Here she first began to experience the deep contemplative prayer that would sustain her throughout her life. On Sunday afternoons she would "walk down to the farthest field that I could, and not see anyone else. . . . I would lie in the grass and look up to the sky. And I always felt that I was looking into heaven . . ." At other times, she remembers "walking through the woods. I would see the sunlight coming through the trees and leaves and it's just beautiful. And I would just walk with God." She marvels that she did not really understand that she was absorbed in contemplation until she was a professed sister:

> I had no clue that what I was engaged in was prayer because what they were trying to teach us at the high school, the aspirancy, was all saying prayers. And that just wasn't my style . . . no one was teaching us [contemplation] because they thought we were too young. But here I was doing it . . . I didn't tell anybody about it because I wasn't saying those [aspirancy] prayers that were locked up in my drawer in my bedroom.

After completing the program, Kate chose to enter the PHJC community. Although she wondered if this decision was "a lazy response to just keep on keeping on," she also knew she was happy and content: "It just seemed like that was a good next step. I thought about it. I felt at home with the Poor Handmaids, and it seemed that this was where God wanted me to be, and I was happy."

DID YOU LIVE LIFE TO THE FULL? YOU BETCHA I DID!

Throughout her religious life Kate Kuenstler had a deep and abiding devotion to the founder of the Poor Handmaids of Jesus Christ, Saint Mary Katharina Kasper (d. 1898). Like Kate, Katharina was born into an agrarian family, and also like Kate she often noticed the presence of God in nature. Despite a challenging novitiate, Kate decided to profess first vows because of several religious experiences she had involving Mother Katharina, whom Kate had invoked for guidance. Shortly after professing vows in August 1970, a near-death experience from an allergic reaction would change Kate's life. In reflecting about it later, she recalled: "I was so closed and quiet and withdrawn. And I remember thinking when I die and God asks me, 'Did you live life to the full?' I want to be able to say, 'You betcha I did!'" Nearly fifty years later, as she lay fighting the cancer that would take her life, Kate said, "And, to be honest with you, I can say that now, I really have lived my life to the full." After recovering from the allergic reaction, Kate pushed herself beyond her comfort zone and soon became adept at public speaking: "One of my favorite things to do is to give presentations to adults on theology or the church or whatever they want to talk about. I love doing that." Looking back, Kate dates her "180-degree turn around" to this near-death experience.

Despite entering at a time when many sisters were leaving their communities, Kate chose to stay. On November 27, 1976, she was just one of two women in her original class of twenty-five to profess final vows. In making the decision, she says, "So I remember sitting there one day thinking, 'Okay, what do they know that I don't know? . . . why am I still hanging onto the ship?'" After thinking it over, she decided, "This was good for my soul. It was the way I was being led and it was very satisfying and rewarding. . . . And so, I thought, 'Well, I'm sorry about those others, but I'm staying because this is where I belong.'"

INNOVATIVE CATHOLIC EDUCATOR

After receiving her bachelor's degree in education from St. Joseph College in East Chicago, Indiana, Kate began teaching second grade in Hammond, Indiana, in 1972. She would stay for five years. Over the succeeding ten years she was deeply involved in various aspects of Catholic education in Indiana, Illinois, and Minnesota. In August 1979 she earned a master's degree in theology from Aquinas College in Grand Rapids, Michigan.

In early 1980 Kate was hired as a consultant in the diocese of Belleville, Illinois, where the Diocesan Education Office had been summarily closed owing to a crisis of diocesan debt. A creative and determined Kate soon developed a "stand-alone" catechist formation program that trained parish directors of religious education and parish catechists. She deliberately designed it so "it did not need the Diocesan Office of Catholic Education, and no priest or bishop. It was set up with a board of directors for the diocese. These were lay people from the different parishes, and they ran it. They were the ones who did the evaluations, the testing and the [staffing] decisions." Her model was so successful that the Springfield, Illinois, diocese soon adopted it. Essentially every parishioner in the southern half of Illinois would benefit from Kate's innovative, cost-effective program.

In June 1981, Kate was hired to develop a catechetical program for the one-thousand-family St. Cecilia Parish in Glen Carbon, Illinois. Over the next four years she managed over two hundred volunteer teachers for a Parish School of Religion that included preschool, elementary, and high school students as well as adults. From 1985 to 1989, after being recruited by the Springfield diocese, she served as director of the Office of Religious Education where she wrote a curriculum that would be used in every diocesan elementary school as well as in the parish schools of religion. Upon leaving the flourishing St. Cecilia's program which she had launched, Kate proudly noted, "I was replaced by five paid professional people. That sounds a little impossible, but it happened. I set up the programs and then they took off with them." Kate also gave frequent workshops to adult catechists and teachers all over the diocese. Publishers of Catholic catechetical resources soon began consulting with her, and she was a writer for the "Seasons of Faith" National Catechetical Series published by Harcourt Religion Publishers (formerly Brown-ROA).[2]

In reminiscing about her ministry to adults in Catholic parishes, Kate realized she had also been sowing seeds for an unsought and unexpectedly prophetic future:

> My background prepared me for my work with parish closings and church clos-ings. . . . And then there was this whole thing of the rights of the laity and canon law . . . realizing that the laity have a voice and that they have been stifled. It has been so stifled and scared off by the hierarchy. And so, my goal was to empower the laity to know they had a right to a voice, that they had a voice, and to help them learn how to use it.

And so it was that Mary Kathleen Kuenstler made a decision that would change not only her own life, but that of thousands of parish-centered Catho-lics in the United States and around the world.

Chapter 3

Canon Law Studies in Rome

In the late summer of 1988, Sister Kate Kuenstler's community leadership asked her to study canon law. For the previous eight years, she had loved designing innovative catechetical programs for two dioceses. She had also loved educating and empowering parishioners to lead those programs and hoped to pursue advanced studies in theology. After consulting with several female canon lawyers, however, and with some reluctance, she agreed to pursue canonical studies. She decided it would be wise to seek practical experience in the field before applying to graduate programs. Providentially, the Fort Wayne–South Bend bishop, John D'Arcy, agreed to hire her in hopes she would agree to return and work for him after completing her studies. From November 1989 through May 1990, Kate worked as an auditor in the South Bend Tribunal Office. Diocesan tribunals mainly handle marriage annulments, and auditors do much of the background work. In Kate's view the auditor essentially functioned "as an executive secretary to the judge. They do everything a judge does except sign the sentence."[1] Kate remembers, "I interviewed, I did testimonies. I did verbatims. I gave my opinion of the case." She then sent a summary to the tribunal judge—who was required to have either a licentiate or a doctorate in canon law—for final adjudication of the case.

This hands-on experience would greatly enhance Kate's ability to navigate the challenges of advanced studies in canon law. An American priest classmate in Rome once told her: "You know, Kate, there's only one priest in this room that has more experience than you do. And yet he doesn't have as much experience as you do. He handed out the mail in the tribunals. You worked as an auditor. You have the most experience of anybody in this room." Bishop D'Arcy offered to pay for Kate's doctoral education. In return he requested that she commit to working for his diocese for ten years. But she tactfully declined, thinking wryly to herself, "I'm not a cheap date." Plus she had enough experience with the vagaries of diocesan appointments to shrewdly consider, "He could be gone when I return, and then what am I into?"

While working in South Bend, Kate explored various doctoral programs before choosing to attend the Pontifical University of St. Thomas Aquinas (*Angelicum*) in Rome, which taught in Italian rather than Latin. She would later meet with US seminarians from the North American College (NAC) who told her, "We just so envy you that you're at the *Angelicum* because we're still learning in Latin at the *Gregorian* and we don't know what's going on. It is not fun."

"PROFESSORESSA KATI"

Kate was impressed that *Angelicum* professors formally acknowledged her prior master's in theology as well as her pastoral experience: "From the very beginning the professors called me, '*Professoressa Kati*'—Professor Kate. . . . So they showed a great respect." The *Angelicum* required four semesters of class work to receive a licentiate in canon law. Another semester of course-work was required if a student chose to obtain a doctorate. This would be followed by whatever length of time it took to research and write a dissertation—usually two or three years. Many classmates were priests sent by their bishops to obtain the licentiate required to adjudicate procedural law in their home dioceses. Others were seminarians taking canon law classes that were required for ordination. Kate remembers having about twenty to twenty-five students in her licentiate class—predominantly priests hailing from all over the world. Few went on to receive doctorates because "the bishop didn't want to pay for it and wanted them home," she recalled. There were "three women at most" studying with her at any given time. One was a lay woman from Naples. Others were sisters, several of whom left after just one semester since classes were often more difficult than anticipated. Kate was often the only woman in any given class.

The first big challenge Kate faced was the necessity of learning Italian. She went to Perugia (near Assisi) for language study two months before classes began. "I got nowhere. But I had a great time," she humorously recalled. The first day of licentiate studies involved four lectures on four different topics. At day's end she painfully remembered looking at her notes only to find "I had four words after four hours of class . . . those were the only ones I recognized. And so I sat there and I thought, 'Okay, Kate, this is not good.'" Trying not to panic, she considered her options: "One was, I'm staying until January when we have our exam and when I fail the exam, I will write the provincial and tell her I'm coming home." Kate's next option demonstrates the determination and creativity that would characterize her future: "The second set of thoughts was, 'Okay, Kate, you did some graduate-level education at Purdue University for children who have learning disabilities. . . . So what did you do for the kids? Do that for yourself.'"

From that day forward *Professoressa Kati* assiduously developed strategies for learning Italian and finding workarounds for classroom comprehension. Her experience in the South Bend tribunal proved invaluable. The tribunal office's color-coded system turned out to be a huge learning aide: "So when we were studying the papers for an annulment, I just thought of the color that I had used in South Bend. I had the experience of using the actual procedural papers, and could think about the color of the paper, and then I knew what the procedure was." She purchased English-language class notes written by students from previous years who were fluent in both Italian and English. She found a Latin-Italian canon law book and another Latin-English canon law book, assuming that if she used these "correctly" she could manage the canons:

> I would listen to the professors teaching in Italian. They were usually working from a certain canon in canon law. And I would find that in my book. Then I would read the English. Soon I was able to follow what they were saying. . . . I began to mark up my canon law book so that I had all these beautiful notes. Even today when I open it up, there's certain things that I knew I wrote that first year.

Kate also listened carefully to Italians conversing with one another on the long bus ride back and forth from her residence near the Vatican. Although it was brutally hard, she did not give up. "I used every little thing I could find, and then I cried. I went home and cried. I had lunch and cried. And then I proceeded to go back over my notes over and over again." She slowly began to learn the Italian she needed.

> I couldn't speak it because I never conversed with anyone. But I understood it. I began to understand the professor a little more every week. I was beginning to write in English. I won't call it a translation, but the meaning of the Italian I was hearing. So by January when we had our exam, I was doing fairly well with the Italian, not good, but fairly well.

Yet the January exams would be a big challenge. She was immensely relieved to learn the exams would be oral. "Praise God. I didn't know how to spell Italian or write Italian or write an Italian sentence, so I could just go in and talk." Once again, she found a clever workaround. She knew her professors were fluent in a number of languages, including English, although they never used English in class. When she sat for each of her four oral exams, the professor would ask one question in Italian from his semester course. And then Kate said:

> I would think about it a little bit and then I would tell them in English what I thought the question was. Then I would answer in English with about three Italian words that I knew added in the middle of it. Because that was really all [the Italian] I knew, and they knew that. After that was done, they wanted to talk about the church in the United States. So I'd spend the rest of the test time having a wonderful discussion about [it]. . . .

To her surprise other classmates had a different experience. "I would watch all these other students go in, come out crying, some white as a sheet, you know, and I'm thinking, oh, what's going on in there?" She discovered, "What was going on was that these other students hadn't done their homework. They hadn't attended class. They didn't understand what was going on." Priest and seminarian classmates had been sent by bishops from "at least 25" countries from around the world. A professor later told Kate "on the QT" that although a given seminarian or priest had failed a class, he would still be given a "diploma" although it didn't signify he had passed. "The bishops sent them, he sent his best people, and they will go home with a degree in canon law, but it won't be like yours," the professor told her. For Kate, "It was the best they could do under the worst circumstances. They can go home, call themselves a canon lawyer and then work as chancellor or head of the tribunal . . . because for them to follow the procedural law, they had to have canon lawyers who had these degrees."

Students were evaluated using a grading system of one to ten, with one being the lowest. When first semester grades came out, Kate anxiously went to the registrar's office to see how she had done: "Oh my God. I had aced the whole thing. I had tens all the way down. I couldn't believe it." And then she thought, "Shucks, I can't go home."

In the ensuing two years *Professoressa Kati*'s facility in Italian gradually improved. At her fourth-semester oral exams, Kate followed her tried and true procedure of translating the professor's question into English and then giving her answer in English. But now she was able to translate her English answer "the best I could" into Italian. She remembers keeping the word she used and the sentence structure very simple "so that [the professor] really could follow me."

COURSEWORK AND THE RIGHTS OF THE LAY
FAITHFUL

Kate remembered a specific focus on marriage law during her licentiate studies because much of the canonical work that takes place in dioceses around the world addresses annulments. She also had courses in international law and, because she was in Italy, Italian civil law. If she had studied in the United States, she would have had courses in American civil law. Several one-hour classes addressed the Catholic sacraments, about which Kate already knew a great deal from her previous ministries. Yet she found that while canon law does address the sacraments, it is "never in a theological way. It's always in a procedural way." For example, in an emergency, such as during a war or in a natural disaster, a laicized or excommunicated priest can administer the sacrament of reconciliation. Other coursework included the development, history, and theology of canon law and what Kate liked to call "the good, the bad, and the ugly of canon law through the centuries." The latter course covered the abuses of canon law in Church history. Kate gave an example: "It would take three weeks to get the [canonical] document from Rome to Paris, for instance. And in the meantime, [Church officials] had retranslated it and had a different decree they were bringing to Paris."

During her second year of study, a course about the temporal goods of the Church was foundational for Kate's future ministry of helping Catholic laity appeal the closure of their vibrant churches. For the first time, she understood the distinction between the parish as a corporation and the parish as a faith community:

> That was one of the things that I'm not sure a lot of priests and cardinals figured out for a long time—the distinction between a faith community and a corporation. Because of this class I realized those are two separate entities, two separate ideas. . . . I've noticed over the last 12 years that bishops use the faith community and all of its aspects to evaluate a vital parish and that's okay. However, they end up saying you don't meet muster and therefore we are shutting down your corporation. And it's two different things. And it's so demoralizing to the laity.

Kate realized that no matter how hard parishioners worked to show the vitality of their parish faith community, the bishop was using a corporate criterion—namely money—for his own evaluative decision-making:

> So the laity do their homework, go through all these procedures, write up all these reports, telling everything that's going on in their parish and how successful it is and how they like it and how it's good for the church. But no matter what they write, it is never going to keep the corporation from being shut down. . . .

When they merge parishes, [the bishop's] intent is to move the money from a financially solvent parish into a non-solvent parish. So that the [diocesan] debt of the nonsolvent parish will be paid by money from the financially solvent parish.

Kate's canonical training opened a way for her to pursue justice on behalf of aggrieved parishioners. While studying Book Two in the 1983 *Code of Canon Law*, she discovered a listing of the rights of the laity that had emerged from the Second Vatican Council. In future years, she would give many talks about "Canon Law and the Rights of the Lay Christian Faithful" throughout the United States. She loved to describe her awakening:

I remember sitting in the classroom in Rome, . . . and I opened the canon law book, and I started reading Book Two. And I'm thinking, do they know what they wrote? Did they really mean what I'm reading here? I couldn't believe it. And I couldn't wait to come back and tell everyone about it. And it's been eleven years now that I've had a chance to start telling everyone about it. And it's one of the most exciting things I can do.[2]

LIFE IN ROME

One reason Kate had been half hoping to return home if she failed first semester was that she was "exhausted all the time because the classes were so intense for me." She also found living in Rome difficult: "There is no system in Rome for buying groceries or paying bills or getting anywhere. It's just the way it is." The commute alone was demanding since the Resurrection Sisters' guest house where she lived was an hour away from the *Angelicum* and required bus and train transfers each way. Transportation strikes could and did occur at any time, often "at least twice a month." Taxi fares were exorbitant, so when a strike was called, Kate had to walk both ways, although (Rome being Rome) she discovered "it took about as long for me to walk it as it did to take the bus." As with most of Rome's religious guest houses, Resurrection guests were expected to observe a strict curfew. Kate soon found this unworkable. She was helped by a woman who became her lifelong friend, Divina Melotti, who encouraged her to find more suitable lodgings. Melotti recalled, "I said to her, there are many houses here that rent rooms. So you will be free to come when you want."[3] Kate also became friendly with Divina's husband, Roberto, and their three children. She was quickly adopted into the family. "She came very often to have a lunch with us mainly on Sunday," Divina recalled. In subsequent years, whenever Kate visited Rome, she stayed with the Melotti family. She visited for the last time in 2018 when—even though physically unwell—she came for Mother Katharina's canonization.

To alleviate some of the intensity of her coursework, Kate found strength, companionship, and spiritual sustenance by worshipping with a predominantly American community located at the Church of St. Agnes in the Piazza Navona. "Every Sunday I would go there, I'd sing in the choir, serve as a cantor, make friends with Americans—there was a group of us. Sunday was my American Day." After Mass she went home for "a wonderful siesta" before returning at 4:00 to pray with a "very nice" charismatic renewal group. In the early 1970s, Kate had been attracted to the charismatic renewal movement because she believed "it was a renewal of the early Church. The Holy Spirit giving the gifts that we had lost over two thousand years and they were coming back. And we really needed those gifts to be able to implement Vatican II so as to become mature Christians, to be able to be disciples and create a community together." Plus she loved the prayer style, "it wasn't a specified, rigid way of praying," and she liked the idea of "the laity having community and praying together in a way that was not dictated by Rome." Yet she had become disillusioned with the US charismatic movement in Springfield, Illinois, when it turned to a more fundamentalist approach: "Women were to be submissive to the men. Women could not be leaders. . . ." The Rome charismatic prayer meetings were very different. Kate attended charismatic prayer sessions at the Pontifical Gregorian University which were especially fulfilling: "We were not dogmatic, but more interested in prayer. And they really supported each other. It was a good experience for me."

Kate came to know many priests and seminarians while she studied in Rome. As one of very few women in a sea of clerics, she befriended a number of seminarians. Her classmates struggled with many challenges, not least of which was the exodus of female spiritual directors and teachers from their seminaries. In 1992 Pope John Paul II published an exhortation, *Pastores Dabo Vobis* (PDV—*I Will Give You Shepherds*) following the 1990 Synod of Bishops on "The Formation of Priests in Circumstances of the Present Day." While the exhortation's theological reflection about the priesthood and priestly formation is inspiring, it is also limited. This is because the theological lens was exclusively male. For example, formation in seminaries is compared to Jesus's teaching the twelve male apostles prior to sending them forth.

It is a community established by the bishop to offer to those called by the Lord to serve as apostles the possibility of re-living the experience of formation which our Lord provided for the Twelve. . . . It should be experienced as a community, a specifically ecclesial community, a community that relives the experience of the group of Twelve who were united to Jesus.[4]

Sadly missing is the contemporary biblical scholarship—already extant at the time—showing that Jesus's Galilean entourage included many women who were also "being formed" in the Gospel alongside their brothers (see Luke 8:1-3).[5] This is significant because although *Pastores Dabo Vobis* alludes to "the suitability of a healthy influence of lay spirituality and of the charism of femininity,"[6] in the training of priests, it essentially bans women from serving as spiritual directors for seminarians and implies that teachers of theology must be male.[7] While the 1983 *Code of Canon Law* explicitly says seminarians must regularly seek out spiritual direction, it did not stipulate that the directors must be priests.[8] When *Pastores Dabo Vobis* was issued, women were already serving as spiritual directors to seminarians in Rome—indeed around the world—and there were female professors of theology teaching in seminaries as well. Now that was changing.

And so it was that Kate found herself counseling—and consoling—many of her younger brothers.

> I was 40 years old and these guys were like 27 or 22 and they were going through a real hard time. [The seminary] got rid of all of the women who were spiritual directors, professors . . . and their [male] replacements weren't that great. They missed having a woman to talk to. . . . So these guys gravitated to me in the Canon Law room. Word got out that I would listen, that I was reasonable, sensible and I had credibility. . . . Every once in a while, someone really needed a longer talk. So we would walk to a little cafe for coffee. I ended up being their spiritual director practically, helping them figure out how to manage living in that new environment.

Aside from a lack of gender balance in the seminary community, the seminarians who sought Kate out were struggling with some very serious issues. Foremost among them was surviving in a dysfunctional and corrupt clerical subculture that permeated Rome as well as their own seminaries. The young men Kate counseled were homosexual and committed to living a celibate lifestyle. They found the behavior of some of their gay classmates deeply disturbing. A small subset of gay seminarians not only disdained celibacy, but cynically targeted and seduced heterosexual classmates. They then publicly shamed them for violating celibacy rules. "These guys who are talking to me—every one of them a homosexual—were livid at this horrible behavior going on. . . ." recalled Kate. When a new seminary rector arrived, many feared homosexuality would be publicly banned. Such a policy would merely drive the reality—and gift—of being differently oriented underground. As a result, in Kate's view, "There would be no control over the abuses." Today the challenges of living a celibate lifestyle within the priestly caste are extensively documented.[9] Nearly every month dismayed Catholics learn more about sexual solicitation in the highest ranks of the clerical system. Yet when

Kate studied in Rome, these abuses were only whispered about. When then-archbishop Theodore McCarrick stayed at the NAC on his frequent visits to Rome, it was common knowledge that he had solicited seminarians and young priests in Metuchen and Newark. After McCarrick was forced to resign in 2018, Bishop Steven Lopes—a former seminarian in Rome—said, "I was a seminarian when Theodore McCarrick was named archbishop of Newark—and he would visit the seminary often—and we all knew."[10]

Another problematic issue for any young man seeking to live a celibate lifestyle is that Rome, in Kate's words, "is a very sexually permissive town. There are prostitutes on every corner and each corner has its own type of prostitute. You can pick and choose whatever you want." Yet even some of the prostitutes were concerned that seminarians were soliciting them for sex. Kate's seminarian friends were deeply scandalized when they discovered that Rome's sexually promiscuous culture extended into the hierarchy: "I have proof of that. They would tell me stories about Vatican people—priests and cardinals, . . . that would curl your hair."[11] Yet Kate also remembered that, "I was surprised that I wasn't so shocked. . . . I didn't like it. I was angry. I was more angry than shocked. . . . But on the other hand, I was so privileged to have these guys [the seminarians] trust me and tell me these things . . . I still hold it in confidence." None of these distressing disclosures led Kate to doubt her calling:

> I had a mission to be a disciple and to help people use their voice and their right-ful privilege in the church, so that they can speak for themselves. None of that was ever affected by this. I've decided to stay and fight within. . . . In a way I wasn't surprised because of some of the things that went on in different dioceses where I worked in the past.

She took heart that while such egregious behavior was "rampant at the Vatican," today Pope Francis is "cleaning house," although "that's why it's so hard for him to do it, because there is such cabal of people, men who are just covering for each other." In her previous ministries Kate had worked with priests and bishops whom she respected and admired: "I found priests and bishops who were upright. They were people who had a mission of ministry to their people, either diocese or parish. And it was fun."

DOCTORAL STUDIES: CARDINAL HUME

For her second year of studies, Kate needed to complete one semester of classes before tackling dissertation work in earnest. At this time there were just seven students in her class. Kate was the only non-Italian. Two classmates were lay women from the Bologna tribunal and the remainder were priests. Her course-work focused on the development of canon law dating from the earliest (third and fourth century) church orders, to the first formal codification of canon law in the twelfth century, and into the present day. She remembers being delighted that one of her professors had actually been an author of the new 1983 *Code of Canon Law* and lectured on that topic. Other overarching themes were how custom precedes law, and the essential principles that underlie canon law itself.

As Kate was finishing her last set of classes, she visited a friend in England. While there, both were invited to tea at the Archdiocese of Westminster. Basil Cardinal Hume's secretary was also in attendance. Kate's friend had told the secretary about her search for a dissertation topic.[12] She had three criteria: It had to be an original topic, it had to be in religious law, and it had to challenge injustice. "I think the cardinal has a topic for you," the secretary told her. Kate's immediate thought was something along the lines of, "Oh right, like Cardinal Hume would even know who I am." To her surprise the renowned Benedictine prelate was looking for someone with Kate's qualifications—especially her concern for justice. He was dismayed that high-ranking churchmen—including Pope John Paul II and Vatican Secretary of State Cardinal Casaroli—had interfered with the Vatican II renewal processes of discalced Carmelite nuns.[13] A minority of Carmelite monasteries were fearful of the changes that could result from a renewal of religious life mandated by Vatican II. As a result, there were deep divisions among the world's Carmelite nuns. A small number of traditional monasteries had enlisted powerful conservative allies who were able to obstruct the legitimate renewal processes of the majority which had been under way for over a decade. Cardinal Hume—who was a spiritual advisor to the Carmelite women—hoped Kate's doctoral work would examine this questionable hierarchical use of authority in light of canon law. As Kate saw it, Hume viewed what had transpired as "an abuse of the true nature of the discalced Carmelites. It wasn't following the true legacy of Teresa of Avila. . . . He wanted to document the story and so did I."

But Cardinal Hume needed to be discreet. "I had to keep his name secret, so that he wouldn't get sabotaged or blackballed in doing his work," Kate recalled. Yet she needed to involve her own leadership in the decision. "I told him, 'I can't accept it yet, but I need to write a letter to my provincial and ask her permission to pursue this controversial topic, especially if it brings a bad name to me or to the community.'" The cardinal "understood completely," so Kate wrote to her provincial, Sister Annemarie Kampwerth, who responded: "But of course you have to do this. We're supporting you one hundred percent. This is wonderful." Kate remembered Annemarie's full-hearted response her whole life long: "I remember feeling 'Thank you God.' They really supported me and what I was doing."

However, other canon lawyers, religious sisters and priests, and church functionaries repeatedly warned her against taking on such a risky topic: "Everybody who knew I was doing it warned me that the Vatican and others—Opus Dei, for instance—and others would blackball me. . . . I would be silenced and wouldn't be able to write the dissertation."[14] Although she found herself somewhat fearful, Kate decided, "Well that's too bad. This has to be told, so I'm going to tell it." Her original research addressed discriminatory clerical and political processes that bypassed the Carmelite nuns' right to exercise their own Spirit-given voice—and experience—in interpreting and adapting their founder's legacy. Consequently, the nuns' efforts to update their rules and customs to better live Teresa's vision in the modern world—as Vatican II had requested of all religious—were greatly impeded. Kate's doctoral exposé of unworthy tactics designed to derail the Vatican II reforms desired by so many discalced Carmelite women provides an important prologue to her future advocacy on behalf of beleaguered parishioners.

Aside from visits to several monasteries of Carmelite women for research purposes, Kate wrote most of her dissertation at Clare House, a farmhouse located on the grounds of the PHJC motherhouse in Donaldson, Indiana. She also spent three months at St. Paul University Library in Ottawa, Canada, because of their excellent English resources on Vatican II and canon law. Her previous theological studies had focused mostly on sacraments rather than religious life or Vatican II ecclesiology. "I was a sophomore in high school when Vatican II occurred and just too young to really know what was going on," she reflected. "So I had to do a real study of it to prepare." She loved every bit of her time researching her topic: "It was exciting. I couldn't wait to get it done. . . . I enjoyed getting up every day and going to work on it because I was on a mission. I knew the story was important and that this was the only way it was going to be told—because the hierarchy wanted to hide it. They really wanted to hide it."

She found it "very distressing" that Pope John Paul II seemed to be taking sides with some of the most conservative elements in the church, such as Opus Dei, and remembers having "to be very careful" about how she wrote about it in her dissertation. At her dissertation defense in 1995, the last question posed was from her director, who was a Spanish Dominican. He asked her views on why Pope John Paul II had supported Opus Dei's intrusion. "How do I answer this in public?" she thought. "I don't want to bad-mouth the Pope." After deciding "I was just going to tell the truth," she simply replied, "That is a very good question." Whereupon her professor quickly intervened, "Well, time's up." A relieved Kate later reflected: "I didn't have to answer the question. But it was a very good question because this strange relationship had been developed and was being promoted by Spanish people in the hierarchy and the Opus Dei people. And why?" Piecing it all together over two decades later, Kate offered these thoughts:

> John Paul was very conservative when it came to women. And I think he didn't know what [sisters'] apostolic work was. But then the Discalced Carmelite nuns came along. And I think he liked them very much. But he thought they should continue the rule of Teresa without any exception. And what he forgot was that law grows, and custom changes, and lifestyle adjusts, and Vatican II took place. And so all of that needed to be considered when you looked at how the nuns were going to live their life. And I think he was brain-washed a little bit by people around him.

Contrary to Kate's worst fears, she suffered no repercussions. She attributes this to the fact that she had meticulously documented every one of her findings. Her dissertation was the first in many years to use all primary sources: "They had nothing to come after me about. One chapter of my dissertation had one hundred footnotes. The professors pointed that out during the defense, and I smiled and said that was a research chapter. . . . And none of it was original to me." One professor on her dissertation panel had a reputation

Figure 3.1   Sister Kate Kuenstler with Pope John Paul II, 1993. Courtesy of Poor Handmaids of Jesus Christ

for being "a devil's advocate" who sharply criticized doctoral candidates. Kate worried: "Oh God, he's on my panel too. What's he going to do . . . God, have him ask good questions." At the conclusion of her defense, she was immensely gratified to find that this professor "was so impressed that he invited me to lunch the next day and we sat and talked about it."

Kate's exhaustive documentation was excellent preparation for her future canonical advocacy for laity: "I always write the truth. And this is true with the parish mergers, et cetera. I use data, due diligence, and documents—that is, physical documents to prove what I'm saying, that support what I'm saying. And that's why they can't go after me. And that's what happened with the dissertation too."

The *Angelicum* printed twenty-five copies of Kate's dissertation. They immediately sold out—which suggests there may have been considerable political angst swirling around Opus Dei and Vatican hierarchs at the time. In 1997 Kate wrote a scholarly article, "The Fractured Face of Carmel," that summarized her work.[15] It would be downloaded from the internet many times. Nearly twenty-five years after receiving her doctorate in canon law, Kate still mourns what happened to the Carmelite sisters: "What broke my heart was that the nuns themselves had this horrible experience of fighting among themselves and not having peace and not being able to form a unified community. And they should have been able to do that, but they were prevented because of decisions made by men in the church."

Sr. Constance FitzGerald OCD, a Carmelite theologian and historian, was intimately involved in the painful events surrounding Carmelite renewal. With the late Sr. Vilma Seelaus OCD, FitzGerald helped Kate with her research and reviewed her dissertation before it was formally submitted at the *Angelicum*. Although FitzGerald doubts that very many Carmelite nuns ever read it, she is grateful for the dissertation's core contribution: "I think its value is that it captures the history . . . it is written down someplace for future researchers. And even though I would add other things, those are minor, considering the gigantic task that she [Kate] had to get her head around."[16]

Reflecting on the lengthy and deeply flawed Carmelite renewal process today, FitzGerald believes the very struggle to suppress the Vatican II voices of Carmelite women has actually given them one: "In the process we have found our voice. We would never be who we are today, speaking the way we do, with a certain kind of calm competence, if we had not been put in the difficult position, over and over again, to say who we are and what we think expresses the Teresian charism today."[17] Although the struggle was long, painful, and threatened to fracture the Order, FitzGerald suggests a deeper source of unity:

There have been terrible disagreements and shocking ruptures throughout our history over the Constitutions of Teresa. What is ironic in this whole debate is that Teresa's written works, along with those of John of the Cross, have always been the major formative influence among the nuns, far surpassing the influence of the Constitutions. It is these writings, which powerfully embody the charism, which have kept the Teresian Carmel alive for over 450 years. . . . We live out of them.[18]

Chapter 4

Catholics Discover They Have Rights

Belleville Debacles and Discoveries

When she returned from Rome in 1995, Kate served as a marriage tribunal judge in the diocese of Wilmington, Delaware. In 1998, she accepted an invitation from then-bishop Wilton Gregory to return to her home diocese of Belleville, Illinois, and work in the marriage tribunal. It was a tumultuous time. Gregory eventually rose to national prominence because of the integrity with which he managed an egregious thirty-year cover-up of clergy sex abuse in Belleville.[1] In 2001 he was elected president of the US Conference of Catholic Bishops and oversaw the development of the bishops' "zero-tolerance" policy for clergy sex abuse. In 1993, a year before Gregory was named bishop of Belleville, the diocese removed its first priest from ministry for credible allegations of sexual abuse of minors. It was the tip of the iceberg. Over the next ten years, Gregory removed fourteen more priests and one deacon. Under Gregory's leadership, according to Alan Cooperman, Belleville "became the first diocese in the country to disclose exactly how much money it has spent over the years on legal fees, counseling and settlements in abuse cases: $3,156,414 from 1993 through 2001."[2]

Shortly after his arrival in Belleville, Gregory publicly announced he intended to personally review the personnel files of all priests to ensure that no allegations had gone undisclosed to the review board. When he reviewed the file of Fr. Raymond Kownacki, he became concerned and turned it over to the review board for further examination. The board voted unanimously to remove Kownacki from the active ministry. He was placed on administrative leave but neither defrocked nor otherwise punished.[3] In 2002, one of Kownacki's victims—James Wisniewski—filed a civil lawsuit against the Belleville diocese. In the legal discovery process it came to light that Belleville vicar general, Msgr. James Margason, had deliberately withheld damning information about sexual abuse—which Wilton Gregory had never seen—from Kownacki's personnel file. Three previous Belleville bishops repeatedly transferred Kownacki to multiple parishes despite documented reports from at least seven victims whom he had sexually abused.[4]

In 2008, the circuit court of St. Clair County found the Belleville diocese guilty of "fraudulent concealment" and awarded Wisniewski $5 million. Margason—who had a canon law degree from Rome and had actually drafted the diocese's sexual abuse policy—admitted under oath that he had known of Kownacki's deviant sexual crimes as early as 1984, but in his words, "withheld this information from the review board."[5] As a canon lawyer and the vicar general of the Belleville diocese, Margason had an obligation to report these grave crimes to the presiding bishop (Gregory) and to Rome.[6] He did neither. Over the objections of diocesan clergy and lay leaders, Gregory's successor, Bishop Edward Braxton, fought the circuit court's 2008 ruling all the way to the Illinois Supreme Court.[7] On July 28, 2011, the court upheld the lower court's ruling and required the diocese to pay $6.3 million to James Wisniewski, $1.3 million over the original settlement owing to accrued interest.[8]

Such was the clerical cast of characters inhabiting Belleville diocesan offices where Kate served for eight years, from 1998 to 2006. She would also meet a vibrant group of Belleville laity who changed the trajectory of her life.

DO CATHOLICS HAVE RIGHTS IN THE CHURCH?

As a result of Belleville's clergy sex abuse scandal, an organization of lay people—then known as the Fellowship of Southern Illinois Laity (FOSIL)—asked to meet regularly with Bishop Gregory.[9] According to the history on its website, FOSIL was founded in 1971 "because of the need and hunger of lay people in the Diocese of Belleville for spiritual renewal and faith education."[10]

> Members of FOSIL are not dissident Catholics or second-class citizens. We're official members of the Catholic Church; our ID card is our baptismal certificate. Vatican Council II placed a special emphasis on the importance for lay people to take their rightful place within the whole People of God. FOSIL members respond to this call. Many are active members of parishes throughout the diocese, serving as lectors, outreach ministers, parish council members, Eucharistic ministers, teachers, etc.[11]

In addition to sponsoring regular educational events, FOSIL conducted an array of advocacy initiatives including eliminating the death penalty, addressing the international priest shortage, and calling for women's equality in the church while countering sexism. Although Gregory at times banned FOSIL from meeting on church property, it is to his credit that he also met with them quarterly for most of his tenure in Belleville. Perhaps the most influential FOSIL initiative was a series of six lay synods which the organization held throughout the diocese. FOSIL noted in its history that these addressed "various Church issues such as the sex abuse crisis, rights and responsibilities of lay people, selection of bishops, and servant leadership."[12]

Lena Woltering, a coolly analytical lay woman, had been inspired by FOSIL's programs. She quickly became a skilled organizer and spokesperson for the group. Woltering well remembers the circumstances surrounding her first encounter with Sr. Kate Kuenstler in 2005: "We were busy trying to get our vicar general [Margason] and our bishop [Gregory] to accept the fact that we are part of the church." But Margason rebuffed FOSIL: "He was using canon law as a club against us," Woltering recalled. "So one day I asked him, 'Well, why don't you come and defend canon law to us?'. . . And he said yes."[13] But after thinking it over, Margason tried to recruit other canon lawyers to meet with the progressive lay organization. They all refused. When he finally asked Kate, she accepted readily. "Little did he know what he was doing," chuckled Woltering, who gave this account of Kate's very first presentation about the rights and responsibilities of Catholics in the church:

> There were about 150 people there to hear her. [Kate] was incredible. She began her presentation by saying "Canon law is your friend." And then she went on and just captivated this crowd of people. Afterwards, she opened up the floor for discussion and questions. She was just amazed at how much these lay people were energized by what she was saying.[14]

As she watched the electrifying effect Kate had on the crowd, Woltering had an idea.

"I raised my hand when she was finished and asked, 'Would you be willing to take this show on the road?'"

"In a heartbeat," replied Kate, all the while thinking to herself, "I'll never see this woman again."

Yet Kate soon saw a great deal of Woltering. For the next two years the dynamic duo gave presentations about lay synods (Woltering) and "the Rights and Obligations of the Laity in Canon Law" (Kuenstler) at twenty-two gatherings in dioceses all over the United States. Woltering was on the board of Call To Action, an independent national church reform organization whose many chapters throughout the United States were eager to hear Kate's message. By 2009, Kate had given a total of thirty-one presentations in ten states.[15] Most venues were filled to capacity, attracting between one hundred and three hundred Catholics.[16] Attendees were amazed to discover that they had rights in the Catholic Church, and that those rights were protected by canon law.

VATICAN II AND CANON LAW: SOME BACKGROUND

Before unpacking Kate's unprecedented national presentations on the rights and obligations of ordinary Catholics, it would be wise to review a bit of the history and theology upon which those rights are based.[17] The 1983 *Code of Canon Law* arose from a new understanding in the Catholic Church that resulted from the Second Vatican Council. It would have major implications for the rights of Catholics in the Church. The ecclesial model underlying the older 1917 Code was that of the Church as a "perfect society" or sovereign state. In this model, the rights of individuals derived from the beneficence of the sovereign—the pope and bishops—not from their inherent dignity as persons. But Vatican II shifted this ecclesial construct to a more biblically and theologically based understanding of the Church as the People of God. In this model, people had rights because of their dignity as persons, not because a sovereign deigned to grant them. The Church essentially moved from a feudal monarchical model, to a more communitarian model in which the Church is understood as a community *(communio)* of believers whose rights and obligations arise from the dignity of their personhood in Christ.

Pope John XXIII inaugurated Vatican II and wished for Church law to reflect emerging conciliar wisdom. Therefore, a revision of the *Code of Canon Law* was already a given even before the Council opened in 1962. In 1983, when the new Code was finally promulgated, John Paul II announced that the Council itself was the key for interpreting and implementing it: "If however it is impossible to translate perfectly into *canonical* language the conciliar image of the Church, nevertheless the Code must always be referred to this image as the primary pattern whose outline the code ought to express insofar as it can by its very nature."[18] Such a shift in understanding had significant implications for Church governance and decision-making, the meaning of which is still emerging today.[19]

The 1983 Code contains two new listings of rights and duties of the faithful. The first (Canons 203–223) includes statements pertaining to the equality of all Christians; obligations and rights arising from governmental modes; rights pertaining to spiritual goods, worship and personal spirituality; rights and obligations with regard to the mission of the Church (association, assembly, etc.); and protection of rights (vindication, due process, etc.). The second list (Canons 225–231) concerns rights of lay persons who are explicitly acknowledged to enjoy the obligations and rights of all the Christian faithful (i.e., just remuneration for services, etc.). Both lists of canons reflect new developments that arose from the teachings of the Council and represent an important new way of thinking in canonical tradition.[20]

It is no secret that Vatican II ideals have not been completely and whole-heartedly implemented. It is also true that the juridic form of the conciliar texts codified in canon law, particularly as they relate to the rights of persons in the Church, have yet to be implemented in such a way as to fully exemplify the *communio* ideal. The "perfect society" model of Church in which the sovereign bestows rights did not disappear overnight. It continues to impede the development of *communio*'s full potential. One needs only to witness the decades-long process of lay people trying to hold bishops accountable for their shocking cover-up of clergy sex abuse of minors to know that this is true.

In a 2011 keynote address given to the Canon Law Society of America (CLSA), James A. Coriden reported that the Church has been unsuccessful in protecting the rights of the Christian faithful: "I haven't found any of our [canonical] writers who think so. All the evaluations I've found indicate that it is a goal not yet achieved, an ideal not yet realized."[21] In a major address at the same 2011 meeting of the CLSA, the respected canonist John P. Beal lamented that concern for rights had become a "peripheral concern" in the Catholic Church.[22] Further, in a prescient statement reflecting the synodal-ity values of Pope Francis, he sharply criticized the failure to meaningfully include laity in Church decision-making:

> Despite all the glowing rhetoric about the equality of the faithful based on baptism and the rights of the baptized in the Church, it is difficult to speak meaningfully about equality and rights in an ecclesial society in which the laity who represent the overwhelming majority of the baptized, are kept aloof from the decisions of some importance which affect them.[23]

Differences in Roman and Anglo-American jurisprudence have also ham-pered full implementation of human rights in Church structures. In Roman law, it is the lawgiver who has the right of interpretation of the law. This is a very different system from the Anglo-American concept in which the courts have the final say in how the law is to be interpreted. Still, Daniel J. Ward has some interesting observations about how the Roman "philosophy of interpretation," if you will, need not be an obstacle to due process. Ward acknowledges that Canon 223 limits all rights by situating them in the com-mon good, thus exemplifying the Roman principle that the lawgiver is the one to moderate/interpret rights in light of the common good.[24] Nevertheless, he points out:

[T]he limiting principles stated within the canons are guiding principles for
executive and judicial authorities to use, no less than the implicit assumptions
underlying the American common law tradition . . . each is articulating the same
basic dignity of the human person as lived within a given society. . . . The results
should not, therefore be dissimilar.[25]

While these distinctions may seem esoteric, it is instructive that despite obvious differences between Roman and Anglo-American jurisprudence, the end
result can be similar. Since implementation of the canons is in fact not done
by legislators, but by executives and administrators who interpret their meaning (as is done by the court system in the United States), the underlying basis
for the American notion of due process remains relevant and justified.[26]

Highly relevant to Kate's empowering mission was the need for the People of God to first claim and own their rights. Failure to understand that one
in fact *has* rights is probably the biggest obstacle to their full implementation in the Church. The Council's shift in understanding of the person gave
new emphasis to their rights which are based on their dignity as baptized
believers in Christ. Since in the past all rights in the Catholic Church were
bestowed by the sovereign, there is a sense in which any rights arising from
a person's dignity must first be "claimed" by that person before they can
become "real" in law. Jesuit canonist John McIntyre explains: "Unless the
people of God really practice these elements of personality and commitment, the fundamental Charter of rights exists only *in spe* (in hope). . . . As
rights to be possessed, the faithful must first claim them in order to make
them real."[27]

This being the case, we should not be unduly surprised that the actual
acquisition of ecclesial rights by the average baptized Catholic has lagged
so far behind conciliar hopes. To exercise one's rights, one must first believe
s/he has them. Since many believers in today's Church still look to Rome
or the local hierarch for decisions which are fully within their purview as
baptized and gifted in the Spirit to make, it is perhaps unsurprising that
passivity often reigns. Kate's nationwide speaking ministry educating ordinary Catholics about the need to claim their rights was desperately needed.
Catholics were waking up, especially in light of rampant cover-ups of clergy
sex abuse and the decisions of too many bishops to shrink parishes to fit an
ever-diminishing supply of priests. The Church as People of God was and is
suffering because too many Christian faithful do not know they have rights
and do not know how to claim and defend them.

Historically, yet another factor affecting the non-acquisition and non-
implementation of the rights of Catholics is the lack of structures by which
those rights may be vindicated when they are violated. In 1991 Beal wrote,
"Conspicuously absent from the revised Code, however, is any provision for

the establishment of administrative tribunals, the need for which was 'everywhere strongly felt' in 1967."[28] A 1987 study, "Due Process in Dioceses of the United States," reported that only 57 percent of 186 US dioceses had any experience with due process cases or had developed due process materials.[29] Possible explanations for minimal utilization of due process procedures included lack of awareness on the part of the faithful about their rights or that processes were available to vindicate them, ambivalent or hostile attitudes on the part of bishops and priests, lack of training and resources for personnel, polarization, reluctance to subject Church activities to outside scrutiny, conflicts of competence, and difficulty in accommodating groups in processes designed for individuals.[30]

Pope Francis's 2021–2024 Synod on Synodality is a hopeful indication that ordinary Catholics all over the world are recognizing that they must become co-responsible for the Church's mission as called for in the Synthesis statement of the 2023 session.[31] The Synthesis called for a review of canon law and other authoritative church documents. The goal is to build more inclusive and accountable structures and ensure the effective exercise of co-responsibility within the Roman Catholic Church.[32]

PARISH RIGHTS AND OBLIGATIONS

Perhaps the foremost academic promoter of the canonical rights of parishes and parishioners is the Rev. James Coriden whose book, *The Parish in Catholic Tradition*, lists the rights and obligations of parishes in considerable detail.[33] Parishes are not administrative units like McDonald's or your local bank, but true churches and, according to Coriden, as such have basic rights.[34] The most fundamental right of a parish in canon law is the right to come into existence, to be acknowledged, and to continue in existence (Canon 374.1). Once a community of faith is formed and recognized, it becomes a "juridic [legal] person" which by nature is perpetual unless it is legitimately suppressed or stops all activity for one hundred years (c. 120.1). To be suppressed, the impossibility of continued life must be clearly demonstrated.[35] Coriden is careful to note, however, that there are limitations on parish rights and obligations:

> In exercising their rights the Christian faithful, both as individuals and when gathered in associations, must take account of the common good of the church, and of the rights of others as well as their own duties toward others. In the interests of the common good, church authority [for example the diocesan bishop] has competence to regulate the exercise of the rights which belong to the Christian faithful (c. 223.1, 223.2).[36]

The Parish in Catholic Tradition appeared in 1997. It was the first pastoral and practical guide for Catholics trying to understand how canon law applied to parishes. Coriden's theoretical guidebook outlined ways of claiming and vindicating parish rights using the administrative recourse procedure. Until Sr. Kate Kuenstler began working with beleaguered parishioners in 2006, however, no one had yet successfully applied these procedures to permanently reverse a bishop's decision to suppress a parish and close its church. Kate's dogged perseverance—and the courage of a charismatic priest and parishioners in the diocese of Camden, New Jersey, as well as groups of parishioners in the dioceses of Syracuse and Cleveland—would soon change all of that. Kate's creative support of an inspiring—and inspired—group of Catholic faithful pioneered a path through canon law where none had existed before.

In the course of her national advocacy, Kate found new and creative ways to help Catholic parishioners access little-known administrative recourse procedures in canon law to appeal imprudent diocesan decisions to merge their vital parishes and sell their churches. But before this could happen, she needed to help Catholics understand that they had rights, what those rights were, and ways they could stand up for themselves.

CANON LAW 101: RIGHTS, RESPONSIBILITIES, AND RECOURSE

When she spoke to large gatherings of Catholics, Kate often began with a frank statement that invariably surprised attendees: "I believe that canon law is a gift to the church, but it's not a perfect gift. Canon law has not been used adequately by the leadership in the church. The Christian faithful have not been informed about what is in canon law. They have not been informed about how to protect their rights that are contained in the law."[37] Her lectures educated listeners about why canon law is important to the church, what it has to do with a life of faith, and the role it plays in the believing community. She helped Catholics begin to think of themselves as integral members of this great *communio* called Church, rather than as "pray, pay and obey" people who blindly follow a ruling bishop. "No Christian is baptized to be a lay person," she told them. "Jesus in the gospel, never called people saying, 'come be the laity,'" she said while observing that the word *laity* "comes from [the Greek word] *laos*, which means 'the people.' We are people who are disciples and followers of Christ." "So why don't we call ourselves who we truly are?" she asked. "Our baptismal identity is discipleship. A fundamental aspect of discipleship is participation in the ministerial life of the community, service through leading, praying, teaching, preaching, and caring for those others." Canon law, she said, "must always serve the religious purpose of the church.

It must help the Christian faithful to proclaim the life and message of Christ to be a communal witness, to the loving presence of God, to be of service to the world today."

An important reason both clergy and laity were—and are—uninformed about their rights is what Kate called the "black hole in the Church," that occurred between 1965 when the Council ended and 1983 when the new Code was promulgated:

Any priest ordained before 1983 did not study this code in the seminary, and they were not formed in the new renewed understanding of who the Church is and how the Church functions using the theology of Church that was formed during Vatican II, basically because it wasn't written. We had the theology, but we did not have the practical application.

The sad result, said Kate, is that "canon law has been misused, unused, and abused." She encouraged Catholics to speak up, sharing that she often heard well-meaning adults ask, "How can I do anything? The Church is not a democracy. Doesn't loyalty to the Church require silence?" This was her reply:

True loyalty to the Church requires us to speak out when we believe the Church is not living up to the ideals and practices of Christ. Do not let anyone make you feel that you are unfaithful when you stand up to protect your rights or the rights of anyone as found in the 1983 Code of Canon Law. Call yourselves who you truly are. You are the Christian faithful, because Christian faithful is your baptismal name.

Kate explained that canon law is meant to protect personal rights, provide avenues of recourse to address grievances, and to resolve conflicts. It is not intended "to make any of these, or produce these," she said pointedly. "Canon law is only the bare minimum of how to live a life of discipleship. It is to be used to lead people to a virtuous life," she explained. "One of the oldest canons of the Church is Canon 1752 which says, 'The salvation of souls must always be the Supreme Law of the Church.'"

Kate underscored an inspiring theological principle in canon law: "All ministry is rooted in one's relationship to Christ and to that [Christian] community, whether the person is ordained or not." She enjoyed telling appreciative audiences, "I don't know if you know it or not, but the word hierarchy does not appear anywhere in the 1983 *Code of Canon Law*. The adjective hierarchical appears only nine times in 1,752 canons." Furthermore,

Gospel leadership is service. *Lumen Gentium* paragraph 18 clearly says, "Those who have been given authority are servants of their brothers and sisters." The concept of *communio* (communion) is key to understanding the nature of the

Church. . . .We do not act in our own name. We act on behalf of Christ, who entrusted to the Church—to us—the threefold duty to teach, to sanctify, and to govern.

Before turning to individual canons, Kate carefully clarified church teaching about the primacy of conscience:

No one can coerce anyone to act contrary to their conscience. We must be free to question, to search, to be on pilgrimage as the people of God. The internal forum—that is one's conscience—is sacred. Canon law addresses only the external forum—the community life, the public life of the Christian faithful. Blind obedience has no place in the code of canon law.

After situating canon law within this historical, theological, and philosophical context, Kate turned to a discussion of a number of specific canons that address the rights and obligations of the Christian faithful. Space considerations do not permit a comprehensive treatment of every relevant canon here, but a sampling is provided below.

The first canon Kate discussed in her lectures was Canon 208, which sets the stage for everything else. It stipulates that because of their Baptism, "there exists among all the Christian faithful a true equality regarding dignity and action by which they all cooperate in the building up of the Body of Christ according to each one's own condition and function.[38] Before Vatican II, Kate explained, "ministry was restricted only to the clergy—bishops, priests, and deacons. Laity were allowed to assist in an apostolate only by invitation. And there was a definite inequality between clergy and everybody else." But, she said, Vatican II taught "there is now a fundamental equality rooted in the sacrament of Baptism, fully recovering the ancient notion of the priesthood of the faithful that had been lost as the years went by . . . and clergy and laity are now called to assist one another in the Church's mission."

Discussing Canon 209, Kate underscored that Catholics have obligations and duties in the church that emerge from their common call to build God's reign on earth as in heaven. These duties do not include blind obedience. Canon 209 reads:

§1 The Christian faithful, even in their own manner of acting, are always obliged to maintain communion with the Church. §2. With great diligence they are to fulfill the duties which they owe to the universal Church and the particular church to which they belong according to the prescripts of the law.

But the Church does not equate to only the pope, bishops, and priests. Rather, "the people are the Church, the Holy Spirit dwells in them, and their goal is God's kingdom," Kate declared. Therefore, "all share in Christ's prophetic, priestly and governing roles. All are called to exercise the mission that God has assigned the church to fulfill in the world. That is your obligation. The canonical obligation."

Canon 212 has three parts, all of which include important under-utilized actions and rights that need to be claimed by the Christian faithful. Paragraph 1 reads:

> The Christian faithful are obliged to follow what the bishops declare as teachers of the faith or what the bishops determined as leaders of the church.[39]

Before situating this canon in its larger context, Kate clarified: "This canon does not mean that an individual bishop is infallible. This canon does not mean that the Christian faithful may not question a bishop." Yet she made clear that "the highest authority in the church is collegial. The college of bishops with the Pope as its head, are to be held in respect because they are the highest authority." While the college of bishops with the pope make laws for the church, Kate also pointed to two time-honored canonical traditions that temper this law: "First, another canon, Canon 27, says custom is the best interpreter of law. That's a very old canon. . . . And it has never been revised." According to this ancient principle "the community knows best . . . the way a law is actually lived out and followed by the people is the best measure of the law's intent. This reflects the belief that the Holy Spirit dwells within the community and guides the community of the faithful." The second canonical tradition that tempers laws made by Church authorities is that "the community's reception or receiving of the law is decisive." In this tradition, Kate explained, "The force of law depends in part on the community obeying the law. When the community fails to observe the law, it often means that the law is impractical or unsuited to that community. And I carefully and very respectfully suggest that possibly the law on contraception fits this very well."

Then Kate turned to Canon 212, paragraphs 1 and 2, which "tell the rest of the story" about how Catholics have both the right and the duty to share their Spirit-given perspectives about "matters which pertain to the good of the church." Canon 212, paragraph 2 reads, "The Christian faithful have the right to make their needs and their desires known to their Bishop."[40] Paragraph 3 goes even further saying,

> According to the knowledge, competence, and prestige which they possess, [the Christian faithful] have the right and even at times the duty to manifest to the sacred pastors their opinion on matters which pertain to the good of the Church and to make their opinion known to the rest of the Christian faithful, without prejudice to the integrity of faith and morals, with reverence toward their pastors, and attentive to common advantage and the dignity of persons.[41]

With a touch of humor, Kate emphasized that the authentic teaching of the church requires ordinary Catholics to speak up when the good of the church is at stake:

> Not only is it your right, but your obligation [to speak up] is right there in canon law. This is the authentic teaching of the Roman Catholic Church. Have you ever heard of that before? It's not rocket science. The Christian faithful have the right and obligation to take part in consultation. They have the right to participate in coming to decisions that affect their lives. If you want something conservative, this is it. Go for it.

She then cited Canon 119, paragraph 3: "What touches all as individuals, however, must be approved by all."

"Hmm," mused Kate. "That is why the 'community of communities,' is the new model of the church, the participative model of the church. And it is why when you find the participative model not happening, it rankles the way it does. It doesn't seem to fit anymore because it doesn't."

Canon 215 reads: "The Christian faithful are at liberty freely to found and direct associations for purposes of charity or piety or for the promotion of the Christian vocation in the world and to hold meetings for the common pursuit of these purposes."

"This includes people who belong to FOSIL, Call To Action, Future-Church and other organizations," said Kate.

Canon 213 is especially significant in our contemporary context of a world-wide priest shortage. It reads: "The Christian faithful have the right to receive assistance from the sacred pastors out of the spiritual goods of the Church, especially the word of God and the sacraments." Kate pointedly criticized the misguided statements made by prelates at the 2005 Synod on the Eucharist:

> Those wonderful bishops and cardinals stood up and tried to argue that receiving the word of God and the sacraments was a privilege of the laity and therefore they did not have to provide it for them. And our wonderful Pope Benedict stood up and said, "I think the canon lawyers of the world would take great exception to that because canon law says the Christian faithful have the right to receive the word of God and the sacraments."

MORE ABOUT ADMINISTRATIVE RECOURSE

On May 17, 2007, in the midst of crisscrossing the country, Kate gave a passionate presentation on "Canon Law and the Rights of the Lay Christian Faithful," to about two hundred Cleveland Catholics. Her presentation was organized by the Cleveland-based nonprofit organization FutureChurch.

Since the Cleveland diocese was in the midst of a parish reconfiguration process, there was considerable anxiety that many vital parishes and churches could close. Clevelanders were especially anxious about newly arrived Bishop Richard Lennon in light of his devastating closure of over eighty Boston parishes. Many doubted Lennon's vision would respect the diocese's nationally recognized "Church in the City" effort to preserve as many parishes as possible in poorer neighborhoods. Most also believed that what the bishop decided—what *any* bishop decided—was the final word. Knowing her audience, Kate went into considerable detail about the rights of laity with regard to parish mergers and church closings. Attendees were surprised to learn that ordinary Catholics had rights and obligations that were named in and protected by Church law, and that parishes also had canonical rights. She spoke in detail about a little-known and little-used process in canon law through which parishioners could exercise their rights and defend threatened parish communities. She said:

> In Canon 221, paragraph 1 it says the Christian faithful have the right to vindicate and defend their rights in a church court. More often than not we know about the rights of the Christian faithful being abused. Most of the time, this is done through administrative decisions made by priests, by bishops or others in authority of the church, such as the chancellor or the vicar general, all of whom can be taken to task. If they step on the rights of the Christian faithful, the way to vindicate and defend one's rights is through the administrative recourse process.

Yet the administrative recourse process had not been put immediately into the 1983 *Code of Canon Law*. One reason, said Kate, was because "the bishops really did not want this oversight." Nor could Church officials agree on what the process should say before the new code was published. Still the administrative recourse process did appear later. Although "it was watered down somewhat," said Kate, "it still has enough teeth to be a very good process to follow." Even so, she emphasized: "For the most part the Christian faithful don't know about this process, and they don't know it's available to them."

For the next ten years Kate Kuenstler dedicated her life to helping hundreds of Catholics use the administrative recourse process to appeal misguided decisions to suppress their parishes and close their churches. She pioneered a successful procedural path for defending parish rights. Catholics slowly began to own their baptismal equality, claiming their rights, and many were able to save their church homes. At the time of Sister Kate's Cleveland address I was working as the founding director of FutureChurch. The organization had just launched a new *Save Our Parish Community* (SOPC) initiative and desperately needed someone who knew canon law and who felt strongly about the rights of the laity. As I sat and listened to Kate's knowledgeable, passionate presentation, I knew we had found that person.

"DO NOT STIFLE THE SPIRIT"—*SAVE OUR PARISH COMMUNITY* INITIATIVE

As more bishops planned to sacrifice vibrant parish communities to address steep financial challenges and the priest shortage, in July 2005 the Future-Church board decided something had to be done and voted unanimously to undertake the SOPC initiative. FutureChurch had been deeply rooted in parish realities since its founding in 1990, when priest and lay leaders in the Cleveland diocese organized to raise awareness about the consequences of ignoring the priest shortage. Twenty-eight Cleveland parishes and religious communities signed a statement saying that access to the Mass was more important to Catholic identity than the gender or marital status of the priest. FutureChurch soon expanded outside of Cleveland, growing to three thousand international members. Many thousands of other parish-centered activists regularly downloaded prayer and action resources from the FutureChurch website. By 2005, the FutureChurch organization was well positioned to help Catholics decide what to do when their vibrant, solvent parish was threatened with closure or merger. The Cleveland-based organization could not have known at the time that Bishop Richard G. Lennon, the architect of Boston's disastrous parish reconfiguration plan, would be appointed the tenth bishop of Cleveland. Providentially, the organization became a hub of canonical information to help Cleveland Catholics appeal mistaken decisions to shutter their beloved parish homes. And Sister Kate helped Clevelanders every step of the way. FutureChurch's *Save Our Parish Community* initiative was "designed to provide educational and organizing resources to faith communities discerning an appropriate response to diocesan decisions to close or merge their vibrant, solvent, and apostolically effective parish." Two Catholic foundations supplied grant funding for the much-needed effort.[42] In coming years, many hundreds of Catholics would download free SOPC resources—including canonical resources prepared by Sister Kate—to learn about their options and access canonical support.

THE INDEPENDENT PRACTICE OF CANON LAW

By early 2006 Kate had served as a judge in the Belleville marriage tribunal for eight years. Although she didn't always agree with him, she thought well of Bishop Wilton Gregory and viewed him as "a mover and a shaker." The two had a good relationship, for "I respected him and he respected me." The same could not be said of Gregory's controversial successor, Bishop Edward K. Braxton. Not long after his June 2005 installation, Braxton used $10,000 from a special ministries fund to purchase an expensive table and chairs for the chancery conference room. He also used $8,000 from the Society for the Propagation of the Faith to purchase five new sets of vestments.[43] After the diocesan finance council protested vigorously and publicly, in January 2008 Braxton returned the funds and apologized. In April 2008, over half of Belleville's priests called for his resignation, and a prominent religious order—the Adorers of the Blood of Christ—asked the apostolic nuncio to intervene.[44] By the time Braxton's difficulties became public, however, Kate had long since left his employ. Citing "personal and professional reasons" why continued employment under Braxton would not work, she resigned in late 2006. Despite being good at her job, she said, "I realized one day that being a tribunal judge was not what I was really called to. I wasn't sure what I was called to, but I knew this wasn't it." The Poor Handmaids community gave Kate a sabbatical year, ostensibly to author a book, but fate (or perhaps the Holy Spirit) intervened.

Approximately one month after beginning her sabbatical, Kate received a telephone call from Colleen LaTray, a parishioner at St. Mary Parish in Jamesville, New York.

"Could you help us save our parish?" she asked.

"Well, I'm not sure I know how to do that, but let's talk," Kate responded.

And so began Sister Kate Kuenstler's independent practice of canon law. At first, she affiliated with Canon Law Professionals, an organization founded in 2000 in its words, "to offer independent canonical services to all members of the Catholic Church."[45] Usually canonical assistance was offered only by canon lawyers employed by dioceses or religious communities. This made it very difficult for lay people to find a canon lawyer who did not have a built-in conflict of interest. Kate subsequently inaugurated her own independent practice, Canon Law Ministries, where she adopted a special title, "Advocate for the Laity." It is to the St. Mary Jamesville story that we now turn.

Chapter 5

Advocate for the Laity—St. Mary Parish, Jamesville, New York

In 2007, when Kate first met Colleen LaTray and her savvy group of parish leaders from St. Mary Parish in Jamesville, New York, she could not have known that over the next thirteen years she would work with scores of Catholic groupings that opposed ill-advised diocesan decisions to close their vibrant, solvent, and ministerially fruitful faith communities. Kate's story is also the story of hundreds of courageous Catholics—and a few good priests—who exercised their canonical rights and resisted their bishop's decision to suppress a beloved parish and demolish the church they had proudly maintained for generations. It is impossible to write about each of the scores of parishioner groups for whom Kate worked as an advocate for the laity. Instead, I have chosen to chronicle the stories of selected parishioner groupings in several key dioceses whose canonical appeals catalyzed the development of Rome's procedural norms about parish and parishioner rights. Their stories also provide a window into destructive downsizing tactics used by US bishops to deal with financial pressures from clergy sex abuse and the worsening priest shortage. While this is Kate's story, it is also the story of the fearless faith communities, priests, Catholic activists, civil attorneys, and journalists who banded together to create a way where previously there had been none.

PARISHIONERS APPEAL DESPITE PUNDIT PREDICTIONS OF FAILURE

In December 2010, the canonical recourse first filed in 2007 by Colleen LaTray and Catholics from St. Mary Parish in Jamesville, New York, became the first parishioner appeal to be granted a full hearing at the Apostolic Signatura, the

Church's highest court.[1] Previously, the lower court—the Congregation for the Clergy—had summarily denied all parish appeals—including eleven from the Archdiocese of Boston and at least one from Camden, New Jersey.[2] With help from Sister Kate and under the passionate leadership of LaTray, in 2007 the St. Mary, Jamesville Appeals Committee filed administrative recourse in Rome. They did so despite predictions from church pundits that parishioner appeals were doomed to fail.

"The Vatican is only concerned about whether proper canonical procedures were followed," said Fr. Thomas Reese, former editor of *America*, a monthly Jesuit publication. "They are not interested in arguments like 'this is a wonderful parish.'. . . They're not going to get into second-guessing pastoral decisions of the local bishops."[3]

Nonetheless, by 2010, determined Catholic groups from at least fifteen dioceses filed at least eighty canonical appeals in Rome, essentially flooding staffers at the Congregation for the Clergy as Vatican offices scrambled to keep up with the influx.[4]

Although Kate guided the canonical process of a substantial, indeed pivotal, number of those appeals, she was determined to stay in the background. She refused all media interviews until 2012 when—in an unprecedented decision—Rome ruled against Cleveland bishop Richard Lennon and twelve Cleveland parishes won their appeals. Kate believed canonical recourses belong to parishioners. Her job was to guide the process. "They're the ones who are the foundation of the faith community. That was very important to me in my studies, in my reflection of canon law on parish issues. The laity are the driving force, not a highly educated canon lawyer. It wasn't my recourse; it was theirs."

On May 21, 2011, LaTray and the St. Mary, Jamesville, Catholics received a precedent-setting decision when the Apostolic Signatura—the church's highest court—reversed the Congregation for the Clergy's earlier decree and ruled that, although the parish could be suppressed, St. Mary Church must remain open as a worship site.[5]

It was the first public victory with which Kate had been quietly involved. Her first actual victory had been won privately the previous October. A strong case can be made that Camden bishop Joseph M. Galante's October 2010 St. Vincent Pallotti reversal is the linchpin upon which subsequent surprising Vatican decisions upholding parishioner appeals, including St. Mary's, depended. Between January and May of 2011—in what Duquesne University canon law expert Nicholas P. Cafardi described as a landmark change—the Congregation for the Clergy issued partial victories to thirteen churches in the dioceses of Allentown, Pennsylvania; Springfield, Massachusetts; and Buffalo, New York. In each case, Rome upheld the bishop's suppression of the parish, but ruled that their churches must remain open as worship sites.[6] At

Figure 5.1   St. Mary Church, Jamesville, New York. Parishioners regularly celebrated sidewalk prayer services before winning their appeal to keep their beloved church from being demolished. Photo by Nate Wales via Wikimedia commons

the time, Charles Wilson, the executive director of the St. Joseph Foundation in San Antonio, Texas, told the *Syracuse Post-Standard* that his organization had handled roughly three hundred cases related to the closing of a parish or church building, and only once had the Congregation for the Clergy ruled in favor of parishioners.[7] A significant change had occurred at the Vatican, but no one knew what was behind it.

An earlier, largely unknown canonical victory shepherded by Sister Kate had paved the way for both the St. Mary's win and those of the other twelve churches. In April 2008, Msgr. Lou Marucci, a brilliant, brave pastor of St. Vincent Pallotti (SVP) parish in Camden, contacted Kate after the Camden diocese announced his parish would merge with a lesser-equipped one, St. Aloysius. Marucci was physically disabled and SVP attracted many parishioners because it was handicapped accessible. Now, all worship would be held at St. Aloysius even though it had unsuitable access. This arrangement was seen as a death knell for St. Vincent Pallotti, as most non-worship-site churches in the Camden diocese would be sold or designated for other uses. Inexplicably, just four months earlier, Marucci had publicly dedicated Pallotti's brand-new million-dollar, ADA-compliant community center. With Kate's guidance, Marucci and SVP parishioners filed a canonical recourse.

Two and a half years later, on October 10, 2010, Galante suddenly reversed himself and decreed that St. Vincent Pallotti Church would become the seat of the newly merged parish, thus assuring its long-term survival.[8] Under Cardinal Raymond Burke, the Signatura had essentially told Galante that a future Pallotti appeal would win, once parishioners were given the official decree which he had been withholding.

The St. Vincent Pallotti victory signaled a dramatic change in Vatican policy. It was the first of many cases that Kate would win, and it is arguably the most influential. The Signatura had exercised its leverage to uphold the norms of canon law and protect parish rights. Something had changed, and the change came from the top. Three months after Galante's unexpected reversal—and shortly before a slew of decisions from the lower court at the Congregation for the Clergy[9] that kept thirteen US churches in the dioceses of Allentown, Springfield, and Syracuse as worship sites—Cardinal Raymond Burke, the ultraconservative prefect at the Apostolic Signatura, told a group of canon law judges from England and Wales that closing a church should be done only "as a last resort." Furthermore, he said a parish's "spiritual patrimony" was the most important consideration, and that it is better for a church to be open for monthly Mass than to be closed.[10] As prefect of the Church's highest law court, Burke was essentially the boss. His St. Vincent Pallotti finesse led to a sea change at the Congregation for the Clergy, which on December 31, 2010—two months after the Pallotti victory—began publishing the first of many January-May decrees ruling that while the bishop could suppress parishes, their churches must remain open for worship.[11] These precedent-setting victories would not have happened without Kate's canonical acumen, an arch-conservative cardinal-prefect who knew his canon law, and the faith-filled advocacy of St. Vincent Pallotti and St. Mary, Jamesville, Catholics.

ST. MARY PARISH, JAMESVILLE—DIOCESE OF SYRACUSE

The story of St. Mary Parish in Jamesville, New York, is significant because it is the first parishioner appeal ever accepted for a full hearing at the Apostolic Signatura. The Signatura would eventually uphold the right of St. Mary Church to remain open for worship although, as we shall see, the pastor and local bishop shamefully resisted that ruling. The St. Mary story begins where most parish suppression and church closure stories begin, with a severe shortage of priests in the Diocese of Syracuse.[12] In 1974, 366 priests served 375,000 Syracuse Catholics in 170 parishes and twenty-one missions. By 2006, 108 full-time pastors served 350,000 Catholics in 161 parishes and fourteen missions.[13] Most had multiple ministries or parishes, and more than forty-five were already beyond the retirement age of seventy.[14] While it is true that more Catholics were moving to the suburbs with correspondingly fewer in urban and rural areas, the main driver of the dramatic changes in Syracuse parish life was the severe shortage of priests. Ironically, in his 2001 pastoral letter "Equipping the Saints for the Work of Ministry," Syracuse bishop James M. Moynihan acknowledged a marked increase in lay ministry with over thirteen hundred men and women commissioned to this role as well as an additional five thousand persons serving as catechists in parishes and schools.[15] Apparently the Syracuse diocese did not sufficiently value keeping parish communities together. Given an abundance of lay people committed to church ministry, it is lamentable that so little creativity was employed to preserve vibrant faith communities. Instead the bishop prioritized a "one priest-one parish" model that was being replicated in other dioceses across the United States.[16]

With the 2001 pastoral letter, Moynihan inaugurated a diocesan-wide pastoral planning process in the seven-county diocese. He asked each parish to meet in pastoral care areas to discuss the situation and submit proposals for reconfiguring in their geographic locale.[17] In the spring of 2007, after the pastoral planning process concluded, the diocese announced a historic reorganization that would eliminate forty churches by 2010. The number of parishes and missions would decrease from 175 to 134 which—according to diocesan projections—would be served by fewer than one hundred priests.[18] Even with the painful reductions, there were not enough priests to staff every parish.

On April 27, 2007, Catholics at St. Mary's Parish, the only Catholic church in Jamesville, were greatly surprised to learn that their century-old church would be shuttered and sold. Their vibrant parish would be merged with Holy Cross Parish in DeWitt, located about fifteen minutes away. Fortunately, LaTray had just read about Kate's "Thruway Tour" of several cities along the New York State Thruway at which she spoke about the canonical rights of Catholics—including the right to appeal parish closures. Sponsored by local chapters of the Catholic church reform organization, Call To Action, activists made sure to invite media outlets in Buffalo, Rochester, Syracuse, Albany, and Binghamton. After reading about Kate's presentation in her diocesan paper, the *Syracuse Catholic Sun*, LaTray immediately sent her a long email describing the plight of St. Mary Catholics. Later, she observed, "This canonical appeal option was a great surprise to me because Msgr. Yeazel [the new pastor] had repeatedly stated at our public meetings that 'there is no appeal process.' Ironically, I read that there was, in fact, an appeal process in the Syracuse diocese's own newspaper."[19]

Kate telephoned LaTray immediately. She told her she would be in the Buffalo area within a month and would be happy to meet with St. Mary parishioners. On May 1, per Kate's telephone advice, LaTray and a determined cohort of parishioners filed a brief appeal to the Syracuse bishop and to Cardinal Claudio Hummes at the Congregation for the Clergy. Normally the appeal to Clergy is sent only after the local bishop has either denied the parishioners' appeal or has not responded for thirty days, but Kate advised parishioners to write Moynihan so as not to miss the filing deadline.[20]

LaTray was a well-educated mother of three, who taught at nearby Le Moyne College, Syracuse University, and the Jamesville-DeWitt School District. She subsequently wrote a lengthier recourse to Hummes. When Kate visited Jamesville, she reviewed her work and provided input. LaTray modeled her recourse on several appeals from the Boston area which she had found on the internet. But like most Catholics, she was unaware of the strict timing regulations guiding canonical appeals. In 2007 hardly anyone knew anything about how to proceed with parish appeals, including Kate herself. St. Mary, Jamesville, was the first case Kate was asked to help with. Looking back, she reflected that although she had a doctorate in canon law, "closing parishes and selling church buildings was not high on the priority list in Rome. So I never really learned about that." Furthermore the documents and canons to challenge a bishop's decision about closing a parish and selling its church were not in any one place. Instead, she said, "They were hidden in many different books. A single canon in Book Three went with a single canon in Book One. You had to find out where all of them were. There was no written handbook, and no directions were given."[21] Even worse, "the protocol was so strict, if you didn't know the protocol or follow it, you lost the case automatically." Given the difficulty accessing scattered canons, one could easily conclude that Rome didn't necessarily want people appealing decisions about their parishes. "One of my professors at the *Angelicum* said just that," Kate confirmed.[22]

LaTray and another St. Mary committee member picked up Kate in Buffalo. On the two-and-a-half hour journey home, Kate reviewed LaTray's multiple-page appeal. "She was very impressed with the document and said it was well done," recalled LaTray, who confirmed that Kate had supported the recourse.[23] Over the next two days, Kate also met with the St. Mary lay leaders who wanted "to pick her brain," although they did not always agree with her suggestions. At this point, no one—including Kate—had a successful track record on Vatican appeals. LaTray remembers, "Overall, I was grateful for Sr. Kate sharing her experience and expertise, but it was a delicate balance between doing what Sr. Kate demanded and how our committee members wanted to proceed. After thoughtful consideration and discussion, we always proceeded with the majority rule as a committee."

On May 26, 2007, St. Mary parishioners filed formal administrative recourse with Cardinal Hummes. Just one year earlier—in a cooperative effort to alleviate pressures from the priest shortage—lay parish leaders at St. Mary had agreed to become a "mission" of Holy Cross. Monsignor Yeazel had led parishioners to believe that they would continue worshipping at their beloved church for the foreseeable future. As they understood it, St. Mary's would remain, technically, a parish. On May 25, 2006, the Syracuse vicar for parishes, the Rev. James P. Lang, sent a letter to the St. Mary parish administrator, the Rev. Andrew E. Baranski, confirming that the parish would become a mission of Holy Cross Parish in DeWitt. However, the exact meaning of *mission* went undefined. In their appeal, St. Mary parishioners argued correctly that *mission* is not a canonical term. This fact would significantly influence the outcome of their administrative recourse to the Vatican. Canon law requires that parish appeals be filed with the bishop within ten days of any decree suppressing a parish. For St. Mary parishioners, the dating for their recourse would be a critical factor, both in its denial by the Congregation for the Clergy and its subsequent success at the Apostolic Signatura.

Throughout 2006, St. Mary Parish leaders participated in the diocesan reconfiguration planning sessions. At an October 16 meeting, four options surfaced for possible worship sites for the parishes in their geographic area. The fourth option suggested that worship sites be located at Holy Cross in DeWitt and St. Mary, Jamesville.[24] Since nothing was finalized, St. Mary leaders were surprised when no further reconfiguration meetings were convened. Therefore, on November 19, 2006, the four members of the St. Mary's Pastoral Care Committee submitted a letter to Reverend Lang. They made a compelling case for why their 350-family worshipping community should remain in Jamesville. The following information is drawn from documentation submitted to the Vatican in 2007 and 2008 by the St. Mary Appeals Committee in its hierarchical recourse opposing Bishop Moynihan's decision to suppress their parish and close their church.[25]

St. Mary Church was the only Catholic church in Jamesville, a small verdant hamlet of about ten thousand people outside of Syracuse, whose population was growing, not shrinking. With the highly regarded Jamesville-DeWitt School District attracting residents, new housing developments soon complemented the more traditional homes that graced the small city's wooded streets. Studies from the school district at the time projected that over the next five years, 70 percent of the district's growth would occur in Jamesville. Over one thousand people were expected to move into the area, and an additional five hundred Catholics could conceivably inhabit the city. The parish was financially stable with assets of $526,000, and $5,400 in cash. It had no debt, annually met its diocesan financial obligations, and regularly exceeded its Diocesan Hope Appeal fundraising goals.

By way of comparison, according to a May 16, 2007, joint St. Mary/ Holy Cross pastoral council meeting, Holy Cross Parish—under its pastor,

Monsignor Yeazel—had an outstanding building loan of $1,050,000, with another $400,000–$500,000 debt tied up in litigation over stained glass windows. The accruing monthly interest fees amounted to $6,500.[26] A *Syracuse Post-Standard* story about Bishop James Moynihan's April 27 decision reported that St. Mary's "territory, assets, debts and records will go to Holy Cross church in DeWitt."[27] Thus began a recurring pattern in parish mergers that Kate encountered again and again. A financially sound parish would be suppressed and merged with a parish that had significant debt. The assets of the wealthier, now extinguished, parish were then used to balance the books of the newly merged entity.

Of greater importance is the fact that St. Mary Jamesville Parish had a thriving ministerial and faith life. Official diocesan records just prior to the announced merger indicate that 535 families were registered and at least five hundred people attended each of the two weekend Masses. The parish also sponsored a successful community-wide food bank—St. Mary's Pantry—to which area churches and community groups contributed. Food was distributed year-round in the greater Jamesville-DeWitt community. In 2006, 476 households comprising 1,349 individuals were served by the ministry. For over twenty-five years St Mary's had provided religious education to both Catholic and non-Catholic children, who walked or were transported by bus during midday recess from Jamesville Elementary located a block from the church.[28]

Middle-school students and confirmation preparation classes were also taught at St. Mary's. Altogether about 230 children participated in the religious education program. The parish's social ministry included both generous support for the Eastern Farm Workers organization, and welcome of a twelve-member refugee family from Somalia. This involved helping the family acclimate, providing furniture, clothing, groceries, and household supplies. A St. Mary ministry fair held in the fall of 2006 yielded 216 volunteer lay ministries, including sick calls to homebound and nursing homes, lectors, Eucharistic ministers, altar servers, hospitality, choir, liturgists, bereavement support, youth ministries, and lay religious education teachers in the religious education program.[29]

Given that this was a vital, self-directed group of faithful Catholics, it is perhaps unsurprising that—after pleas to keep their church open fell on deaf ears—St. Mary parishioners followed the lead of similarly beleaguered Boston Catholics. On June 28, 2007, parishioners began a twenty-four-hour vigil to keep the Syracuse diocese from locking their church.[30] For the next six months they occupied their church and held communion services on Sundays and feast days with consecrated hosts supplied by sympathetic priests. On January 30, 2008, as Bishop Moynihan and titular pastor Monsignor Yeazel looked on from a distance, the Onondaga County Sheriff's Office ordered vigil attendees to leave. Yeazel then removed the tabernacle, crucifixes, liturgy books, and consecrated hosts.[31] Thenceforth St. Mary Catholics gathered every week in front of the church, at what they called their "sidewalk parish," for worship and celebration together. This weekly sidewalk parish would continue for several years.

With Kate's assistance, a second administrative recourse was filed to the Congregation for the Clergy, this time against Yeazel for failure of fiduciary responsibility. Although Kate advised committee members that this recourse was unlikely to succeed, LaTray reports that "a few committee members wanted to send a message even if the chances of a favorable outcome were slim." A key issue was the management of St. Mary endowment monies which, as long as the initial recourse was undecided, had to be left unspent. Yeazel had repeatedly declined parishioner requests for an accounting of parish monies, as well as a $100,000 endowment bequest given by former St. Mary's pastor Father John Daley.[32] At a May 7, 2007, meeting Yeazel allegedly told St. Mary parishioners that he would be willing to sell the church for $1.[33] This second recourse to Clergy asked for restoration of weekend Masses, monthly financial reports, and full disclosure about the endowment and appropriate maintenance of the church to be managed by the Building and Grounds chair. A window into the heartfelt sense of betrayal on the part of distraught parishioners is found in the concluding paragraph of the recourse:

> For the last seven months we have proven our ability to sustain and manage the Saint Mary's parish through 100% involvement of the laity and without assistance from a priest or member of the diocese. All we are seeking is a priest to say Mass and perform sacraments. We do not understand why Saint Mary's, a vital, financially solvent, and growing community should be closed, since we are not a burden on the diocese.[34]

On August 5, 2008, the Congregation for the Clergy rejected the St. Mary Appeals Committee's original recourse and upheld the bishop's "suppression of the Parish of St. Mary and the subsequent closing of the Mission Church."[35] It did so on the grounds that "the suppression of the parish in question is well outside of the time limits required by law for its licit presentation."[36] The Congregation for the Clergy considered May 26, 2006, as the date of the bishop's decision, even though he had signed no formal suppression or church relegation decrees at the time, as required by canon law. Since the St. Mary parishioner recourse was filed over a year later, after parishioners were told their church would be closed, the Congregation considered it outside the procedural time limits and rejected it. It was also rejected on the merits, saying the bishop's reasons for suppression and closing "were sufficient." A month later, on September 9, 2008, the St. Mary Appeals Committee received a letter from Bishop Moynihan informing them that their second recourse against Monsignor Yeazel for failing his fiduciary responsibilities was also denied after the Congregation ruled it had no jurisdiction in the matter and referred it back to him as Moynihan was Yeazel's immediate superior.[37]

ST. MARY APPEAL TO THE APOSTOLIC SIGNATURA

Undeterred, on August 26, 2008, intrepid St. Mary's parishioners, led by LaTray, sent a letter via the Vatican's US embassy to Cardinal Raymond Burke at the Apostolic Signatura, announcing their intent to appeal the decision of the Congregation for the Clergy. On November 7 the Signatura secretary, Bishop Frans Daneels, replied, clarifying that LaTray would henceforth be identified as the recurrent party and that she would need to use a Rome-based canon lawyer (also called a "procurator advocate") to pursue the St. Mary recourse. He advised her of the need to submit a deposit of 1,550 euros (roughly $2,000 at the time), and he sent a list of approved canon lawyers.[38] These Rome-based attorneys had their own fees and would bill separately. Attached to the letter was a detailed document explaining the procedures for appealing to the Apostolic Signatura. A section at the end explained how appealing parties with reduced financial means could request gratuitous legal assistance and/or a waiver of the deposit.[39] St. Mary Catholics had sufficient means and soon acquired the services of a procurator-advocate—Carlo Gullo—who was qualified to practice before the Apostolic Signatura.

In December 2008, LaTray—with input and guidance from the Save St. Mary's committee—responded to ten questions sent by Advocate Gullo as he prepared his appeal.[40] Much of the information had already been included in the original recourse to Clergy which Kate had vetted. Worthy of note is Gullo's inquiry about the incidence of sexual misconduct by priests and if the scandal had impacted Mass attendance. The reply from the Appeals Committee referred Gullo to their May 31, 2008, letter to the Congregation for the Clergy referencing a newspaper report about a list of forty-nine priests from the Syracuse diocese alleged to have engaged in sexual misconduct. While St. Mary's had not seen any decline in Mass attendance because of the scandal, they asked, "Is this the reason why the Syracuse diocese is closing financially solvent and liquid parishes like St. Mary's Jamesville to cover the pending and future losses affiliated with the sex abuse scandal?" Kate would later report: "Every case that I sent to Rome had at least one sentence in it mentioning the sex abuse cases and the need for money . . . Rome would not hear of it at first. A shift only came much later—several years after Pope Francis was elected."[41]

On January 27, 2009, Carlo Gullo filed his "Brief for the Appellants" for consideration by the Supreme Tribunal of the Apostolic Signatura.[42] In it he carefully documented why the original recourse should not have been denied on procedural grounds based on dating. For one thing there was no decree signed by Bishop Moynihan on May 25, 2006. There was only a letter from the vicar for parishes which notified some parishioners of the change of name to *mission*. Furthermore, Gullo cited numerous canonical experts to show that a *mission* is a "quasi-parish" and equivalent to a parish in canon law. Therefore, St. Mary was a parish until April 27, 2007, and parishioners had, in fact, submitted their recourse within the procedural time limits.

Acknowledging the legitimacy of a presumed decree date of April 7, 2007, advocate Gullo went on to cite the substantive reasons why St. Mary Parish should not be suppressed. He submitted documentation of the parish's solvency, vitality, and ministerial effectiveness. He quoted Pope Benedict XVI's April 17, 2008, response to questions from American bishops helping young people develop an intimate relationship with God: "And where is this learned? In the family, certainly, in school but especially in the parish. . . . And here a lot remains to be done at the level of preaching and of catechesis in the parishes." Gullo argued that St. Mary Church met none of the "grave reasons" needed to relegate it to profane use before it could be sold. Parishioner documentation revealed that some church property had already been sold for $60,000 a year earlier. Worse, titular pastor Monsignor Yeazel continued showing the church to prospective buyers even as the appeal process was unresolved. Gullo asked for suspension of any movement to sell the church and that Bishop Moynihan "be declared provisionally responsible for custody of the goods of the parish, while reserving the right to petition for damages."[43]

Once the recourse to the Apostolic Signatura was filed, there was nothing to do but wait. The St. Mary Appeals Committee remained very busy, however. Minutes of their February 9, 2009, meeting reveal a discussion of various fundraising options, that finances were "sound," and that the committee had spent $8,000 on the appeal so far. Options for seeking redress in New York civil courts did not appear promising, and parishioners were urged to "stay the course and allow the canonical appeal to mature to a decision." The "Civil Committee" reported, "We are proud that we have handled ourselves in a 'Christian-like' manner. This means acting within canon law, not engaging in attacking behavior, and always being truthful in our dealings with others."[44]

"THE SMOKE OF GOOD JURISPRUDENCE"

In August 2009 a new bishop, Robert J. Cunningham, was appointed to lead the Syracuse diocese. The St. Mary Appeals Committee soon wrote asking him to reconsider the actions of his predecessor. They shared their desire "to initiate a positive dialogue regarding the recourse placed at the Apostolic Signatura by the St. Mary's parishioners."[45] Specifically they requested that St. Mary's become "a model of a laity-led parish," possibly "involving a Parish Life Coordinator and shared pastoral care as an alternative to the one priest, one church philosophy."[46] Cunningham replied on September 25, expressing his opinion that "appropriate consultation and study" had already taken place and it was necessary to await the Signatura decision before proceeding with further dialogue. He assured the committee that "the Syracuse diocese will follow canonical precepts," and encouraged members to "register and faithfully attend another parish."[47]

On November 4, 2009, Carlo Gullo relayed much-anticipated news. The Signatura's promoter of justice had ruled that their appeal could be reviewed for consideration by the Apostolic Signatura, since it was found to have "the smoke of good jurisprudence," a standard Latin phrase meaning there was sufficient probable cause for it to be considered by the court.

UNPRECEDENTED FULL COURT HEARING AT THE APOSTOLIC SIGNATURA

In December 2010, the St. Mary committee received unprecedented news that their case would be heard on February 12 by the full panel of Supreme Tribunal judges. Peter Borré said in a media interview, "This is highly significant because it's the first and only case to my knowledge from an American parish group that's made it all the way to be granted a full court hearing."[48] A cofounder of Boston's Council of Parishes, Borré cited eleven parish appeals from Boston which had all been denied. A "cautiously optimistic" LaTray told the *Post-Standard*, "Our decision to appeal has been confirmed every step of the way. . . . We know we have a strong case. We are financially solvent, growing, located in an expanding community, and have a strong active ministry."[49]

A month later, the Congregation for the Clergy began issuing surprising new decrees ruling that while bishops in Allentown, Pennsylvania, and Springfield, Massachusetts, could suppress eleven appealing parishes, they could not close and sell their churches.[50] The tide had somehow turned, at least partially.

Church reform advocates at FutureChurch were quick to realize that such "split decisions" could slow the wholesale dismantling of viable parish communities. Citing civil efforts to tax closed churches,[51] the organization noted: "If the Vatican upholds similar parishioner appeals now pending in Cleveland and elsewhere, diocesan bishops will be less inclined to suppress small, vibrant and solvent parishes especially if they are forbidden to sell buildings and land that could now be subject to property taxes."[52] Meanwhile the St. Mary hearing at the Apostolic Signatura had been postponed from February 12 until sometime in May. In March, parishioners from another Syracuse parish, Holy Trinity, learned that their church would also remain open, making this the twelfth "split decision" from the Congregation for the Clergy.[53] In a portent of things to come, a spokesperson for the Syracuse diocese gave a decidedly sour grapes quote to the Associated Press: "All it says is it (Holy Trinity) is designated as a church building. It is still a church . . . we don't have to reopen the church."[54]

SIGNATURA DECREES THAT ST. MARY'S CHURCH, JAMESVILLE, MUST REMAIN OPEN

On May 21, 2011, the highest court in the Catholic Church ruled that St. Mary Church, Jamesville, could not be closed and sold. The Apostolic Signatura decree rejected the Congregation for the Clergy's decision that St. Mary parishioners had not acted within the procedural time limits for filing their appeal and therefore their recourse was valid. However—as in similar rulings in Allentown and Springfield—it upheld Bishop Moynihan's original merger of St. Mary Parish with Holy Cross Parish.[55] The high court cited church law that "the reasons and motivations (for mergers and suppressions) are to be just, not on the other hand grave."[56] In other words, canon law leaves "just reasons" for merging parishes to the discretion of the bishop. But it requires a different standard to deconsecrate and sell a church. These decisions require "grave reasons, not only just ones," the ruling pointed out. Furthermore, the high court noted that since the decision to close and sell St. Mary Church rested "simply upon a proposed general pastoral restructuring," it was necessary to "differentiate carefully between the process of restructuring [the parishes of the diocese] and the determination concerning the canonical status of the sacred buildings."[57] Therefore, regarding closure and sale of St. Mary Church, the Signatura ruled, "The decision of his Excellency the Bishop of Syracuse is invalidated because on the legal merits it violated the provisions of canon 1222 p.2."[58] This canon pertains to the need for "grave cause" and "the consent of those who legitimately claim rights for themselves in the church" and stipulates that "the good of souls suffers no detriment thereby."[59] Insofar as the standard of "grave cause" to close and deconstruct St. Mary Church was not met, and insofar as a community of the faithful was committed to preserving their church and would suffer detriment should it be closed, the St. Mary parishioners were upheld in their appeal. Because the Signatura's decision was based on the legal merits and not procedural issues, the sentence was definitive, with no further possibility of canonical appeal.[60]

On Tuesday, May 24, ecstatic St. Mary parishioners gathered outside the church, hugging each other as they heard the news. "We are so grateful to God," said former St. Mary trustee Tony DeBottis. "It took too long to right a wrong," he said, "but when you're right, you are right."[61] As she read the Vatican decree on the steps of the church, LaTray said, "I was overcome with emotion . . . especially when I read the part of the decision based upon merit. I remember two other committee members standing on either side of me, putting their hands on my shoulders for support."[62] Winning a decision based on merit was very important, said LaTray, because "Sister Kate had always prepared for us to receive the same type of decrees that other prior churches had experienced . . . there were a few churches who 'won' based on procedure only and the diocese then corrected the procedure. The churches always ended up closed as a result."[63] The parishioners hoped this would not be the case with St. Mary Church, Jamesville. Three months later, when St. Mary appellants received a full translation of the Signatura ruling, they were advised by canon lawyer Gullo to ask Bishop Cunningham to immediately reopen the church for worship, as this was far from certain.

SYRACUSE DIOCESE BALKS BUT LOSES APPEAL

In fact, getting Bishop Cunningham to open the church for regular worship proved very difficult. It would be thirteen months before he permitted a Mass to be celebrated at St. Mary Church.[64] Even then, the Mass was held in the middle of the day with very little advance notice. In the interim, the diocese decided to appeal the decision from the Apostolic Signatura.[65] On September 12, 2011, having received no official communication from the diocese, the St. Mary's Appeals Committee signed a letter to Bishop Cunningham asking for "the immediate and effective reopening of the church of St. Mary's (in accordance with canons 1214, 1218-1219) so that our rights as [the] faithful are not further injured."[66] On September 21 the bishop sent a surprising response which essentially rejected the Signatura's final ruling: "It appears that the petition is based upon the belief that the Signatura has acted definitively and conclusively in this matter," he wrote. The bishop had decided to pursue the matter further with the Signatura:

> Significantly grave reasons exist to support the full amalgamation of St. Mary's with and into Holy Cross Church. Therefore, I believe that the Congregation for the Clergy and the Sacred Signatura will uphold our application of Canon 1222.2 to St. Mary's in Jamesville. I am taking the appropriate actions to initiate

this further review. Therefore, no further action related to this matter will be taken until the matter is fully concluded.[67]

Cunningham's action led to yet another round of canonical jousting, but he was on the wrong side of canon law. On November 18 the Apostolic Signatura ruled that the bishop's revised decree was "illegitimate on its merits," affirming its original decision that St. Mary's could not be sold, and must remain open for worship. St. Mary activists planned a Christmas prayer service to celebrate the positive outcome of the appeal on Tuesday December 20, 2011. A day earlier, LaTray told the Associated Press: "We are hopeful that we will reopen," and noted that the Syracuse diocese had assured them it "would follow the precepts of canon law."[68] On December 21, 2011, LaTray received a letter from Archbishop Frans Daneels at the Apostolic Signatura which said, "The Supreme Tribunal has made clear that the church of St. Mary retains the canonical status of a sacred building dedicated to divine worship to which the faithful have of access for that purpose (cf. can. 1214). Said status presupposes that some form of worship will actually take place within the church."[69] Yet Daneels carefully pointed out that "the extent of that worship—both its type and its frequency—is generally not determined by the law and therefore remains within the discretion of the competent authority, that is, first of all, the parish priest of the parish which has responsibility for the church in light of the specific circumstances, including the fact that the church of St. Mary has not been designated the principal church of the merged parish." Before relaying his confidence that "a serene solution can be reached in due time," Daneels mentioned that none other than Cardinal Burke himself "had the opportunity to explain the Segnatura's [*sic*] decision to the Bishop during his recent *ad limina* visit to Rome."[70]

Unfortunately, no "serene solution" would ever be reached. Although St. Mary Catholics had saved their church from the wrecking ball, their hopes and expectations for a return to regular weekend Masses never materialized. Monsignor Yeazel opposed the idea of regular Masses at St. Mary Church even though several area priests had offered.[71] In this he had the support of Bishop Cunningham. On January 10, 2012, Cunningham issued a public statement promising that "from time to time" church services would be held at St. Mary Church and that weddings and funerals could also be celebrated there by members of Holy Cross Parish. He also carefully stipulated that as St. Mary was no longer a separate parish, the church building would not be open to the public and regularly scheduled services would not be held there.[72]

As the pastor of the newly merged parish, Monsignor Yeazel was the "competent authority" to determine what worship would take place at St. Mary, Jamesville. On January 20, 2012, he met with two representatives from the St. Mary Appeals Committee, Jack and Regina Clinton, in hopes of "extending an olive branch," and bringing "peace, healing and reconcilia-tion."[73] A summary of the meeting notes prepared by the St. Mary committee reveals that Yeazel reported Cardinal Burke had told Bishop Cunningham that he could not sell the church building, but that it could be used for other purposes such as a food pantry. Furthermore, according to a disingenuous Yeazel, none other than Cardinal Burke had said there could be no Sunday Mass at the church and that the building should remain locked all the time.[74] As a possible solution, Yeazel had the bishop's permission to make St. Mary Church into an oratory which would allow it to be open several times a week for prayer. This could include the presence of the Eucharist, benediction, novenas, and extended hours. In return, he expected the St. Mary community to discontinue Sunday sidewalk prayer services and stipulated that Holy Cross must initiate all prayer services. Likewise there could be no unauthor-ized services, especially communion services, and no sit-ins or occupation of the church beyond the stated hours. He further announced that Holy Cross would sell the rectory and its contents, probably at auction. Furthermore, since the church building was the property of Holy Cross Parish, he, the pas-tor, would determine its use. As to timeline, Yeazel told the Clintons that he would restore gas and electric utilities that same week, and complete needed repairs and cleaning over the next several months, with a view to opening the oratory around Easter. He concluded by stating he felt he was reaching out to the degree he could, which was "more than the bishop wanted or was required to do."[75]

Evidence of the severe distrust between Yeazel and St. Mary activists is found in the fact that on the very same day—January 20, 2012—other members of the St. Mary Appeals Committee were meeting with the New York State attorney general to explore civil options with regard to church finances. There were reasons. The church building superintendent had told the Clintons that money from the sale of the rectory would be used to repair the roof of the church. Yet prior documentation submitted to the Vatican during the appeals process revealed that the $60,000 sale of the parish ball field was to have been used for the roof repair, yet Yeazel had never authorized it. In fact, even though the canonical recourse was in process, he had initially sought to have the $60,000 check made payable to Holy Cross rather than St. Mary. The purchasers refused and made the check payable to St. Mary instead.[76] As a result, the church now had water damage in the loft, and mold in the basement. Perhaps Yeazel expected the Vatican to uphold the bishop's decision to sell the church and therefore delayed repairs. In any case trust had been lost. This is reflected in a January 22 email from LaTray to the Gullos: "Unfortunately there has been a pattern and series of unfulfilled promises leading to feelings of mistrust with the pastor at Holy Cross."[77]

After the disheartening January 20 meeting with Yeazel, the St. Mary committee wrote a lengthy, scathing letter to Bishop Cunningham informing him that the monsignor's proposals were "totally unacceptable to us as recurrents."[78] Citing their rights in canon and civil law, they reiterated "the urgency of reopening St. Mary's promptly to ordinary worship to meet the spiritual needs of the faithful of Jamesville and of surrounding areas." As to canon law, the letter said, "the establishment of an Oratory may only be done through a decree by the bishop of the diocese." In civil law, the proposals were understood to be inconsistent with their rights as beneficiaries "whose interests must be protected by those functioning as trustees of the St. Mary property." In addition, the committee requested "a full financial accounting of assets transferred to Holy Cross in 2007," and reflected the belief that "we have been grievously damaged by your failure to comply with two Signatura decrees, many months after the fact." A concluding statement threatened, "Failing a satisfactory agreement, we are ready to proceed both under canon law and under civil law." Copies were sent to Monsignor Yeazel and Christopher Wiles, the assistant attorney general of New York State.[79]

On January 31, 2012, Bishop Cunningham replied, and this time he was supported by both canon and civil law. With regard to the assets of the parish he noted: "As the Diocese has previously indicated [your] attorney may easily reach our diocesan attorney. A conversation with Mrs. Simmons will clarify the meaning of the New York State Religious Corporation Law including the question of the corporate membership. The New York Court of Appeals has recently reaffirmed the law in this manner."[80] Noting that the merger of St. Mary Parish with Holy Cross had been upheld by the Apostolic Signatura, he advised, "Your pastor is now the primary recourse in the pastoral care of Holy Cross Parish which encompasses the territory of the former Jamesville parish."[81] Furthermore, he said his decree regarding the use of St. Mary Church had been published and contained "the full extent of my intentions for the use of St. Mary's church building."[82] A closing sentence suggested that his decree detailing the proposed use of the church had recently been confirmed by Rome.[83] In late February, the committee received a letter from the Congregation for the Clergy dated February 3, 2012, relaying that Bishop Cunningham had sent them a copy of his January 10 press statement "to the effect that the church will remain open for sacred worship, albeit in a limited capacity, for various liturgical functions."[84] Therefore, Clergy found the bishop had executed the Signatura decree that St. Mary Church must not be reduced to profane use, and furthermore, "The provisions made are deemed consistent with the provisions of can. 1214 CIC. With this disposition, the Dicastery considers the recourse definitively concluded."[85]

Slowly, the St. Mary Appeals Committee began to realize that further discussion with the bishop was unlikely to yield hoped-for outcomes. Advisors with legal expertise had also counseled them that pursuing civil recourse would be expensive and unlikely to succeed.[86] On February 19, committee member Christopher Prosak wrote a conciliatory letter to Monsignor Yeazel asking to meet again to "further discuss your proposal," and "come to an amicable resolution, one that creates the pastoral harmony we both seek."[87] But the monsignor was having none of it. On February 24 he sent Prosak a perfunctory reply and referenced Cunningham's January 31 letter saying, "The contents of the Bishop's letter stating that the latest Signatura correspondence indicates the solution to be followed is his sentiment and mine."[88]

In the months that followed, relationships between Yeazel and the Appeals Committee reached what can only be called a nadir. The adversarial state of affairs was further stoked by evidence that Monsignor Yeazel was trying to declare St. Mary Church unsafe, with a view to demolishing it. In March 2012 a company hired by the diocese at Yeazel's behest recommended structural repairs of $250,000, even though the building had been judged to be sound just one year earlier when the Signatura found there were no grounds to demolish it on the basis of irreparability.[89] In response, the Appeals Committee sent a letter to Cunningham on April 24 to say that "multiple sources" had made them aware that the diocese was considering demolishing St. Mary Church. The letter also expressed appreciation that Cunningham had "taken a stand against this tactic and recommended that Holy Cross make necessary repairs toward the reopening of the church."[90] On April 25, the Town of DeWitt inspected the church at the request of the diocese, in LaTray's words, "for the pastor's intended purpose of demolishing St. Mary's church building."[91] Whereupon the Town of DeWitt "verbally informed the diocese that the building is not condemnable and then put coding information in writing."[92]

After the city said the church building was not condemnable, Yeazel finally gave in. On Sunday July 22, 2012, as St. Mary Catholics gathered for their usual Sunday sidewalk prayer, he sent a verbal message to say he did not plan to sell or demolish their church. Over the next two weeks long-awaited repairs were at last completed in preparation for the use of the church. The St. Mary Appeals Committee requested that Mass be celebrated on August 15, the Feast of the Assumption.[93] On August 13, the *Syracuse Post-Standard* carried news of the milestone.[94] As LaTray remembers it, "The church was packed with standing room only and many more parishioners were standing out on the sidewalk on the street."[95] Yet after the Mass, she learned "Msgr. Yeazel was so upset with the success in numbers, that he said to his own staff that he would never hold a Mass at St. Mary's again."[96]

On August 29, members of the St. Mary Appeals Committee sent an exuberant letter of thanks to Yeazel: "An overflow crowd celebrated the simple liturgy. Participation was heartfelt and joyous. It was truly a memorable occasion. There must be some way we can capture this spirit. We should meet soon to exchange ideas and work together toward this attainable goal. Thank you on behalf of the St. Mary's faithful."[97] Bishop Cunningham was copied. Unfortunately, Yeazel never responded to the letter, and subsequent requests to meet with the pastor and/or the bishop were not granted.[98]

Given Monsignor Yeazel's failed efforts to demolish the church even after the Vatican said this could not happen, it is easy to see why the St. Mary Appeals Committee did not trust him—their purported pastor—to have their best interests at heart. This apparent betrayal, as well as Yeazel's subsequent refusal to grant permission for three longtime St. Mary parishioners to celebrate a baptism, a funeral, and a wedding, led to a spate of new appeals to Rome. Over the next two years the St. Mary committee—through their advocates, Carlo and Alessia Gullo—asked the Congregation for the Clergy, the Roman Rota, and as a last resort Cardinal Raymond Burke at the Apostolic Signatura, to intervene and allow their church to open for worship. In every case they were told that these curial departments were not the competent authority to consider their requests. They were referred back to Monsignor Yeazel and Bishop Cunningham.[99] Considering Yeazel's attempt to flout the Vatican's mandate and demolish St. Mary Church, one can only wonder at the lack of prudential judgment on the part of Bishop Cunningham. True to his word, Yeazel did not schedule any other Masses at St. Mary. Neither did he keep up with ongoing repairs. On November 30, 2014, faithful St. Mary Catholics appealed to Cunningham to intervene and allow them to affiliate with a new pastor—perhaps from nearby parishes—who "understands the value of St. Mary's and who will take care of St. Mary's, both spiritually and physically."[100] They noted that the church remained locked, opening only for an hour's prayer service or Eucharistic adoration once or twice a year. A copy was sent to Yeazel.[101] Their requests went unheard.

In the ensuing years, Monsignor Yeazel, supported by Bishop Cunningham, adopted a minimalistic, not to say vindictive, practice of allowing Masses or prayer services just once or twice a year at St. Mary Church, often on short notice. Except for rare occasions the church remains locked and shuttered to this day.[102] Yet the St. Mary faithful stayed together as a community. Over one hundred people attended a September 2016 Mass, one of the few held since 2012. "We had so many people attend, it just shows the community is here," said Francis Nelson, a member of the Appeals Committee.[103] The priest presider, Fr. Louis Segliuzzo, agreed, "I could see that they were really kind of gathered together as an assembly, a congregation."[104] When asked if she would do the appeals process all over again, LaTray replied,

When I was very young, I was taught "When you see a wrong, try and right it." Everything about the potential closing of a vibrant, financially solvent church in

a growing community seemed wrong, since it was primarily volunteer parishioners who cared for and ran the church. The number of Catholic parishioners was
declining across the country and the world but not at St. Mary's. The closure
decision did not make any sense from a Christian standpoint.[105]

Although all of St. Mary's liquid assets were taken after the parish was
merged, LaTray takes comfort in the fact that "they were not able to bulldoze
the church as was the case in other parts of the country."[106]

Chapter 6

Making a Way Where
There was No Way

ST. VINCENT PALLOTTI PARISH—DIOCESE OF
CAMDEN, NEW JERSEY

The pastor and people of St. Vincent Pallotti (SVP) parish engaged in a multi-year struggle to save their parish and its church from utter destruction. Their victory became the linchpin upon which succeeding successful appeals turned. Sister Kate's canonical creativity and her well-timed letter to Cardinal Raymond Burke, the prefect of the Apostolic Signatura, literally made a way through canon law where previously there had been none. This victory is important because for the first time, Rome's Apostolic Signatura essentially ruled that Camden bishop Joseph Galante's "intent" to merge and close St. Vincent Pallotti Parish was not equivalent to a formal decree to merge and close, and that this formal decree must be supplied to parishioners if they are to exercise the canonical right to pursue recourse. Yet this victory would not have happened without the integrity and brilliance of SVP's courageous pastor, Msgr. Louis Marucci, whose persistence, combined with Kate's canonical expertise, finally convinced Roman officials to look twice at the misguided decisions made by too many US bishops who seemed to view parish communities as businesses rather than spiritual families. The SVP victory came at no small cost. There are many heroes in the SVP story, not least of whom is Monsignor Marucci himself.

The parish of St. Vincent Pallotti in Haddon Township, New Jersey, was formed in 1963 from five surrounding parishes. As the parish grew, its largely blue-collar Catholics worked hard to pay off the building debt. When a new first-time pastor, Msgr. Louis Marucci, arrived in 2002, he brought an unusual dynamism. Parishioners described their parish as having "a rebirth" after his arrival. Weekly Mass attendance tallied 32.7 percent (981 of nearly

3,000 parishioners), well above the national average of 23 percent, and well above nearby St. Aloysius Parish which stood at only 16.6 percent.[1] But SVP parishioners proudly noted: "Attending Mass at St. Vincent Pallotti is not simply sitting in the pew for 50-60 minutes and leaving the building. It is total involvement and participation."[2]

Marucci deeply believed in the concept of stewardship as a way of life, and inculcated that belief in his parishioners. The parish paid all of its bills and regularly led the diocese in support of the bishop's annual appeal. He asked his people not only to focus on treasure but on time and talent as well:

> I require all the parishioners to commit to at least one ministry for at least one year. And if it is not life-giving, it's not a death sentence. They can try something else, and they're welcome to engage in more ministries. But it was opening that door and allowing them to get engaged, that created that parish to be, I think, as vibrant as it was.[3]

When Marucci arrived, there were exactly three altar servers, two lectors, and a small woman's club. The parish trustees, pastoral council, and finance council existed in name only. The new pastor's energetic leadership quickly reinvigorated all three critical functions. A trained harpist, Marucci's passion for all things musical encouraged parishioners to start a music ministry which, along with a newly formed Art and Environment Committee, greatly

Figure 6.1   St. Vincent Pallotti Church in Haddon Township, New Jersey, ca. 2005. Renamed St. Joseph the Worker Parish in October 2011. Photo courtesy Friends of St. Vincent Pallotti

enhanced Sunday worship. People soon signed up to become ushers, greeters, Eucharistic ministers, and sacristans. Committees to help the homebound and assist the impoverished attracted scores of volunteers. A Youth Ministry program focused on spiritual and social development for middle and high school students. By 2008, the vibrant community offered thirty-seven active parish ministries through which Catholics could exercise and grow in their faith.

SVP attracted worshippers from thirty-four zip codes in New Jersey, Pennsylvania, and Virginia. Parish leaders observed: "They feel as if this is a church where the congregation extends themselves to make them feel welcomed. The Pastor not only greets everyone but also wants to know everyone."[4]

ABOUT MONSIGNOR MARUCCI

Louis Marucci is an unusual pastor. For one thing, the middle-aged priest gets around in a motorized wheelchair. He was diagnosed with multiple sclerosis in 1987, just six months after being ordained a priest for the diocese of Camden. In a May 2008 interview with the *Philadelphia Inquirer* he described his disability as both a cross and a crown.[5] The cross is a devastating and unpredictable chronic disease that attacked his body's immune system. After rigorous rehabilitation, he regained the use of his arms and was eventually able to live independently, albeit in a tricked-out motorized wheelchair. For Marucci, the hidden crown is that his illness has deepened his relationship with God. He describes himself as "tremendously, tremendously blessed . . . had it not been for the MS maybe my life and priesthood would have gone along in a very different path . . . but you know, when you have a need for God you have a need for God."[6] The disability also provided an unexpected opportunity for study. The monsignor proudly points to four master's degrees including a master of arts in philanthropy and development, and a master of science in church management. He also earned a doctorate in ministry, specializing in medical moral end-of-life issues, and is currently working on a second doctorate, this time in organizational development and change.[7]

For the first part of his priesthood, Marucci served primarily in administrative positions at the Camden diocesan offices. In 1999 he became the director of development, with a mandate to create a comprehensive development structure for the diocese. He would later hold this position simultaneously with that of pastor of SVP, an assignment he accepted in 2002. Marucci proved to be a very able development director for the Camden diocese. In one year he more than doubled donations to the bishop's annual appeal, going from $2.2 million to $5.8 million. By 2005, with Marucci's skilled leadership, the bishop's annual appeal generated nearly $8 million annually from faithful donors.[8]

In April 2004, Joseph Galante was appointed the seventh bishop of Camden. He decided to restructure diocesan administration and began changing all of his predecessor's appointments. Three years later Marucci left his diocesan position to devote his full energies to being the pastor of SVP. As he remembers it, there "wasn't any kind of animosity" between him and Galante when he departed: "The bishop just wanted his own organizational system."[9] A year later, the relationship between this gifted priest and his bishop would be strained to the breaking point. Ethics and transparency in fundraising—two values Marucci holds sacred—led a passionate pastor and his outraged parishioners to oppose their bishop's imprudent decisions all the way to the Vatican's highest court.

A DIOCESAN PLANNING PROCESS GONE AWRY

The courageous advocacy of SVP parishioners and their intrepid pastor begins with their good faith participation in a Camden diocese planning process conducted between 2004 and 2008. After his arrival in 2004, Bishop Galante met with individual parishes over a period of fifteen months. Six pastoral priorities for the diocese were identified. In the fall of 2006, the diocese launched a planning process called "Gathering God's Gifts" with a goal of revitalizing parish life.[10] Each parish was asked to create a Pastoral Planning Team tasked with evaluating their parish's vitality and—using previously endorsed diocesan pastoral goals—to plan the future pastoral activity in their parish. The Phase I process was short-lived.

On January 6, 2007, Galante began a massive reconfiguration of Camden parishes (Phase II) by calling a diocesan-wide meeting of delegates from each parish's Pastoral Planning Team. After some confusion—largely owing to the fact that earlier, carefully considered parishioner input was nowhere in evidence—it soon became apparent that the new function of the parish planning teams was to reconfigure parishes rather than to plan pastoral activity.[11] Parish delegates were told that owing to age, retirement, sickness, and death, a decline of 50 percent of available priests was projected for 2015 compared to 2006 numbers. Fewer than eighty-five active priests would be available in 2015 to serve the diocese's five hundred thousand Catholics.[12] Parish planners were now asked to plan pastoral care according to the number of priests that would be available for their geographic locale. A Diocesan Planning Commission was introduced, and planners were given a manual which included data specific to each parish within their deanery. A deanery is a group of parishes, usually in the same geographic area, that is presided over by a "dean" who is normally a priest. In coming months parish meetings would yield information to be shared at regional meetings. Regional deliberations would then filter up and inform decisions to be made at deanery meetings. Deanery input would then be followed by meetings at the diocesan level between Bishop Galante and the Diocesan Planning Commission.[13]

Parish planning teams were given five models to consider:

1. Merger. Two or more parishes close and become one new parish.
2. Cluster. A pastor has responsibility for two or three parishes with added staff at each parish.
3. Priest team. A team of priests with designated moderator assumes pastoral care of several parishes
4. One-priest-one-parish. A single parish with its own pastor.
5. Director of parish life with a sacramental priest. A deacon, religious, lay minister assumes pastoral care of a parish with priests appointed as canonical pastor and sacramental minister.

In February and March 2007, the SVP parish planning team participated in three regional meetings with two of the nine other parishes in Deanery III. The goal was to create and submit a reconfiguration recommendation that required just six full-time priests for the deanery compared to the eleven that served it at the time. After extensive discussion and planning the SVP cohort, which included Holy Saviour Parish in Westmont and Christ the King in Haddonfield, chose a cluster model which would require two priests to serve the three parishes. In mid-May all members of the ten-parish cohort that comprised Deanery III met to review the final report to be submitted to the Diocesan Planning Commission. Deanery III successfully met the goal of reconfiguring with six priests. Three parishes (the SVP cohort) chose to cluster, two chose to merge, three chose a one-priest-one-parish model, and two chose the director-of-parish life model.[14]

But at a September 29 diocesan-wide meeting in the presence of Bishop Galante, the teams learned from the Diocesan Planning Commission that most of their carefully considered plans had been rejected. No plans involving clustering were approved. Neither were plans that involved lay administrators. Only one-priest-one-parish or merger models were approved. This led SVP parish leaders to conclude: "It became evident that merger was the only pre-conceived model that the Bishop would accept."[15]

One could reasonably wonder why the diocese even offered five potential models to parish planners if only two were acceptable. Furthermore, planners were quick to observe that, of the five models initially offered, only the merger model directly impacted the temporal assets of the parishes. This would therefore "provide an opportunity for the bishop to accumulate parish assets."[16] In a merger, the assets and liabilities of both parishes are combined, and the new parish becomes responsible for all assets and debts of both. In some instances, parishes owed the diocese back due assessments and/or loans. In the merger model, the assets of a wealthier merged parish could be used to pay off the diocesan debt of a poorer parish. In their canonical recourse to Rome, SVP parishioners wrote they "are most concerned that this entire process was nothing more than a means to obtain the temporal goods of the parishes and had no direct bearing to Phase I planning of pastoral priorities."[17] They decried a flawed planning process wherein "the Parish plans were arbitrarily dismissed at the level of the Diocesan Planning Commission and Presbyteral Council levels."[18] Worse, SVP leaders alleged, "these plans were arbitrarily dismissed because the cluster model did not provide the opportunity for the bishop to obtain the temporal goods he desired."[19]

SOME PLANNERS WALK OUT; OTHERS GO BACK TO DRAWING BOARD

At the same September 29, 2007, meeting, the Diocesan Commission announced an even more surprising change. Despite months of reconfiguration meetings based on the need to reduce the number of priests in each deanery, parish planners were now told that priest numbers were no longer a primary driver or indicator to be used in reconfiguration. A new planning process would begin and now the primary indicator was creating "vibrant and dynamic" parishes. The implicit assumption that many Camden parishes were not already vibrant and dynamic was not lost on those in attendance. According to the SVP planners present, "This abrupt change in indicators was a huge upset and annoyed numerous members of the parish planning teams in all the deaneries throughout the diocese. At this point, a number of participants walked out of the meeting and did not return."[20] In addition, said SVP observers, "those members who continued on to the Deanery level meetings began to question the purpose of the planning, concerns related to a lack of transparency on the part of the Bishop and the Diocese, and if the entire purpose of planning was merely an attempt to absorb parish assets."[21] There was additional speculation that the abrupt change had occurred because a shortage of priests is not a canonically defensible reason for suppressing a parish or closing a church.[22] Since Bishop Galante had a doctorate in canon law from Rome's Pontifical Lateran University and was presumably aware of canonical precepts, such speculation is not unwarranted.

Parish planners were instructed to begin a new planning process and given a series of questions to reflect upon. Some, including SVP, were required to begin planning with parishes in their geographical area even if these were outside their deaneries. When Monsignor Marucci and Carmela DiMaria, the chair of the SVP planning team, attended the first meetings of Deanery II, they were dismayed to discover that a proposal for St. Aloysius Parish to begin planning with SVP had already been submitted—without their knowledge—to the Rev. George Seiter, dean of Deanery II. The fact that Seiter was also the pastor of St. Aloysius Parish suggested to more than a few that a preconceived plan involving the two parishes existed at the diocese.[23] Previously each parish grouping was told to submit its plan to the diocese directly. Now the Diocesan Planning Commission required the entire deanery to vote on the plans to be submitted. For Deanery II, this meant that fifty-six delegates would vote to decide which configurations to submit.

Over the next three months, the parishes in Deanery II met in three regional groupings to consider various parish configurations. As the meetings progressed, according to a recourse subsequently submitted to Rome, "the configuration of St. Aloysius Parish and Holy Maternity Parish merging with SVP parish, with SVP as the parish seat, moved consistently to the top of the list of preferred deanery merging configurations."[24]

On December 4, 2007, a final, formal vote was held in which fifty-four of fifty-six deanery delegates voted to merge Holy Maternity, St. Aloysius, and SVP, with SVP as the parish seat.[25] The SVP campus was selected as the worship site because of its spaciousness, ample parking, new buildings, vibrant ministries, disability access, closeness to Holy Maternity and St. Aloysius parishioners, and financial stability.[26] Just three days later, on December 7, 2007, Marucci dedicated a new million-dollar addition to the SVP campus, including a new rectory, memorial hall, and parish offices. Marucci had initially asked Bishop Galante to preside, but was advised to dedicate the new facility himself, as the bishop was not available.

With the reconfiguration decision made, the merging parishes were asked to complete reports about the vibrancy of their configuration. As a final step, planners were to attend a meeting at the selected worship site to complete Diocesan Planning Commission forms. A significant glitch arose when the dean of Deanery II and pastor of St. Aloysius Parish, Rev. George Seiter, failed to respond to telephone calls and messages from the SVP planning chairperson. St. Aloysius did not participate in any meetings with the other two parishes to create the final document. They only submitted input a few hours prior to the final gathering at SVP.

Seiter would be roundly criticized by both Holy Maternity and SVP planners for his lack of professionalism and for providing "a poor example of transparency and cooperation."[27] As a result, SVP and Holy Maternity planners completed the final forms themselves and submitted them to the diocesan facilitator, Mr. Rod Herrera, and to Seiter on January 8, 2008. These were then submitted to the Diocesan Planning Commission. In the first round of planning, each parish had received a copy of the dean's summary report. But when the SVP planning team requested a copy of Reverend Seiter's summary report, they were told that it would only be made available to the Diocesan Planning Commission, not to the parishes.[28] These events led SVP parishioners to become concerned "that the Rev. Seiter was manipulating the process." They also expressed "serious concerns about allegiances between the bishop and his deans, since none of the deans' parishes was suppressed or lost their status as a parish site when the final decisions of this phase were proclaimed."[29]

A SHOCKING ANNOUNCEMENT

In an April 3, 2008, video posted on the diocesan website at 1:30 p.m., Bishop Joseph Galante announced his intent to decrease the number of parishes in the diocese of Camden, from 124 to 66.[30] He described the closings as "radical" in their scope, and indeed they were "among the largest ever undertaken by a U.S. diocese."[31] The new restructuring consisted of thirty-eight merged parishes, three clusters involving six parishes, and twenty-two stand-alone parishes.[32] To the shock and dismay of Monsignor Marucci and SVP parish leaders, Galante announced his intention to merge SVP, Haddon Township, and St. Aloysius in Oaklyn, New Jersey, at the St. Aloysius site.[33] Camden's bishop had ignored the nearly unanimous decision of Deanery II planners which named SVP as the parish seat. Instead, the parish, its church, and its brand-new state-of-the-art, handicapped-accessible facilities were slated to be merged at St. Aloysius, with no indication that they would be used in the future. Marucci first heard the announcements at a priests' gathering at the cathedral earlier that morning. He well remembers what happened after the SVP decision was announced:

> Some of the priests around me gasped when they heard it. I didn't stay for the rest of the meeting. I was sitting in the middle of the aisle because there was no place for me to sit in my wheelchair. I just turned around and rolled out the cathedral door. There was a reporter there who asked me a question. I said, "No, I don't have any comment at this time." And I went back and immediately called and asked to appeal that decision. Everybody was caught off guard because that was not what the deanery delegates proposed.[34]

One SVP parishioner, Ed Pierzynski, told a Camden newspaper that he was convinced the press announcement was mistaken. "They put it backwards. Everybody's got this wrong," he thought.[35] But there was no mistake. John Canuso described his stunned reaction to the *Philadelphia Inquirer*, "I can't tell you it was as bad as my daughter dying, but it was pretty bad." Canuso had given $400,000 to the SVP building fund. The spacious newly dedicated parish hall had been named for his daughter, Joan "Babe" Canuso Fischer, who died in 2005 at the age of forty. "This is Babe's legacy," he said. "I have to keep that alive."[36] One week later in the *Camden Courier-Post* Marucci connected his experience with multiple sclerosis to learning that his parish was slated to close: "One physically took the breath out of me, the other spiritually took the breath out of me."[37] In the midst of the turmoil the monsignor asked his congregation to maintain their respect of the bishop and to be in communication with the people of St. Aloysius. His sermons counseled: "Don't let the issues you may have with religion destroy your faith [in God]. Be accountable in your faith: reverent and respectful." Yet, he said his "greatest pain in all of this is the hurt of the parishioners."[38]

DIOCESAN BID TO ACQUIRE ASSETS AND VIOLATION OF DONOR INTENT

In the coming months Marucci did not hesitate to comment when the media came calling. It was important for the public to know that the delegates from Deanery II had overwhelmingly chosen SVP as the premier worship site. Plus he says,

> I was so driven to do this because I had been the director of development at the diocese. And I would always say that the appropriate response to a gift from a donor is stewardship of the donor's gift. . . . As a professional development officer, I never wanted to be put in a position that violated donor intent. It violates the ethical principles of the Association of Fund-Raising Professionals.[39]

Yet Galante's intent to close SVP and sell the church property had put Marucci—and the diocese—in exactly the position of ignoring the intent of hundreds of SVP donors, like John Canuso, who had pledged over $1 million to build the new facilities at the parish. Aside from being a violation of canon law, this violated civil laws in New Jersey.

Irate parishioners immediately raised this issue with Monsignor Marucci, who in turn raised it with the bishop. Marucci quickly sent a letter to Galante listing serious reasons why he should reconsider: parishioner concerns about potentially fraudulent activity because the bishop had granted permission to construct the new memorial hall and chapel . . . and ethical issues around restricted gifts and responsible stewardship toward donors. He also stated that the SVP closure plan looked as if the diocese was attempting to absorb SVP assets, "as this is the only parish incorporated under the name of the

Diocese of Camden." Finally, he cited a "lack of sufficient knowledge by the Presbyteral Council." Marucci then requested that the bishop implement other possible options, such as clustering SVP and St. Aloysius together, allowing SVP to remain a stand-alone parish, or permitting SVP to remain a worship site.[40]

Galante responded the same day. He referred to what he viewed as a "bottom up" planning process for the merger. He suggested that (and this is the actual sentence), "A review of the data that went into this recommendation should sufficiently provide you with the information that went into this decision to provide the concrete data that you seek."[41] As for the selection of the worship site, he said he had "leaned heavily on the advice of the Diocesan Planning Commission and very especially on the wise counsel of the Presbyteral Council." He expressed his wish that Marucci would "lead your people to be supportive of this decision for the good of the new parish."[42]

On April 7 Marucci again asked Galante to reconsider, reprising original concerns about restricted gifts and the requirement to respect donor intent. He relayed serious questions raised by parishioners that led them to believe that the diocese was closing their vibrant parish as a strategy "to absorb assets that belong to the parishioners." He enclosed a letter from John D. Wilson, an attorney who was also the president of the SVP Parish Council, who noted he had been contacted by other attorneys and parishioners concerned about the deed associated with the parish. It showed that the Diocese of Camden was the property owner of the thirty-five-acre tract of land upon which the SVP parish facilities sat. This is unusual. In most parishes, the land upon which the church stands is owned by the parish, not the diocese. When SVP was built, a complicated zoning issue led the diocese to hold the deed to the property. Located on the same thirty-five-acre tract of land were Pope Paul VI High School, a large parking lot maintained by both the school and the parish, and a convent. The assessed value of the entire complex was $27.2 million, making the potential sale of the SVP campus far and away the most valuable of all Camden parishes slated for closure.[43]

It is likely that the diocesan high school, Pope Paul VI, figured prominently in the decision to close SVP Parish. The thirty-five-acre tract could not be subdivided. The only way the bishop could acquire all of the assets was to sell the land and properties. The diocese already controlled the high school. Only SVP Parish stood in the way of selling the property. In June 2008, two months after Galante's reconfiguration announcement, the diocese publicly announced a plan to build a new high school in Gloucester County.[44] SVP parishioners learned that 29 percent of Paul VI's students traveled from Gloucester County to attend high school at the SVP site. Another diocesan high school—Camden Catholic—was located just three miles away, leading many to wonder if the bishop planned to merge the two diocesan schools at the Camden campus once the new Gloucester County high school was built. This would free up the Paul VI campus, allowing the diocese to acquire many millions of dollars once the patrimony from the sale of SVP building assets was separated out for the newly merged parish at St. Aloysius. In May 2008, Marucci had asked Galante directly about rumors that the diocese had plans for the thirty-five-acre property. Galante denied them saying, "You give too much credit to the diocese."[45]

THE BISHOP AND THE BROKER

The concerns of SVP parishioners about diocesan acquisition and sale of church properties were not unfounded. In July 2008, a story about Galante's connection to a recently indicted church real estate broker appeared in the *Camden Courier-Post*. Raffaello Follieri was a twenty-nine-year-old Italian businessman and chief executive of the Follieri Group, a company whose mission was to buy and redevelop Catholic church properties. On June 24, 2008, New York federal prosecutors accused him of wire fraud and money laundering. In October 2008 he pled guilty and was convicted of fourteen counts of money laundering, subsequently serving over four years in prison.[46] He spent up to $6 million of investors' money to finance an extravagant life-style, including a Manhattan apartment, expensive clothing, gourmet meals, and chartered jets for getaway vacations with his Hollywood girlfriend, Anne Hathaway.[47]

In 2007 Galante—who had himself worked for seven years as an under-secretary at the Vatican—sold his townhouse in North Wildwood, a Jersey Shore beach town, to Follieri.[48] This led SVP leaders to wonder if Follieri was currying favor with their bishop, who was planning to close nearly half of the churches in the diocese. The total value of soon-to-be-vacated parish properties in the diocese of Camden was estimated at $89 million.[49] Although diocesan spokesperson Andrew Walton assured reporters that the diocese had only become aware of the fraud accusations after the sale of Galante's Jersey Shore property, there were other concerning connections. In 2004 Galante received a call from the office of the Vatican Secretary of State. "He was told about the work of the Follieri Group and the fact that they worked specifically with church organizations that they did development that would benefit the community," said Walton to a reporter from the Associated Press.[50] In 2005, the Follieri Group purchased a rundown parish and abandoned school complex in Atlantic City in the Camden diocese, which was led by Galante at the time. Walton also told the press, "Not only did [Follieri] have the approval of the Vatican, but dioceses and bishops were encouraged by the Vatican to work with Follieri Group."[51]

Angelo Cardinal Sodano was the Vatican secretary of state at this time. His nephew, Andrea Sodano, was a vice president of the Follieri Group. In 2004, Cardinal Sodano had promoted his nephew's business interests with potential backers at a company launch party held in Manhattan.[52] In November 2006, at their annual fall meeting in Washington, DC, US bishops voted 222–2 to ask the Vatican to amend church policy and allow dioceses with more than five hundred thousand Catholics to sell or mortgage properties for up to $10.3 million without Rome's prior approval. According to those supporting the change, the previous limit of $5.1 million was cumbersome in the current real estate markets. At the same meeting Follieri and Andrea Sodano hosted a hospitality suite at the Capitol Hill Hyatt Regency Hotel where the bishops met.[53]

In a 2006 investigative piece for the *National Catholic Reporter*, journalist Joe Feuerherd quoted Follieri about the two factors that led to the company's interest in US real estate:

> First, he said, "The [sex abuse] scandal in America [where] dioceses were paying a lot of money to pay[off] the lawsuits" would necessitate the sale of church property. Next, he said, the changing demographics of the church . . . mean that "a lot of the schools and churches that were full of people in the beginning" are now largely unused.[54]

Feuerherd described the real estate industry as "hyper discreet," with sales records that do not become public until well after deals are finalized. Furthermore, "Even then, in some jurisdictions, religious institutions are exempt from some disclosure requirements. Dioceses and religious orders, meanwhile, are notoriously reluctant to discuss their business dealings, especially when senior Vatican officials are involved."[55]

As it turns out, more than one "senior Vatican official" was involved. Most pertinent to Kate Kuenstler's long-shot quixotic quest is Monsignor Giovanni Carrù who, upon the insistence of Cardinal Sodano, was appointed undersecretary at the Congregation for the Clergy in 2003.[56] As an undersecretary, Carrù managed all correspondence including mail, faxes, and documents from bishops and dioceses around the world. According to investigative journalist Jason Berry, "Carrù was instrumental to Follieri and Andrea Sodano in identifying prospective churches to buy and resell. The Follieri-Sodano scheme was roughly analogous to insider trading on Wall Street, albeit with fewer regulatory oversights."[57] After reviewing FBI documents provided under the Freedom of Information Act, Berry found that "Follieri wired Andrea Sodano more than $800,000 for services the FBI investigation deemed worthless. Follieri wired $387,000 in payments via the Vatican Bank to a Roman Curia lay worker, Antonio Mainiero, who was part of the scheme along with Carrù . . ."[58] FBI agent Theodore Cacioppi told the *National Catholic Reporter*, "We considered these people unindicted coconspirators."[59] He further "likened the payments to bribes paid to the three men—[Andrea] Sodano, Mainiero and Carrù."[60] Even so, Carrù would serve at Clergy until 2009 when he was appointed archaeological superintendent of the catacombs.[61] When SVP parishioners eventually appealed to the Vatican's Congregation for the Clergy, it was Carrù who read their correspondence and it was Carrù who often wrote back.[62]

THE BISHOP SAYS NO, NO, AND NO

On April 15, 2008, parish trustee John Canuso sent an exhaustive report to Bishop Galante on behalf of "The Friends of St. Vincent Pallotti" (FOSVP). He included data from tax maps, municipal ordinances, and the Camden fire marshal demonstrating that St. Aloysius could not "physically or legally handle the merger as the sole worship site."[63] One serious issue was that St. Aloysius Church had room for only four hundred worshippers. The seating could not accommodate the 446 people on average who would attend Sunday Mass in the newly merged community. The jammed worship space also risked violating fire marshal regulations, especially on Christmas, Easter, and other holidays when a markedly larger attendance was a given. Nor did the limited seating capacity allow for future growth. A significant legal-zoning issue was that St. Aloysius was landlocked and had only fifty parking spaces. Camden zoning ordinances required one parking space for each four seats, plus several more depending on the number of on-site church officials and employees. When the rectory and all-purpose hall were also considered, the zoning requirement could easily demand over 150 parking spaces to accommodate parish events and over 446 worshippers. Canuso estimated St. Aloysius would have to purchase four to six adjacent properties to comply with zoning regulations at an estimated cost between $1 to $1.5 million.[64] On-street parking was very limited around St. Aloysius, so holidays would be a nightmare. Handicapped accessibility at the church was also limited. On the other hand, SVP could easily accommodate eight hundred worshippers at one time, had a spacious four-hundred-car parking lot, and all entrances and facilities were handicapped accessible.[65] On behalf of the FOSVP, Canuso again entreated Galante to make the parish a worship site and told him, "The only possible way that this merger can physically occur is that SVP loses greater than 50 percent of its parishioners, which we cannot let happen."[66] In ensuing months Monsignor Marucci and the FOSVP wrote five times to ask Bishop Galante to reconsider closing their parish.[67] A June 3 letter specifically requested mediation. All requests were denied.

ATTEMPTS TO DISCREDIT THE PASTOR

Rather than listen to those most affected by his decision, Galante tried to malign the integrity of Monsignor Marucci. He implied that the diocese had never actually approved the building of the SVP Parish's new facilities and falsely accused Marucci of prior knowledge that their parish would be suppressed before he launched the $1 million capital campaign. On April 12, 2008, parishioner Judith A. Williams questioned Galante about why he was closing her parish. The bishop told her that Marucci "did not have permission to erect a million-dollar building."[68] The bishop was being disingenuous. In a follow-up letter to Williams, Marucci told her that Galante was "absolutely correct" that the bishop had not approved $1 million for the new facilities. But he had approved $650,000 for a rectory, enclosed walkway, and Memorial Hall Chapel. In an October 24, 2005, letter, the chief financial officer had approved $650,000 for the entire project with the understanding that parishioner John Canuso would incur all additional costs beyond $650,000. The bishop, the chief financial officer, and diocesan attorneys had all signed off on the project. In their subsequent canonical recourse to Rome, the FOSVP provided exhaustive documentation of correspondence with the diocese detailing the history of the building project beginning with the previous bishop, Bishop DiMarzio. Sadly, neither Galante nor diocesan officials ever attempted to correct the persistent, false rumor that the diocese had not approved the new SVP facilities.

SVP parishioners quickly wrote hundreds of letters protesting Galante's decision. The bishop responded with a letter dated Friday May 9, 2008. He defended his decision, citing what he saw as a consultative process and the advantages of St. Aloysius as the worship site. Responding to concerns about the needs of disabled members of the SVP community, Galante promised to appoint a special blue-ribbon committee to review the facilities of both parishes in order to "ensure that those needs will be met."[69]

SEEKING RECOURSE IN ROME

After Galante announced he intended to shut down SVP Parish, Marucci called a meeting of the Parish Council and opened it to any parishioner who wished to attend. Over two hundred people arrived. He asked to suspend the regular order of business because "I wanted to hear from the parishioners, what they wanted to do and how they wanted to respond."[70] Parish leadership shared various scenarios including "to accept this and move on, to request mediation, or to appeal to the bishop to reverse his decision." Marucci remembers, "I was trying not to be biased in any way, shape or form, [and]

I wanted to hear from them."[71] As a result of this meeting, the FOSVP was formed as an independent group. Marucci had quickly realized, "They needed to have some entity so that we weren't using parish funds. And there was going to be a time that I was going to be silenced and they could continue to take it further."[72] The group also decided to take their case to the media. But Marucci cautioned, "I would not let the [SVP] congregation do anything that would violate or demean the bishop or his office. We would only pursue our rights as canon law allows."[73]

After Galante's shocking announcement, Marucci asked the diocesan chancellor, "Can I appeal this?"

He was told, "You can't appeal it because there is no administrative act."[74] This response came even as Kate was concurrently working with hundreds of appealing parishioners in Syracuse, Camden, Cleveland, Buffalo, Springfield, New Orleans, Grand Rapids, Kansas City, Kansas, and Miami.

In canon law a bishop must issue a formal decree [administrative act] to suppress a parish. Before selling the church, he must issue a second decree which "reduces the church to profane use"—essentially making it no longer a sacred space. At this time the canonical regulations and procedures governing parish mergers and church closings were obscure at best. Usually the Vatican simply signed off on whatever any given bishop chose to do. Rome did not issue formal guidelines for parish closings until 2013—well after Kate's dogged canonical expertise had helped hundreds of Catholics in at least seven dioceses launch the formal appeals that ultimately preserved their churches and parishes. It is likely that Kate's work—and the sheer volume of appeals—prompted the Congregation for the Clergy to finally create written guidelines first issued in 2013 and again in 2020.

In Camden, Bishop Galante had devised a workaround. He announced he would not issue formal decrees until the mergers were completed. This could easily take two years or more. Canon law requires that canonical recourse begin within ten days of the bishop issuing a formal decree. Without a decree no recourse could theoretically be filed. Galante's plan denied parishioners their right to appeal and seek recourse in Rome. He appointed priest conveners—who were not their pastors—to move forward with mergers, obviously hoping opposition would evaporate as time went on. On June 3, 2008, Marucci wrote to Galante to formally request mediation and asked for a written decree. The bishop denied both requests. He wrote that until efforts to address SVP concerns were completed (presumably referring to the blue-ribbon committee) he believed "other conciliation issues are neither timely or beneficial [sic]." He then chided Marucci for requesting a decree since "I have consistently and clearly stated publicly and in my communication to priests that new parishes will not be established formally by decree for at least 12-24 months."[75] Throughout the summer of 2008, SVP parishioners repeatedly asked Galante to release the results of his vaunted blue-ribbon committee comparing the suitability of St. Aloysius and SVP worship sites for handicapped access. Galante delayed responding, despite receiving their letters of July 9 and July 22 requesting the promised report.[76]

MONSIGNOR LOU MARUCCI INTERVIEWS SR. KATE KUENSTLER

As it became increasingly evident that Bishop Galante had no intention of reversing himself, Marucci went in search of a canon lawyer. He knew he needed someone who would be independent and was not employed by any diocese: "Someone that would not necessarily have to respond to undue pressure by a bishop . . . I was afraid maybe a bishop calls another bishop and says, 'You know I want you to make this person back away.'"[77] A friend (who also happened to be a bishop) referred him to Canon Law Professionals, an independent organization with whom Kate was affiliated at the time. In an interview before hiring her, Marucci remembers telling her "point blank" that they were stepping into uncharted waters to address a side of the church that "wasn't being honest and authentic."[78] He was looking for "someone who can provide the canonical counsel needed to address this appropriately according to church law." Furthermore, he needed legal counsel that would not be forced to withdraw prematurely out of obedience to an ecclesiastical superior: "I asked her to assure to me that if she engaged in this process, would she be free to carry it through to the end, no matter what the end was," Marucci recalled. After assuring the monsignor that her religious superior would not interfere, Marucci remembers that Kate laughingly told him, "I like your style Monsignor because you are asking the right questions."[79]

SVP Parish leaders quickly contracted with Kate to guide them in claiming their canonical rights. Ginny and John Hargrave were active parishioners at SVP. As chair of the finance committee, John worked on the SVP appeal and Ginny volunteered in the parish office. She describes Kate's approach this way:

> She was extremely receptive, extremely personable. I could tell she had done this kind of thing before. She wanted to hear all sides. She had a great sense of humor which helped–especially because she knew we were going through a very stressful time. She wasn't under the bishop's thumb either. She is just one of those people you meet and like.[80]

Marucci's instinct to protect Kate's confidentiality proved prescient. He was called into a meeting with Galante and other high ranking diocesan personnel including the chancellor.

"They asked me point blank who my canonical advisor was. And I said, 'I will not release that information.'

And they asked 'Why, what do you have to hide?'

I said, 'I don't have anything to hide. That hasn't anything to do with our conversation. I am not going to divulge who my canonical advisor is.'"

To this day the monsignor chuckles: "At the time, an extremely intelligent priest, who happened to be a canon lawyer and my former pastor while I was in the seminary, was living in residence with me at St. Vincent Pallotti. I knew that all in the room assumed he was my canonical advisor. But it was Kate that was the lawyer."[81]

FOSVP FILE ADMINISTRATIVE APPEAL TO ROME

By mid-August, SVP parishioners still had not received the promised report from Galante's blue-ribbon committee charged with evaluating handicapped accessibility at the two parishes. Therefore, on August 18, 2008—with Kate's guidance—the FOSVP filed a formal petition for administrative recourse with Cardinal Claudio Hummes, the prefect of the Vatican's Congregation for the Clergy. The recourse was sent to the papal nuncio Archbishop Pietro Sambi, who relayed it to Rome via the diplomatic pouch. A copy was also sent to Bishop Galante. In addition to opposing St. Aloysius as the merger site, the petition questioned Galante's failure to issue a decree, which "blocks our right to appeal his decisions." Citing a lack of transparency and their bishop's failure to consider donor intent and naming rights for their recent million-dollar renovation, SVP petitioners said to Hummes, "We pray that you will issue a protocol number for our petition so that our future correspondence to you can be collected in an orderly manner."[82] Diocesan spokesperson Andrew Walton immediately told the *Camden Courier-Post* that church law would not allow it. "Right now there is nothing to appeal because there is no new parish," he said. "Appeals are reserved for the time at which there's been a decree."[83] Walton would soon be proven wrong.

On August 25, Bishop Galante released the results of the blue-ribbon committee study recommending that "the diocese use the facilities at SVP as a premier worship site focusing on the disabled population in South Jersey."[84] The next day he announced he would allow the SVP church to remain open "to be a worship site to ensure that the parishioners within the configuration will be fully served." But parish leaders were underwhelmed. They saw the new plan as a death knell for SVP, as many non-worship-site churches in the Camden diocese were eventually sold.[85] Furthermore, a decision relegating their church to a secondary worship site would mean losing their canonical rights as a full-fledged parish. "It still leaves us open to being closed," said Ed

Pierzynski for the FOSVP. He also announced the group planned to continue with their canonical recourse.[86] SVP leaders immediately wrote to Galante to first express their appreciation that he now wanted their church to remain open to serve the disabled. They again formally requested mediation asking to become either the primary worship site or a stand-alone parish. They also requested a copy of the bishop's decree if he intended to move ahead with the merger.[87] On September 16, 2008, Galante responded at length defending his decision. He refused to issue a decree.[88]

HAMMERING OUT A NEW CANONICAL APPROACH

When SVP leaders decided to hire Kate, Marucci remembers, "I spent hours just talking, making notes, talking, making notes with Kate before we even brought a committee together." He described their working relationship as "a marriage that worked very well." Marucci was a stickler about respecting the office of the bishop, particularly since parishioners from other Camden parishes were engaged in protest tactics that he found distasteful and disrespectful.[89] "Kate was never disrespectful," he recalled. "She herself also thought that being disrespectful to the office would always backfire. Our intention was to exercise the rights of the faithful, as canon law permits, without disrespecting the bishop's office. She provided strong direction on what was permissible and what was not." Still, Marucci wanted SVP leaders "to be able to test [the bishop's] decision based on what the law of the church allows us to do."[90]

Yet just what "law of the church" was being violated in the present case was not entirely clear. Marucci remembers Kate telling him, "You could have the strongest case in the world, but the question is, did it violate law or not? If it did not, it's not the merit of the case that really matters, it's the question of whether the law was violated or not. We'll have to work together to see how the law was violated."[91] She further explained that while the rights of public juridic persons such as parishes are clearly identified in canon law, bishops at the Second Vatican Council had differing opinions about how these rights could or should be defended. This aspect never formally found its way into canon law, she said. Therefore, "You have to really pick at the law in order to defend these rights," she told him.[92]

Together Kate and Marucci hammered out an astute approach that eventually created precedent-setting jurisprudence. Marucci's background in theology and biomedical ethics with a concentration in medical moral theology complemented Kate's expertise in canon law and theology. They had many spirited discussions. "One of the things I shared with Kate is that prudence is the virtue that drives all the other virtues," Marucci reminisced.[93] "And we had a conversation about this one day because we chose to frame the administration recourse by arguing that the bishop violated the requirement to use prudence when he makes an administrative act." One major hurdle had to be overcome. Marucci had noticed that Galante based everything he was doing on *intent*. "The first four words of every announcement he made was 'It is my intent. It is my intent. It is my intent.'" He thought to himself, "There is something odd about the fact that he always uses those four words." Another dilemma was puzzling: "If the bishop chooses not to go to mediation and the bishop chooses not to reverse his intention, then how do you exercise your rights if there is no decree?" Marucci's collaboration with Kate soon helped him understand that "you cannot appeal an intention because an administrative act has not yet occurred. You can only appeal an administrative act; you cannot appeal a thought."[94]

Kate's visits with Marucci involved "long, long conversations" about how to proceed. Through those conversations, particularly surrounding the issue of prudence, Marucci asked Kate to review the diocese's merger manual, which was given to priest-conveners as the process to merge the bishop's intended merger plan. This led to an important breakthrough. Marucci stated:

> What bothers me about all of this is that it just doesn't seem ethical because, it seems as if your hands are tied. You cannot mediate or dialogue about this intention of the bishop . . . eventually you have to follow this document [merger manual]. And none of the pastors are involved in the leadership of the merger. It is an outside person—the priest convener who is not a pastor. So the bishop is saying you have to follow this protocol, but there is never anyplace in here that says the people can really disagree.[95]

After paging through the manual, Kate inquired if she could take it with her. The monsignor supplied a copy. Several days later, she telephoned him with good news: "I believe that we can find the way that the law might have been violated." Kate explained that in her opinion there were two things at issue: "A Bishop is required to act with the virtue of prudence when he is making an administrative act." The second issue relates to a canonically required thirty-day waiting period. In Catholic canon law, for administrative acts that are particular law (e.g., diocesan decisions about merging parishes or relegating churches), the law does not become obligatory until thirty days after the day of promulgation.[96] This is the timeframe within which concerned parties may seek canonical recourse with the ecclesiastical superior for any given administrative act. Kate further explained that what was being asked for in the Camden merger manual is what would normally happen after an administrative act is declared. She told Marucci, "If this manual is being required after [the bishop's] intention, and what canon law requires after an administrative act are one and the same, then isn't [the bishop's] intention, really an administrative act? . . . Let's ask for clarity on this."

"And that's how that door opened," said Marucci. "We were asking for clarity on whether the bishop was using his knowledge of the law to circumvent really the rights of the people to file the administrative recourse."

SECOND PETITION TO VATICAN YIELDS UNPRECEDENTED RESPONSE

After receiving Galante's September 16, 2008, letter rejecting their request for mediation and a decree, SVP parish leaders wasted no time in submitting a second letter to Cardinal Claudio Hummes requesting him to intervene on behalf of their right to pursue an appeal. They used the canonical approach painstakingly hammered out by Kate and Marucci. Their September 20, 2008, letter took issue with Galante's "refusal to issue the formal decree for the merger of our parish at the parish of St. Aloysius" and said forthrightly, "We hope that the Bishop's knowledge of the law is not being used as a vehicle to prevent us from implementing our right to appeal his administrative decision as the church allows."[97] The petition developed a salient argument based on Canon 8.2 which pointed to the fact that Galante's "intent" was actually an administrative act promulgating particular law and should therefore be eligible for parishioner recourse: "To wait until all of the matters relating to merger are finalized, makes any recourse impotent. This is clearly not the intent of the Church when it provided the recourse process to the parishioners."[98]

SVP leaders requested Hummes to intercede by doing one of the following: either instruct the bishop to immediately issue a decree so that "the parish of St. Vincent Pallotti will be able to begin the Administrative Recourse in a timely manner as the law provides," or inform the bishop that it is understood that he has issued "the promulgation, particular law decree . . . since the bishop is already acting from a final decision that is not open to change and that is to be implemented by a priest convener. Thereafter the parish of St. Vincent Pallotti will be able to begin the Administrative Recourse in a timely manner as the law provides."[99]

The Congregation for the Clergy replied almost immediately, which (as will be seen) hardly ever happens. On September 30, 2008, Marucci received a surprising response from none other than under-secretary Monsignor Giovanni Carrù, indicating Rome had accepted their canonical argument:

Please be advised that this Congregation has understood Bishop Galante's announcement of April 3rd, 2008, as an administrative act, albeit not written, against which you have taken recourse. The matter remains under study and the time limits in the case have been extended until December 28, 2008.[100]

Therefore, the SVP recourse could proceed. Marucci recalls Kate being "thrilled beyond measure" that her canonical expertise had opened a door. "She was so beside herself. It was huge for her. I remember her saying, 'Nothing like this has ever been done before. You don't understand. Nothing like this has ever been done before.'"[101] At the same time he remembers quietly asking himself, "How did I get myself into this mess? All of my life I have been obedient to the church."

EXHAUSTIVE FIVE-VOLUME RECOURSE SENT TO CONGREGATION FOR THE CLERGY

Carrù's September 30 response from Clergy indicated that the FOSVP had until December 28 to submit formal recourse against Galante's administrative act suppressing their parish. A select cohort of FOSVP parishioners swung into action. Five volumes totaling several thousand pages were eventually submitted each with its own subset of carefully developed arguments and exhaustive documentation. Marucci well remembers the lengthy process: "Kate and I worked on that document. She wrote it, I rewrote it. . . . She wrote it through the lens of a canon lawyer. And I wrote it through the lens of the pastor and a director of development who was really concerned of the donor intent violation. The committee members researched and wrote many of those arguments too."[102] He especially respected Kate's expertise: "She made sure that all of our i's were dotted, our t's were crossed, and that all of our timelines were appropriately respected. She was sterling in that regard."[103] Kate appreciated how meticulous Marucci was: "I remember Kate saying to me, 'Monsignor, you are one of the most detail-oriented people I've ever met in my life.'"[104]

On December 12, the Feast of Our Lady of Guadalupe, the FOSVP submitted their five-volume appeal to the Congregation for the Clergy along with a cover letter to Monsignor Carrù, and a lengthy twenty-eight-page, single-spaced, letter to the prefect, Cardinal Claudio Hummes, summarizing the main points of their recourse. This document included salient facts, issues in canon and civil law, and carefully footnoted details about hierarchical recourse. It listed over thirty relevant canons pertaining to decrees, administrative acts, and the differing procedures a diocese must use for suppressing a parish and closing a church.[105] A final segment of the Hummes letter had this subheading: "The Process of Taking Recourse." Here SVP petitioners (directed by Kate) listed the sixteen canons that had guided their recourse.

Copies were sent to the apostolic nuncio, Archbishop Pietro Sambi, Bishop Joseph A. Galante, and Archbishop John J. Myers of Newark, New Jersey, who was the local metropolitan for New Jersey.[106] In their cover letters to each prelate, SVP petitioners were at pains to say: "We regret that we must use the Administrative Recourse Process. We would have preferred to settle the matter at the local level."[107]

THE BISHOP TRIES A TRANSFER

As the SVP recourse was being considered at the Congregation for the Clergy, Bishop Galante tried to transfer Marucci. At a meeting attended by the bishop, the priest personnel director, and the judicial vicar he was informed that he would be transferred. Marucci pushed back: "I don't believe you have the authority to do that," he said boldly.[108]

Marucci vividly remembers that Galante "kept saying to the judicial vicar (who had the *Commentary on the Code of Canon Law* on the table), 'Tell him, tell him.'"

But Marucci would have none of it. "I said, 'No, I want to hear it from the bishop. I want the bishop to tell me that he has the authority to transfer me while administrative recourse has been engaged.'"

Galante repeated his order: "Tell him, tell him."

Marucci again demanded to hear the order from the bishop's own lips. Realizing they had reached an impasse, Marucci announced, "Well look, I actually anticipated that you were going to try to engage this particular tactic. You need to know that I've already asked for clarification on this law from [papal nuncio] Archbishop Sambi. So you can either wait for the clarification of the law, or act in ignorance of the clarification requested."

The priest personnel director then asked the monsignor, "How do we know that you've asked for clarification and that you're not lying?"

Marucci remembers his pointed reply, "I just looked at him and said, well that's insulting because I don't lie. And furthermore here's the letter." He handed Galante his letter to Archbishop Sambi seeking the requested clarification.

The bishop opened the letter, read it, and abruptly announced, "This meeting is over." Since Galante was still holding onto Sambi's letter, Marucci said: "That is my property. I would like to have it back." He proudly remembers, "I stayed on at St. Vincent Pallotti for another two years."[109]

In retrospect Marucci speculates that Galante "knew he did not really have the authority to transfer me, so he kept asking the judicial vicar to say it, rather than have it come from his lips. Down the road he did not want the failure of an argument that he had removed a competent pastor."[110]

A WAITING GAME, AND CAMDEN CATHOLICS KEEP ORGANIZING

Once the appeal was filed, there was nothing to do but wait. In March 2009 and again in June 2009 the FOSVP received word from the Congregation for the Clergy extending the time limits until September 2009.[111] Kate was very encouraged by the Congregation's extensions: "She saw all of those as positive signs, but she did keep reminding me that nobody had won a case yet," Marucci wryly recalled.[112]

Even before Vatican bureaucrats began their deliberations about the SVP recourse, other Camden Catholics had been organizing to oppose Galante's decision to close nearly half the parishes in their diocese. On May 8, 2008, forty Catholics from a newly formed coalition, "The Council of Parishes of Southern New Jersey," demonstrated outside St. Charles Borromeo Church where the bishop was meeting with diocesan priests.[113] Patty Gioffre of St. Anthony's in Waterford Township felt duped. "He's tearing the hearts out of all these little communities. As long as we can remain fiscally soluble and keep our outreach to the community, we should be able to stay open."[114] A week earlier, seventy-five parishioners from St. Mary Malaga, a rural church of just 250 families, had prayed the rosary and picketed: "There is no such thing as merging. It's closing," said Leah Vassallo, a longtime parishioner. "The real reason he is doing this is because he thinks larger parishes are more vibrant. Where is that true? People aren't likely to go to a bigger church, farther from home."[115]

On Sunday June 29, 2008, the FOSVP sponsored their own prayerful witness. Following the noon Mass, parishioners planted hundreds of homemade crosses on the lawn of their parish. In a press release, parish leaders said the crosses were intended to represent "the burden of the current situation imposed on the parishioners by the bishop's intent."[116] Nearly a year later FOSVP spokesperson, Ed Pierzynski, publicly explained how helpful cross-parish internet communications had been and why the FOSVP recourse was so important: "[P]eople are really starting to see what others are doing and are quickly moving. That's why our case with the Vatican is critical. If they do decide to let us remain a parish, it opens the door for other parishes. But we're also afraid, if they don't let us [stay open], that this will close the door for other parishes."[117] In a May 13, 2009, media story describing the "nerve-wracking" wait, Pierzynski speculated,

Last week [in early April] . . . the *Catholic Star Herald* said he [the bishop] was going over to meet with seminarians. Our feeling is that, since they extended the review period, he probably was summoned. It's more than a coincidence.[118]

THE BISHOP MAKES HIS CASE

As print and TV media in Camden and Philadelphia gave extensive coverage to protesting Camden parishioners, the diocese made its own case for why such drastic downsizing was necessary. "I couldn't leave it to my successors," Galante told the *Philadelphia Inquirer* on May 17, 2009. "It would have been irresponsible." The day before, just two new priests had been ordained for the Camden diocese. Furthermore, the bishop said, 41 of the diocese's 162 parishes "could not pay their basic bills," such as utilities, insurance, and health benefits.[119] Camden parish leaders sharply disputed the diocese's dire financial description. A blogger for the Save St. Mary Malaga website wrote: "Many if not most of the churches that Galante seeks to close are financially solvent."[120] It is not unknown for diocesan leadership to paint a bleak picture of parish finances when any given bishop decides he wants to close parishes. For example, before attempting to close fifty-two Cleveland parishes, Bishop Richard Lennon reinstated loans that had been forgiven by his predecessor. Thus he could claim diocesan parishes were in arrears, when many were viable until saddled again with long-forgiven loans. It is clear, however, that the parish of SVP was neither in debt nor financially moribund.

CONGREGATION FOR THE CLERGY UPHOLDS GALANTE—WITHOUT READING SVP RECOURSE

On September 25 and November 4, 2009, SVP leaders wrote to Cardinal Hummes requesting an update about their status, specifically asking for "clarification of the application of the time allotment in canon law if it applies to our case at this time. We need to be assured that our responsibility to protect our parish . . . is protected as canon law provides."[121]

In a November 10, 2009, letter, the secretary for the Congregation for the Clergy, Archbishop Mauro Piacenza, informed SVP leaders that "no recourse is considered operative at this time."[122] Piacenza noted that Bishop Galante had kept SVP as a worship site and said, "Since your original letters to this Dicastery of 27 April 2008 and 20 September 2008 sought to take recourse against closure and merger it would seem that the object of your recourse has been fulfilled." Decisions about the pastor and location of the offices of the merged parish "fall within the direct competence only for the local bishop and therefore outside of the scope of a canonical recourse," he told them.[123] There were significant errors in the Congregation for the Clergy ruling. Most striking is that the dicastery had based its decision on the September 20, 2008, letter from SVP leaders requesting a decree rather than on the actual five-volume recourse submitted on December 12, 2008. The Congregation appears to have ignored the exhaustive recourse documentation so carefully prepared by diligent SVP parishioners.

As is usually the case, the Vatican ruling was communicated to the bishop before the letter reached SVP leaders. On December 3, 2009, their ruling was announced in the diocesan paper, the *Catholic Star Herald*, and on the Camden diocesan blog.[124] Galante called Marucci into his office on the very same day. Marucci remembers being upset about the announcement: "I thought it was disrespectful not to allow the parishioners to be informed first. . . . I actually challenged the communications office for being that disrespectful."[125] When he met with Galante, the bishop told him: "The Congregation for Clergy has rendered their decision and ruled in my favor. I have the authority to transfer you and I'm exercising that right."[126] Marucci didn't argue: "Kate and I knew this day was coming . . . that there was going to be a day that I would be silenced." Still he valiantly replied, "Bishop, because this to me is a matter of social justice, this case will now move to the Signatura. I'm telling you this out of respect to you." Marucci still remembers Galante's response:

> Louie you're a very, very smart man. You're one of the brightest priests in our diocese, and you know that when you take this case to the Signatura, your case is no longer against me. It's against the Congregation for the Clergy. . . . If you want to file recourse against a Vatican congregation to the Apostolic Signatura, you can do whatever you want to do, but I am free to act however I see fit.[127]

To the profound distress of SVP parishioners, Marucci was transferred to St. Andrew Parish in Gibbsboro, New Jersey. He would continue to live at SVP for the next two years as St. Andrew was not yet equipped to accommodate a handicapped priest. In June 2010 he was appointed the pastor of St. Andrew.

APPEAL TO THE APOSTOLIC SIGNATURA

On November 30, 2009, SVP leaders sent a lengthy reply to Archbishop Piacenza formally requesting that the Congregation for the Clergy address the serious errors in their ruling. On December 3 they sent a similar letter to Cardinal Hummes.[128] If the Congregation chose not to address these errors, SVP leaders asked the dicastery to "immediately forward all documentation to the Apostolic Signatura, the Court of the Church so that the Appeal process could begin in the time allotted by Canon Law."[129] Canon law stipulates if a ruling by an ecclesiastical superior or office is based on an error, the ruling is not valid. This was the nub of the SVP appeal to the Signatura. On December 6, Marucci wrote a pointed letter to the apostolic nuncio, Archbishop Pietro

Sambi, expressing grave concern noting, "At no time did the parishioners of St. Vincent Pallotti agree that their Juridic Status be compromised and/or suppressed." He questioned how the Congregation's November 10, 2009, letter could "summarily claim *'the object of your recourse has been fulfilled'* based on information that preceded the submission of 12 December 2008 recourse. . . . The object of the recourse has NOT been fulfilled, nor even addressed," he said.[130]

NEARLY THREE HUNDRED SVP PARISHIONERS SUE THE CAMDEN DIOCESE

After the Congregation for the Clergy upheld Galante's decision to suppress their parish, SVP leaders decided they had no choice but to seek justice in the civil courts. On January 28, 2010, 284 SVP parishioners filed suit against the Camden diocese seeking a settlement of more than $1.4 million, plus interest. In a highly significant development, Superior Court Judge Faustine Fernandez-Vine ruled the SVP lawsuit could proceed despite the traditional reluctance of civil courts to take on First Amendment issues involving the separation of church and state.[131]

SIGNATURA RESPONDS—SLOWLY

On March 10, 2010, having heard nothing from either Piacenza or Hummes at Clergy, SVP leaders sent a letter to then-archbishop Raymond Cardinal Burke, the prefect of the Supreme Tribunal of the Apostolic Signatura, apprising him of the error on the part of the Congregation for the Clergy and the history and timeline of their recourse. Burke is an ultra-conservative American archbishop emeritus of St. Louis, where he had served from 2003 to 2008 before his transfer to the Signatura.[132] SVP leaders wrote: "[W]e respectfully petition you directly to accept our appeal before the esteemed tribunal of the Apostolic Signatura. We once again seek information related to the process, procedures, allotted timeline, and materials required, that are necessary to initiate the appeal."[133] They informed Burke that Bishop Galante had removed their pastor despite the expectation that "no new administrative decisions were to be made until the entire matter came to a conclusion." In closing, astute SVP leaders wrote, "Finally we regret to inform you that we have had to pursue protection by the civil court for violations against donor intent. . . . These donor-restricted funds were not given for general operating use, but were given for restricted purposes, and have numerous naming rights attached."[134] On April 10, SVP trustee Richard Hatch, the first of fifteen signers on FOSVP correspondence, received a courteous reply and information about administrative recourse procedures from Bishop Frans Daneels, the secretary of the Apostolic Signatura. Daneels stipulated that the recourse must be submitted "within the peremptory time limit of sixty days."[135]

On April 19, 2010, SVP leaders initiated formal recourse at the Apostolic Signatura via a letter to the prefect, Burke. To document that their appeal had been filed within canonical time limits, the letter listed dates on which letters and follow-up letters were sent to appropriate Vatican offices. It included a four-point synopsis of their November 30, 2009, letter listing errors made by the Congregation for the Clergy. Number one on the list was Clergy's grave misrepresentation of the September 20, 2008, letter from SVP leaders, upon which it had apparently based its decision:[136] SVP leaders then listed the substantive reasons for their recourse, including that the Congregation's decision was based on an "objectively false positive judgement," and therefore the ruling was invalid. Furthermore the Congregation's administrative act had affected the public juridic person of SVP Parish which "should be seen as *an extremely serious act.* A juridic person, the parish, that canon law says has a right to perpetual existence was seriously compromised by the Congregation for Clergy and its error for its decision" (italics in original). Two other grave reasons for recourse included violation of US civil law, specifically contradiction of donor intent, and violation of parking and zoning ordinances if St. Aloysius Church site was named as the new parish seat. SVP leaders attached summary arguments about civil law violations and requested that a list of approved [Vatican] legal advocates be sent immediately.[137]

THE APOSTOLIC SIGNATURA DEMURS

On May 27, 2010, the SVP appeal was rejected "at the threshold" by the Apostolic Signatura, "since the decree has not yet been issued by His Excellency, the Bishop of Camden." The ruling advised that SVP petitioners could bring recourse to the full Congress of the Signatura within ten days.[138] But (as often happens) SVP leaders did not receive the Signatura's decision until June 14. On June 23 they notified Bishop Daneels of the time discrepancy, filed recourse against the Signatura's May 27, 2010, ruling, and requested further direction.[139] They did not have long to wait. In a letter dated July 10, 2010, the Signatura issued a second decision rejecting their recourse again, noting that Galante had not issued a decree. Yet in closing, Daneels's cover letter pointedly noted: "This decision is without prejudice to the possibility of your having recourse (c.f. canons 1734-1737) against the decision of the Bishop of Camden, if and when it is issued."[140] Canons 1734–1737 address how one might pursue administrative recourse against a bishop.[141]

Marucci remembers "Kate was doing back flips" over the Signatura's response. She told him, "They're not accepting the case, but I really think they're giving the bishop the opportunity to make this right. He would be foolish not to make this right because then this case would move into the public forum through the Apostolic Signatura, and I don't think he would risk losing in the public forum."[142] Three months later—after a polite and pointed intervention with Cardinal Burke by Sr. Kate Kuenstler—Bishop Galante finally made up his mind.

A WATERSHED MOMENT: SISTER KATE WRITES TO THE PREFECT OF THE APOSTOLIC SIGNATURA

As Marucci and the ever-steadfast SVP leaders waited, Kate took it upon herself to write a letter to Burke: "I don't think you want to get involved in restricted gifts/canonical advocate juridic issues," she advised him. "This will not bode well in the public forum."[143] She informed him of the many skilled civil lawyers guiding the SVP lawsuit and that Galante would likely lose: "We're near the end and he's not going to make it [win the civil case]," she warned. "If you want to save the good face of the bishops of the United States, you can change that in a minute by telling Bishop Galante he cannot sell this church and that he must keep it open."[144]

Two weeks later, on October 10, 2010, Bishop Galante reversed himself and decided that SVP Church would become the seat of the new parish. "He must have checked with his civil lawyers on restricted gifts and found out the weakness of his argument and that we were right," said Kate dryly.[145] Looking back nearly a decade later, Kate marveled, "I got Burke on my side, which is unheard of. He would deny it today. . . . And that [involvement] saved this church, this parish. All the while I'm shivering in my boots and thinking, 'Oh my God, what did I just do?'"[146] Two years later—after the Vatican had upheld the appeals of hundreds of parishioners in Allentown, Buffalo, Syracuse, Springfield, and Cleveland—Kate described her intervention with Burke as a "watershed."

> In 2010 I successfully argued the distinction between a parish and a church to the Apostolic Signatura in an appeal against the negative decree, given by the Congregation for the Clergy to one of my clients [SVP]. . . . This was the watershed case that influenced a change in the attitude of the Apostolic Signatura and ultimately the Congregation for the Clergy.[147]

In an announcement in the *Catholic Star Herald*, the Camden diocese said that the bishop had originally chosen St. Aloysius as the parish seat because the bishop wanted to keep a parish on or near the White Horse Pike. Ed Pier-zynski, vice president of the FOSVP, graciously told the *Camden Courier-Post*, "It came to a logical conclusion, and it was amicable between us and the diocese. It was never about us versus them. It was always about what provides the best solution for both parishes."[148]

A year later, on October 12, 2011, Bishop Galante formally established St. Joseph the Worker Parish at the SVP site following the merger of SVP and St. Aloysius, with SVP as the parish seat, and St. Aloysius as a worship site. This is what Monsignor Marucci and Sister Kate had requested from the very beginning. Clair Blake from St. Aloysius acknowledged "some hardships" in the merger process, but said "both parishes are (now) ready to move forward as one, as St. Joseph the Worker Parish." A member of the SVP core team, Frank Liberi, echoed Blake's optimism: "There are a lot of strengths from both churches, that we can draw from," he said, adding that the core members were a "dedicated team" that "seemed to gel together really quickly."[149]

Four weeks earlier, parishioners at St. Mary Malaga—who had held months-long vigils at the church—learned that Galante had reversed himself and would allow their church to open "on an occasional basis" for weddings, funerals, and other "paraliturgical exercises."[150] This partial victory followed similar rulings in other dioceses wherein the Congregation for the Clergy allowed bishops to merge parishes, but upheld parishioner appeals to keep their churches. Despite early diocesan hype about how reconfiguration would strengthen parishes, the Camden merger process had the opposite effect. Mass attendance suffered a substantial decline after Galante announced he would close nearly half of the diocese's parishes. Attendance went from 114,000 in the fall of 2006—thirty-six months before the merger announce-ment—to 100,000 in the fall of 2010.[151]

Meanwhile in June 2010, Marucci became the new pastor of the multi-ethnic community at St. Andrew Parish, an appointment he still holds. Ginny Hargrave remembers it as a traumatic time for SVP parishioners. "We were bummed because, even after this whole appeal and becoming the seat of the parish, we were still losing our pastor. It was pretty upsetting."[152] SVP parishioners threw a farewell party for Monsignor Marucci "that was just incredible," she recalled. At first the monsignor had objected: "I've been to these things, and nobody comes." But hundreds of parishioners attended. "I mean, unless you were away, it was the whole parish," recalled Hargrave.[153] Today, Marucci has no regrets: "I have to tell you, God's hand works in miraculous ways because St. Andrew parish is a really great fit for me and the congregation," he said. "Furthermore, it was good for the parishioners of St. Aloysius and St. Vincent Pallotti to have a pastor that was not involved in the canonical appeal."[154]

Looking back, Marucci remembers Kate's succinct analysis of his role in the SVP saga: "You saved this parish, but you know, you were the sacrificial lamb," she told him.

Marucci laughed and said, "A pastor, if he's going to be a good shepherd, may have to be the sacrificial lamb from time to time."

"Had it not been for you being willing to do that," Kate said, "this parish would have lost its canonical rights."[155]

At one point during this difficult process, Marucci remembers accidentally crossing paths with Galante at a regional meeting. The two were in a private area. After exchanging greetings, he asked: "Bishop, I want to ask you a very sincere question, nor do I really want you to answer it today. I just want you to think about it, reflect on it, and pray over it. Throughout this entire ordeal, do you truly believe that you have been your best self?" Galante did not respond, and Marucci remembers simply rolling away in his wheelchair. Years later, a retired and failing Galante—who was now receiving kidney dialysis—attended an installation ceremony for a bishop in another diocese to which Marucci had also been invited.

As they left the ceremony, Galante—who was now also in a wheelchair—called Marucci over. "Lou, I have thought, prayed, and reflected significantly over the question you asked me a while ago," he said. "And the answer is no. I was not being my best self. And would you forgive me?"

Marucci's quick, compassionate reply is characteristic of the man and of the priest: "Bishop, I cannot . . . I already forgave you a long time ago." He then explained to his bishop:

> When you live life through my set of lenses, when you take a breath of air in and lose the ability to exhale it out, and you are faced with the possibility of death daily, you always need to be your best self. When I put my head on the pillow at night, all I desire is that I have done everything according to the way God calls me to live. At times, it means speaking forth for social justice. At other times it means extending mercy and forgiveness to others. Through prayer, I realized long ago that God desired me to extend forgiveness to you, for both of our spiritual lives.[156]

Bishop Joseph A. Galante then asked Msgr. Louis M. Marucci for his blessing which he gave. These were the last words spoken between the two priests.[157]

Chapter 7

In the Diocese of Cleveland, Catholics Rise Up

While the St. Vincent Pallotti and St. Mary, Jamesville, stories focus on individual parishes, the next three chapters narrate a fierce, diocesan-wide, grassroots struggle to preserve beloved urban parishes serving poorer communities in the Diocese of Cleveland. In the spring of 2009, Sister Kate's expertise guided the initial canonical recourse lodged by Catholics in over twenty parishes. That same expertise went on to help pastors, pastoral ministers, Cleveland's Presbyteral Council, and countless laity to understand and claim their canonical rights. On March 7, 2012, after what Catholic pundit Rocco Palmo described as "the most ferocious and bitter parish planning face-off the Stateside church has seen in the last quarter century," their perseverance paid off.[1] Rome ordered Cleveland's Bishop Richard Lennon to re-establish parishes he had wrongly closed and reopen their churches. It was an unprecedented victory. For the first time, the Vatican ordered a bishop to restore a large number of suppressed parishes as well as reopen their churches. In doing so, the Vatican powerfully upheld the rights of Catholics in those parishes to have an appropriate voice in determining their future. Kate decided to write a canonical *Commentary* on the Cleveland rulings which was published on March 29, 2012. In it she noted: "Both the Congregation for Clergy and the Apostolic Signatura now make a clear distinction between the legitimate reasons to merge parishes and legitimate reasons to close a church."[2] She clarified that a shortage of priests, diocesan financial challenges, and demographic issues are insufficient reasons to close churches, even though nearly every US bishop had claimed all three as justification for downsizing their dioceses.

A TALE OF TWO BISHOPS

Founded in 1847, today the diocese of Cleveland is the twenty-third largest in the United States, serving nearly 613,000 Catholics in 185 parishes in an eight-county area of Northeast Ohio.[3] In 2006—three years before a drastic downsizing—it was home to nearly 800,000 Catholics in 231 parishes, just four fewer compared to 1970.[4] Catholic Charities Cleveland has one of the largest diocesan systems of social services in the world.[5]

The source of what Palmo called Cleveland's "ferocious parish planning standoff" is rooted in the dramatically differing ecclesiologies of Cleveland's ninth bishop, Anthony M. Pilla, and his successor, Richard G. Lennon. Pilla was a native son who valued participative decision-making and supported creative solutions to preserve parishes serving poor urban neighborhoods. Lennon was a lifelong Bostonian who prioritized clericalism over collaboration with lay leaders and, I would argue, a comfortable economic security over mission to the marginalized. For twenty-five years Cleveland's Catholics had been influenced by Anthony Pilla's wide-ranging vision, collaborative decision-making style, and heart for the poor. It is no surprise, therefore, that they resisted the lesser—not to say polar opposite—vision of his successor.

Cleveland's proud tradition of social justice activism and service to the poor was strongly encouraged by Bishop Pilla. A native Clevelander and the child of immigrants, Pilla led the diocese from 1981 until 2006 when he retired for health reasons. He was widely respected by Catholics and non-Catholics alike because of his commitment to serving marginalized communities in a city which annually vied with Detroit as the poorest in the United States.[6] Under Pilla, the Cleveland diocese worked diligently to uphold parishes in struggling neighborhoods. In 1993 the diocese created *The Church in the City*, an initiative to link suburban and rural parishes to their poorer counterparts in the inner city. This nationally known effort led to partnerships between eighty-five parishes and schools, and resulted in numerous practical projects such as building and renovating homes, promoting regional planning, raising grant monies to promote a vision of regional unity and city revival, and fostering life-giving faith-sharing relationships.[7] In 1996, Pilla addressed civic leaders at the Cleveland City Club about the moral implications of regional sprawl for poor urban communities.[8] He shared his experience of growing up in Cleveland, which became a touchstone for his pastoral care of the city and its people:

> My own father came to this country with a nickel in his pocket. Growing up in the city, I know well the struggles he faced and so many others like him. . . . Today we, their sons and daughters, are called to build and rebuild not so much buildings and streets as lives and relationships, one by one.[9]

In addition to working with civic leaders, Pilla was known for working with other faith communities to address the poverty that afflicted his hometown: "The bishop's vision never was strictly a Catholic vision," said Rabbi Ben Kamin of *The Church in the City*.[10] "The moral implications of it apply to anybody. I would like members of our community to study it and consider what we need to do to become involved in it." Pilla also invited Rev. Dr. Kenneth Chalker, Methodist pastor of First Church in Cleveland, to join the *Church in the City* effort.[11] The two became fast friends with Pilla, dining at Chalker's home on more than one occasion.

Rick Krivanka, director of the Pastoral Planning Office during Pilla's tenure, describes Pilla's approach: "The heart of *The Church in the City* was the relationships. Bishop Pilla would say, 'You know, nothing happens between strangers. Between friends, all kinds of things are possible.'"[12] Krivanka observed how much both urban and suburban parishioners benefited from their newfound relationships: "One of the bottom-line outcomes was the suburban people; realizing how much they were being formed in their faith by being with the inner-city people. . . . Everyone thinks it is monetary model. The rich give to the poor. Well, there's different kinds of rich and there's different kinds of poor." What actually emerged, said Krivanka, was "that people were getting together in ministry. . . . Can we do things ministerially and socially in worship and community building?" He attributes this to the wisdom of his boss: "You know that was in Pilla's being—he knew you had to feel and live in that relational sense to appreciate one another."[13]

As in most dioceses across the United States at this time, Pilla's tenure in Cleveland was marked by a shameful denial of the clergy sex abuse scandal.[14] To avoid liability, attorneys representing the diocese used hardball tactics to interrogate victims.[15] To change this despicable practice, Pilla removed his longtime legal adviser, Auxiliary Bishop A. James Quinn, and appointed a lay task force to evaluate the diocese's treatment of alleged abuse victims. Quinn—who was trained in both canon and civil law—had become a national lightning rod after publicly suggesting church officials could send files of priest sex abusers to Rome's Apostolic Delegate "because they have immunity [from legal discovery]."[16] On Holy Thursday, 2002, however, in a gesture of repentance, Pilla won widespread praise when he knelt and publicly washed the feet of a woman who had been raped by a Cleveland priest.[17]

In February 2004, Pilla was forced to fire his friend and chief financial officer of twenty years, Joseph A. Smith. An FBI investigation revealed that the accounting firm Smith had contracted with on behalf of the diocese had directly or indirectly made off-the-books payments to Smith and to companies with whom he was affiliated.[18] The investigation and trials were covered extensively by the Cleveland media and led—unsurprisingly—to pervasive concern about the use and misuse of diocesan funds. In September 2004, the diocese hired a new chief financial officer, John Maimone, who sought to restore a measure of credibility. He appointed three respected professionals to the Diocesan Finance Council and took steps to make financial information more accessible to ordinary Catholics. Despite the bad publicity, parish contributions to the Cleveland Catholic Diocese Foundation were on track to reach a $23.1 million goal by September 2005.[19]

Although Pilla's legacy was undeniably tarnished by clergy sex abuse and financial scandals, he would be remembered for his pastoral sensitivity and sincere belief in empowering lay people to live up to their baptismal giftedness. In his 2022 eulogy, the Rev. Edward Estok elaborated on Pilla's motto, "Live on in my love," and how it became, at least for a time, a lived reality for Cleveland Catholics.

> As the years went by, we witnessed our brother Anthony's commitment to "live on in my love" grow into a veritable pastoral plan with structures and strategies within the church. He said, "togetherness and collaboration, must be the foundation of our mission and the basis of our hope." He loved "the process" that slowed things down so that everyone affected by a decision would have the chance to catch up and jump on board.[20]

Pilla strongly supported lay leadership, and believed the formation and education of lay ecclesial ministers—who were largely female—should be conducted in collaboration with the seminarians of the Cleveland diocese.[21] In 1991, Pilla's diocese created the Center for Pastoral Leadership, an innovative ministerial initiative in which future lay ministers and priests would be educated in a collaborative setting that would better prepare both to work together in the future. Kathleen Haase Falbo served as Cleveland's director of the Office of Pastoral Ministry. She was nationally known for helping to establish early certification standards for lay ecclesial ministers. Since 1985, the Cleveland program has certified four hundred laity for ministerial leadership in the diocese.[22] Pilla also supported alternative models for parish staffing, especially in the face of a steady decline in the numbers of priests.[23] At his retirement in 2006, thirteen Cleveland parishes were staffed by parish life coordinators, including women religious, deacons, and lay men and women. Innovative pastoral teams led other Cleveland parishes. Lisa Frey, a pastoral minister at the Church of the Resurrection in Solon, Ohio, estimates that during Pilla's tenure there were five or six parishes led by pastoral teams which shared responsibility for parish ministries. "It was an amazing and growing experience for me," she recalled.[24]

"AS THE PARISH GOES, SO GOES THE FAITH OF THE PEOPLE."—BISHOP PILLA[25]

Pilla's participative decision-making style and belief in "slowing things down" so everyone had time to "jump on board" was reflected in how diocesan offices functioned. Specifically, a consistent effort was made to get widespread buy-in before launching diocesan projects. This is especially true for Cleveland's Pastoral Planning Office, which coordinated the design of the *Vibrant Parish Life* process first promulgated by Pilla in a pastoral letter issued in February 2001. In his pastoral, Pilla outlined challenges that threatened parish vibrancy including "the effects of [demographic] growth in some areas, decline in others, fewer priests and religious, and the increasing inability to hire lay ecclesial ministers in the places where they are needed and wanted." The consequences of doing nothing, he said, would result in a "day when we will be a Church in decline because our parishes and our ministries have become weakened by fewer staff and diminished resources. This would be a great loss for our people."[26]

Diocesan statistics revealed that between 1970 and 2005, the number of priests in the Cleveland diocese decreased by 27 percent. Of the 296 "active" Cleveland priests (below retirement age of seventy), just twenty-nine were under forty. Presuming five ordinations per year, projections indicated that by 2015 there would be fewer active diocesan priests than the then-extant 233 parishes.[27] Although numbers of deacons, lay ministers, and religious serving parishes had increased, sacramental responsibilities rested with priests alone. For Pilla, moving forward with the *Vibrant Parish Life* process included two criteria:

1. Use parish staff personnel and material resources more collaboratively, creatively, and effectively, and reduce the overall staffing burden for priests and other parish ministers that was previously necessitated by separate efforts.
2. Increase shared leadership, collaboration, and the fullest use of gifts among laity as well as clergy and religious.[28]

In his pastoral letter, Pilla envisioned alternative models of parish leadership that would accommodate the unique sacramental duties of diocesan priests while allowing for fruitful lay ministerial initiative:

[T]hese alternatives may include shared assignments that include parish ministry as well [as] other ministries (e.g. chaplaincy, diocesan ministry); assigning a pastor or priest to more than one parish; placement of a deacon, religious or lay person to serve as Parish Life Coordinator; or the assignment of a pastoral team (priests, deacons, religious, lay persons) for two or more parishes.[29]

Perhaps the greatest difference between Pilla's vision for parish reconfiguration and the one mandated by Lennon in 2009 is that Pilla deeply respected the collaborative involvement of priests and lay leaders closest to each situation: "This respect mandates that any process involve initiative at the local community level. I do not believe that true parish life can be imposed from an outside authority. . . . [I]t must be discerned in faith and be embraced voluntarily with the heart."[30] Consequently, in his 2001 pastoral—some five years before Richard Lennon arrived in Cleveland—Pilla wrote forthrightly:

> My resistance to formulating an aggressive and sweeping plan for parish consolidations or closings is that, rather than "fixing" a fundamental problem or strengthening the faith of the people, the actual result is that people experience tremendous pain and alienation. I do not believe that building *Vibrant Parish Life* can be legislated. It must involve initiative at the local community level and be embraced willingly with the heart by those most affected. This demands local leadership.[31]

In January 2006, Pilla wrote to the Vatican and requested to retire before seventy-five, the mandatory retirement age for bishops. He cited health reasons.[32] It seems likely that the stresses of dealing with the ongoing legal proceedings over the financial scandal contributed to this decision. In April 2006, the Vatican accepted his request and announced the appointment of Boston auxiliary bishop Richard G. Lennon to Cleveland. Unfortunately, Lennon neither shared nor understood Pilla's wide-ranging vision. The outcome was tragic. As predicted, "tremendous pain and alienation" reverberated throughout an already hurting Cleveland diocese for the duration of Lennon's term.

RICHARD G. LENNON

When he was appointed to Cleveland at age fifty-nine, Richard Lennon was already known as the architect of Boston's devastating church closings after Cardinal Law hastily departed. Less well known were problematic issues that arose over Lennon's record as Boston's vicar general and moderator of the curia. According to Rocco Palmo, Lennon's record was marred by "controversies over decisions and methods which have been met with pain and sadness among the clergy and people of the archdiocese."[33] *Boston Globe* columnist Brian McGrory said people in the Cleveland Diocese may need to forget about participatory processes: "He's very authoritative, conservative and not particularly imaginative."[34] On the other hand, Ken Hokenson, a cabinet secretary for fundraising in the Boston Archdiocese who worked with Lennon for eleven years, described him as "an outstanding priest" and a "brilliant leader." "He's the only man I know who can quote canon law from memory," Hokenson told the *Akron Beacon Journal*.[35] The bishop fancied himself an expert in canon law—he read voraciously and had compiled a library of over three hundred books on the topic. Yet he had no formal education in the discipline.[36] This proved pivotal to Sister Kate's success in guiding canonical appeals from courageous Cleveland Catholics.

Richard Lennon grew up in Arlington, Massachusetts, a suburb of Boston. He attended St. James the Apostle Church, where he served as an altar boy and was known for being quiet and working hard at his studies. He suffered from a severe stutter which he finally overcame when in the seminary. After ordination in 1973, Lennon ministered as a parish priest for fifteen years. In 1988, despite the absence of formal training, Cardinal Law appointed him to the Archdiocese's Office for Canonical Affairs, where he advised diocesan priests on canonical matters.[37] He was appointed rector of St. John Seminary in 1999 and was consecrated auxiliary bishop in 2001. In December 2002 he was appointed apostolic administrator after Cardinal Law fled the diocese in disgrace. At the time of his episcopal consecration in 2001, the *Boston Globe* wrote: "Lennon's willpower, analytical bent and capacity for hard work have helped him surpass colleagues of greater charisma or careerism and build a reputation as a man who presses past obstacles where others might stop."[38]

David Clohessy, director of Survivors Network of Those Abused by Priests (SNAP), sharply criticized Lennon's appointment, accusing the new bishop of using hardball tactics with victims.[39] BishopAccountability.org later documented that, despite his initial denials that "he knew 'zero . . . nothing' about the extent of sexual abuse by clergy," Lennon in fact possessed a "deep and detailed knowledge" of clergy sex abuse cover-ups in the Archdiocese.[40] During the 1990s Lennon oversaw payment for psychiatric treatment and other expenses for Boston's accused priests. He also handled laicizations and advised Cardinal Law on abuse cases that involved other dioceses.[41]

As noted in chapter one, Lennon's time as apostolic administrator was notorious for the wholesale closure of viable Boston parishes in a misguided attempt to staunch the flow of red ink from sex abuse lawsuits. In April 2003, Boston's new ordinary, Cardinal Sean O'Malley, appointed him as vicar general of the Archdiocese. In that capacity Lennon oversaw the closing and selling of churches to raise money. But the initiative fell far short of the Archdiocese's projected net revenue of $200 million. As of 2008, after closing or merging seventy-five parishes, the Archdiocese had netted only $62.7 million.[42] The sale of east Boston parish, St. Mary Star of the Sea, in November 2006, is one shocking example of what went wrong. After refusing an earlier offer of $2 million from a non-Catholic denomination, the Archdiocese sold St. Mary Church for $850,000 to a commercial photographer, Michael Indresano. Just twenty days later, Indresano resold the church for $2.65 million to an evangelical sect, the Universal Church of the Kingdom of God.[43] Cardinal O'Malley ordered an investigation and discovered that in January 2006, in an apparent attempt to avoid selling Catholic property to any non-Catholic denomination, Richard Lennon had recommended the Indresano sale to the Archdiocesan Board of Consulters.[44]

This disregard—not to say disdain—for the ecumenical respect encouraged by Vatican II would later play out in Cleveland when Lennon declined to continue the cordial relationships with interdenominational leaders so carefully cultivated by his predecessor.[45] Meanwhile, Cardinal Sean O'Malley was desperately trying to quell the uproar in his Archdiocese resulting from Lennon's disastrous parish reconfiguration plan and the part he played in clergy sex abuse cover-ups. Such were the "controversies" that followed Richard G. Lennon when, on April 5, 2006, he was appointed the tenth bishop of the Diocese of Cleveland.

ACCLIMATING TO CLEVELAND—OR NOT

As Richard Lennon tried to acclimate to Midwestern ways, Cleveland Catholics became aware they were dealing with a very different style of leadership. For one thing, their new bishop was not accustomed to collaborative decision-making. Nor was he particularly interested in meeting with political leaders or his interdenominational counterparts. It didn't take long for the Cleveland diocese's executive director of Catholic Community Action, Len Calabrese, to conclude that his organization's highly regarded political advocacy was simply "not on [Lennon's] radar screen." Calabrese believed Lennon had "a totally different ecclesiology" compared to the one from which the diocese had ministered for twenty-five years. When a colleague tried to convince Lennon to meet with Cleveland public officials who could be sympathetic to the diocese's social justice efforts, Lennon "just looked at him and said, 'Politicians, public officials, why would I want to do that? Can you even be Catholic and be a public official?'"[46] In a wide ranging 2010 profile in the *Cleveland Plain Dealer*, several prominent interfaith leaders lamented that Lennon had "unraveled the interfaith and ecumenical work of his predecessor, Bishop Pilla."[47]

Diocesan priests soon noticed that not only was their new bishop unaccustomed to collaborative decision-making, he had little use for his predecessor, even going so far as to publicly belittle Pilla's legacy. The Rev. Bob Begin, a pastor who had also worked with the Catholic Commission, lamented,

[Lennon] never sat down once with Bishop Pilla to talk about the diocese. A native son, bishop for 25 years, who was renowned throughout the country for

The Church in the City, with the largest diocesan social action office in the whole country and he never sat down once with him.[48]

Calabrese was also dismayed by Lennon's public disrespect of Pilla. "People would bring up things: 'You know we've done it this way'. . . and he would reply, 'Yeah, that's another Pilla thing that didn't work,' or 'That's another Pilla thing we've got to change.'"[49] As Lennon began visiting Cleveland parishes for the first time, Krivanka heard disturbing feedback from parish leaders: "Someone would say 'Bishop, welcome to our parish.' And he would say 'It's not your parish. It's my parish.' And that kind of thinking is deeply problematic," said Krivanka.[50]

The new bishop was also less than comfortable with the many female lay ecclesial ministers serving in the diocese. There were numerous reports that he specifically requested that only parish priests and deacons be present when he visited any given parish. He also instructed the diocese's nationally recognized lay ecclesial ministry office to stop accepting candidates—who were largely female—into their three-year formation program. The lay ministers and women religious I interviewed for this book did not know why the bishop chose to do this.[51]

OF MISSION AND MONEY

When Lennon took the reins, the Cleveland diocese was in much better shape financially than Boston. It was in the black and had increased revenue by $6.4 million to $269 million in 2006. Catholics gave a record $106.1 million, the highest since 2002 when the impact of clergy sex abuse was first felt. Still, the diocese reported that 45 percent of its 231 parishes were operating in the red, many because a $26 million parochial school deficit had forced them to dip into savings and/or delay capital expenditures. Yet Chief Financial Officer John Maimone said the finances of the diocese and most parishes were not in crisis.[52]

In fact, the number of parishes operating in the red had not significantly changed for a number of years.[53] Under Pilla, about 60 percent of parishes were able to pay regular assessments to the diocese. Of the remaining 40 percent, many received subsidies and others had back-due assessments forgiven.[54] Pilla's philosophy was to keep Catholic parishes and schools going in urban regions for as long as possible. He prioritized mission over money. Calabrese recalls more than one conversation in which Pilla would reflect: "Why would you want to close parishes? . . . They're the presence of the church in a community and they're serving people in all kinds of ways."[55] Begin recalls a conversation about the early struggles of St. Colman Parish, a

West Side lifeline for immigrants and poor folk for over forty years: "[Pilla] said, 'When you can't keep on going, just come and let me know and we'll see what we can do.'"[56] In 2000, two Sisters of St. Joseph, Carol English and Lucy Dragonetti, were serving St. Colman as pastoral administrators. Begin, who was sacramental minister at the time, relishes the story: "Carol and Lucy went to Bishop Pilla and said, 'This is the Year of Jubilee, [the previous priest] never paid his assessments all those years before we took over. Will you forgive those?' And he [Pilla] did."[57]

Pilla's successor took a markedly different approach. Begin summarizes: "He evidently read a book on franchise management. He makes his decisions as if parishes are franchises. If there's enough room in one church [for all] to worship, why have more than one? A particular mission, ethnicity, none of those things means anything if the customer base can be satisfied by one church."[58] Lennon's corporate philosophy—sadly shared by too many bishops in other US dioceses—was soon reflected in dramatic changes to Bishop Pilla's *Vibrant Parish Life* process.

A PLANNING PROCESS DERAILED: VIBRANT PARISH LIFE PHASE II

On February 27, 2006, as Cleveland Catholics were adjusting to January's announcement of Anthony Pilla's resignation, the diocese's Office of Pastoral Planning and diocesan leaders rolled out the second phase of the *Vibrant Parish Life* process. This phase envisioned "sharing priests, deacons, parish life coordinators, lay ecclesial ministers and other parish staff, as well as actively engaging the gifts of all the baptized." Two "major concurrent steps for parishes" were identified:

1. Providing a comprehensive education about current and future realities in our diocese, especially regarding parish staffing and the implications of having fewer priests.
2. Discerning cluster partners, and then working together in a long-term relationship of collaboration to plan and provide pastoral care for these communities.[59]

The first phase of *Vibrant Parish Life* was devoted to training parish leaders, conducting self-studies, educating parishioners, and parish networking with an eye to future collaboration. After a January 2005 report and consultation with parish leaders identified a need for comprehensive educational resources about what it called "current and future diocesan realities," an exhaustive Resource Manual was developed for the second phase.[60] Parishes were asked to form two subcommittees, one for ongoing education, and one to discern proposals for cluster partners. Each parish was asked to discern two or three possible cluster configurations of up to five parishes each.[61] These configurations would then be submitted in order of preference to the diocese for review by a team of diocesan and parish staff members. This group would prepare a first draft of proposed clusters for all parishes in the diocese and send them back to the parishes for feedback. A second draft and consultation would then ensue with final cluster partners to be named by April 2007 after being approved by the parishes and the bishop.[62] Parish clusters would then work together in what was expected to be a "long term relationship of collaboration." The introductory materials carefully noted:

> In forming this relationship, each parish has its own parish identity, canonical status, and financial accountability. A cluster of parishes will address the future staffing and reconfiguring of parishes to meet pastoral needs for the next 5-10 years. In some cases over time, these collaborative efforts may lead to addressing the merging, consolidating, or closing of parishes to strengthen and sustain the long-term mission and ministry of the Church.[63]

Although the February 2006 planning materials acknowledged that collaborative efforts "may lead" to the possibility of mergers and closing "over time," there is little to suggest that the *Vibrant Parish Life* team—or anyone else in the diocese—anticipated Bishop Lennon's elimination of fifty-two Cleveland parishes just three years later. Notably, the 2006 introductory materials envisioned cluster partners as retaining their own canonical status and identities, a fact Krivanka repeated to the *Akron Beacon Journal* in October 2006: "Each parish will continue to have its own identity, canonical status and financial accountability," he said.[64] "This is a proven model that has been successful in dioceses across the country that have faced issues like fewer priests to serve parishes."[65] In February 2007, when Lennon announced the initial plan for cluster configurations, the Rev. Paul Rosing, a member of the *Vibrant Parish Life* committee, told the *Akron Beacon Journal*: "This is not about closing parishes. It's not about any major change that is going to affect any particular church or parish in the immediate future. It's about planning for one, two, five, 10 years in the future and how we're going to continue to keep parishes vibrant and vital."[66]

Yet in May 2007, when Lennon sent letters to parishes finalizing each cluster configuration, he issued "challenges" requiring twenty-three of the diocese's sixty-nine clusters to downsize by merging parishes and closing schools. Citing "migration to the suburbs, finances, and a worsening clergy shortage," Cleveland's new bishop decided that as many as twenty-three to forty-eight churches would close.[67] Hardest hit were churches in the city of

Cleveland proper where the *Cleveland Plain Dealer* staff reported at least twenty-five parishes were asked to downsize, as well as parishes in Cleveland's inner-ring suburbs, and urban cores of Akron (four to five closures) and Lorain (seven to nine closures).[68] Over the next fifteen to eighteen months, one-third of clusters were required to recommend which of their parishes and schools would close. The remaining clusters were simply asked to collaborate to better share resources.[69] Given Lennon's autocratic leadership style, it is perhaps unsurprising that he apparently decided on the "challenges" without the knowledge of clergy members of the *Vibrant Parish Life* committee on which Rosing and other pastors served.[70]

And so began eighteen months of turmoil, interparish altercations, and widespread dismay on the part of Catholics in the Cleveland diocese. The diocese hoped the eighteen-month cluster conversations would allow at-risk parishioners time to adjust, give their input, and begin moving through the inevitable grieving process. In derailing the original intent of the *Vibrant Parish Life* process, Lennon introduced the same contentious methods that led to so much turmoil in Boston, where Seitz noted that skeptical parishioners "compared [the cluster process] to the reality television program 'Survivor,' in which participants rely on guile and physical skill to avoid being voted 'off the island.'"[71]

For Krivanka, it was an integrity-testing moment. According to the diocesan manual and training given to cluster leaders, the clusters would be given another opportunity to weigh in after the bishop and diocesan officials made decisions based upon their initial recommendations. But it was not to be. He recalls a "defining moment of my life" sitting in Lennon's office:

[A]nd the bishop said, "Well, why would it go back to them?" I said, "Bishop, that's the process we presented, it's a back-and-forth conversation." And he says, "No, I'm the Bishop. It's my decision. Once they submit those proposals, I'm just going to decide." When he did that, and the mentality was, "No, I just decide," that fundamentally changed the spirit and integrity of the process.[72]

Krivanka agonized over Lennon's failure to appreciate the need to allow sufficient dialogue: "It was the killing of the conversation that I found very difficult. . . . His actions violated values that were foundational to my life's work."[73] Krivanka had worked for many years under a boss with a very different approach: "[Bishop Pilla] understood we needed to have time for the back and forth, for walking together, so people would have a voice and take some ownership for the outcome."[74]

ORGANIZING TO DEFEND PARISH RIGHTS

In late December 2007, just before the diocese first announced proposed cluster partners, FutureChurch sent a special mailing to over a thousand local supporters; hundreds of pastoral ministers, priests, and lay leaders; and members of the Diocesan Pastoral Council and *Vibrant Parish Life* Committees. Recipients were invited to a February 27 lecture given by William Clark SJ on his recent book: *A Voice of Their Own: The Authority of the Local Parish.*[75] The mailing included FutureChurch's "Do Not Stifle the Spirit" statement, which contained information about a parish's canonical right to exist, named eight best practices for preserving vibrant parishes, and offered information about alternative parish staffing models. A cover letter asked recipients to share information with parish leaders. It touted the organization's new Save Our Parish Community organizing packet that "provides proactive resources to preserve vibrant parishes, claim parish rights and resist unjust closures in the event . . . that any diocese decides to close vital, solvent parishes without the consent of parishioners."[76]

Over 200 people attended Clark's lecture and heard him explain how "the local Church possesses the proper type of authority essential to the life of the whole Church."[77] The institutional structure is needed and so is the "living tradition," but they become exclusively hierarchical if input from the laity is weak or without the intimacy of face-to-face discussion of the lived experience. "Look at the face of the Church," said Clark, "and you will see the Face of God."[78]

Founded in Cleveland in 1990—where its national offices are still located—FutureChurch and its board and staff were deeply concerned about parishes in the Cleveland diocese, twenty-eight of which had supported the organization's founding vision. In December 2007, FutureChurch cofounder, the Rev. Louis J. Trivison, asked for a meeting with Bishop Lennon to introduce the organization and to discuss the "Do Not Stifle the Spirit" statement. The bishop agreed, and on January 30, 2007, three FutureChurch leaders, including this author, met with Lennon and several diocesan staff.[79]

It did not go well. FutureChurch raised concerns about findings from a 2003 national study showing that 40 percent of merged parishes lost parishioners, whereas parishes kept open with "parish directors" (basically parish life coordinators) were more likely to increase parishioners.[80] Lennon said FutureChurch materials were too focused on the priest shortage. Three times he repeated that Cleveland parish reconfigurations were not about the priest shortage but were about finances and demographics. Yet his arguments soon belied his words. "When two priests are serving 10,000 people in the suburbs and 14 priests in a small radius in the city, I have to think about what to do," he said.[81] Schenk suggested that Cleveland's urban parishes could be kept open with parish life coordinators and pointed to the reality that urban parishes anchor whole neighborhoods in poorer parts of the city. At the time, thirteen Cleveland parishes were led by parish life coordinators. The author had been told by one of them that 95 percent of the thirteen were in the black.[82]

Unfortunately, Lennon did not support his predecessor's practice of appointing parish life coordinators to sustain urban parishes. Instead he implemented a one-priest-one-parish model that was becoming increasingly popular with bishops across the country. He also discontinued the use of parish pastoral teams. In March 2009, after he closed fifty-two urban and inner-ring suburban parishes, only two parishes would be led by non-priest pastors.

On May 17, 2007, just two weeks before Lennon issued his "challenges" proposing to close up to forty-eight parishes, Sister Kate Kuenstler gave a stirring presentation in Cleveland on the canonical rights of the Lay Christian faithful at a public program sponsored by FutureChurch.[83] She began by explaining why canon law is important: "Canon law is to protect personal rights. It is to provide avenues of recourse. It is to be used to redress grievances, and to be a means for the resolution of conflicts." Before Vatican II, said Sister Kate, "there was nothing written about the laity's rights and obligations in the law of the church." But today, she explained, "the Christian faithful have a juridic personhood. They have official standing in the church and the *Code of Canon Law* protects that standing." In light of the soon to be announced parish clusters, Kate focused on the administrative recourse process as an important means of defending parish rights:

> Administrative acts are issued by those with executive authority in the diocese—bishops, vicar generals, chancellor, superintendent of schools, directors of diocesan offices. . . . [T]he one who claims to have been injured by an administrative action can make recourse for any just reason, to the higher superior of the one who took the action. If such a person [for example] uses their office to change the juridic status of a parish without just cause, this can be taken to the administrative process. . . . So if it's a Bishop then you petition the Congregation for Clergy at the Vatican. If they will not take the case, then you take it to the Vatican Signatura, the Supreme Court in the Roman Catholic church.[84]

Few listening that evening anticipated that in just two short years, a dozen Cleveland parishes would have administrative recourse appeals pending in Rome at the Congregation for the Clergy. Virtually every one of the Cleveland appeals relied at some point on Sister Kate's canonical expertise. At the end of the program, the FutureChurch executive director (this book's author) announced that *Save Our Parish Community* canonical resources had already been delivered to at least fifty-five parish leaders. She also encouraged the nearly two hundred attendees to share information with their own parish personnel.

NORTHEAST OHIO PARISHES RESIST

Over the next eighteen months, as recommendations from each cluster trickled in, Northeast Ohio media dutifully reported which parishes had been "voted off the island."[85] In June 2008 Historic St. Peter's was the first to announce publicly its intent to oppose the recommendation that it merge with St. John Cathedral.[86]

By February 2009 a total of ten parishes—Historic St. Peter's, St. Barbara, St. Casimir, Immaculate Heart of Mary, St. Jerome, Our Lady of Good Counsel, Our Lady of Perpetual Help, St. Malachi, St. Stephen, and Sacred Heart in Akron—had publicly announced their opposition to being closed even before Richard Lennon's final decisions were delivered on March 14, 2009.[87] Local political leaders also weighed in. "If you have something that's working, I don't know why you would fix it," Councilman Joseph Cimperman said in October 2007 after learning that the Historic St. Peter's—one of the most vibrant and socially active parishes in the city—would be closed.[88] Over the

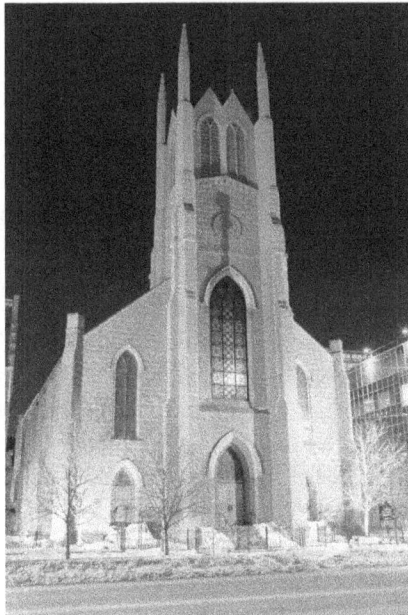

Figure 7.1   A winter night's view of the exterior of the Historic St. Peter Church in Cleveland, Ohio. ©2009 Peggy Turbett

next two years Cleveland City Council members worked diligently to expand the number of churches designated as historic landmarks. "I'm not about to lose these churches to the wrecking ball," said Councilman Mike Polensek.[89] "We're not only abandoning the faith in the city, but also demolishing our history and heritage."

For eighteen months, long-suffering Catholic leaders ordered to downsize their parishes had reluctantly participated in a cluster mandate no one wanted. Richard Lennon's March 14 official letters announcing he would close an unexpectedly high number of fifty-two parishes were met with outrage and dismay. The bishop had ignored the recommendations of at least nine clusters and closed parishes that representatives said should remain open: St. Colman, St. Ignatius, St. Patrick, West Park, Sacred Heart in Slavic Village, and St. Wendelin, all in Cleveland, as well as St. James in Lakewood, St. Mary and St. Joseph in Lorain, and St. Mary in Akron. Catholics at three landmark churches—St. Colman, St. Ignatius, and St. James in Lakewood— were stunned to learn their parishes and churches would no longer exist. "He ignored the cluster committee," said an astonished Rita Gaertner, president of the St. Colman Parish Council. "Sixteen months of meetings. All that work. We don't want to be bitter. But we can't understand. Where is the logic?"[90] Carol Romansky was typical of a number of St. Colman parishioners who actually lived in suburban communities outside the city but came to St. Colman for Mass and to serve its disadvantaged community. "The suburbs are isolated from the poor," she said, noting how inner-city neighborhoods had taken the biggest hits in the downsizing. "Would Jesus have stayed in the suburbs?"[91]

FutureChurch quickly issued a media statement decrying the closure of viable urban parishes and asked the diocese to employ alternative staffing models approved by church law. Their statement pointedly observed: "Bishop Lennon is following the same corporate downsizing model used recently in other dioceses, such as Camden, Allentown, and Scranton. FutureChurch's *Save Our Parish Community* project is providing advocacy support and resources to struggling parishioners all over the country."[92] The organization sent an email blast to hundreds of supporters in Northeast Ohio with a link to free resources to help Catholics discern a way forward. Scores of parishioners from at least twenty parishes downloaded educational, prayer, discernment,[93] and organizing resources. An email chain of nearly forty Northeast Ohio activists was created from those who had downloaded resources. FutureChurch sent regular updates about canonical appeal procedures. An early e-blast said: "Working with an expert in canon law, FutureChurch has put together two new resources geared specifically to the Cleveland reality. These can help people decide whether they wish to proceed further with appeal plans or not." The "expert in canon law" was none other than Sr. Kate Kuenstler who, as was her method, preferred to work anonymously. Years later she explained to a rapt FutureChurch audience why anonymity was important:

> Over the years, bishops and others always wanted to know the name of the canon lawyer who was helping the laity. I always stayed anonymous because recourse to the Congregation for the Clergy is recourse from the laity themselves. I did not want the use of my name and my canon law degree to diminish the authentic role of the laity who are the essential actors in this most difficult process of taking recourse against their own Bishop.[94]

It was also a fraught time in church politics—the Holy See's highly controversial Apostolic Visitation of Institutes of Women Religious in the United States of America had just been announced—and it was wiser for Kate to remain behind the scenes as she had successfully done in Camden.[95]

Kate drafted a sample letter to Bishop Lennon so those who wished to appeal could quickly send it within the ten "useful days" allotted by canon law.[96] Initial estimates from FutureChurch and others indicate that at least twenty-one appeal letters were sent to Bishop Lennon, although just eleven were publicly identified by the *Cleveland Plain Dealer*.[97] Many letters came from Catholics whose parishes were closed against cluster recommendations. Kate's sample letter suggested three possible reasons for requesting mediation and recourse:

1. The salvation of souls of our parish will be put in grave harm if this decision is carried out.
2. We do not believe your decision was taken with the required prudence required in canon law.
3. The diocesan procedures for reconfiguration were not followed.

She further advised activists:

> Be sure to make clear what of the bishop's announcement you are taking recourse against. You need to state clearly what you want instead. This could be the cluster recommendation you sent originally to the bishop. This is what your process in the cluster originally decided would be best, based upon the data and facts you gathered to make such a decision.[98]

Lennon's letter to the parishes was boilerplate, giving similar reasons for the closures such as "demographics, finances, and priest trends."[99] It is commendable that the Diocese of Cleveland—unlike Camden and later the Archdiocese of New York—provided parishioners with the official decree they would need to appeal.[100] The diocese also helpfully specified that letters to appeal Lennon's decision must be received by March 27. Yet there were

egregious canonical mistakes. The bishop had failed to issue a separate decree
for closing the parish church. Further, the merger decrees were boilerplate,
rather than individualized for each parish. This did not become clear until
2012, when the Vatican ruled in favor of the twelve parishes that had pursued
and won their appeals.

Over the next three weeks, Kate provided explicit canonical guidance
in anticipation of Lennon's probable denial of parishioner appeals. She
encouraged activists to gather data and address any specific issues named
in each of their decrees. She created a helpful document that carefully outlined the process of appealing to the Congregation for the Clergy—including sample letters and examples. An updated version of this document
—now known as "Canonical Appeals Recourse Process"—is still regularly
downloaded from the FutureChurch website and would subsequently guide
Catholics in other dioceses—nationally and internationally—in pursuing their own appeals.[101] In the spring of 2012, Regina Dilego wrote to
FutureChurch:

> I want to share with you that North American Martyrs has received notification
> from the Congregation for the Clergy in Rome. . . . They have decided in our
> favor! Your information essentially allowed me to compose focused documents
> that appear to have done the job. I downloaded the *Canonical Appeals Process.*
> I cannot thank you enough.[102]

Once the appeal letter to the bishop was sent with proof of delivery, Lennon had thirty days to respond. If he did not respond, canon law stipulates
that he effectively denied the appeal. Activists then have fifteen days to petition the Congregation for the Clergy via the apostolic nuncio in Washington,
DC. Kate strongly advised parishioners to use the time between their initial
letter to the bishop and receiving his response (or not), to gather information
to counter the bishop's reasons for closing their parish with reasons why the
parish should remain a juridic person in the law. At the time, the odds of
winning an appeal to the local bishop—or to Rome—were not good. Michael
Dunnigan, a canon lawyer at the St. Joseph Foundation which, like Sister
Kate, offered pro bono canonical help to Catholics, told the *Cleveland Plain
Dealer*: "Unfortunately, it's an uphill battle. I can't think of an instance in
which a bishop changed his mind or was persuaded to change his mind."[103]
St. Joseph Foundation director Chuck Wilson said, "The law grants a lot of
discretion to the bishop. The odds are stacked against the parishioners. The
bishop will prevail, and I think that's too bad."[104]

SAINT COLMAN AND SAINT IGNATIUS APPEAL TO BISHOP, AND HE LISTENS

With the unexpected news that Bishop Lennon wanted to close their churches, Catholics from two large, iconic West Side parishes quickly swung into action. St. Colman was built by Irish immigrants, most of whom eventually moved to the suburbs. The cluster had recommended closing St. Stephen, a smaller nearby parish, and keeping St. Colman open, especially in light of its vigorous outreach to poor people in the neighborhood. In 2009, St. Colman counted thirteen hundred households in a community where the average income was below $20,000. The parish was (and is today) a haven for immigrants hailing from twenty-five different countries who daily knock on its doors in search of legal and financial assistance. "If this parish weren't involved in bringing good news to the poor, I would not spend a lick of energy trying to keep it open," pastor Bob Begin told CNN. "But because it is bringing good news to the poor, then I have a responsibility to guard and defend this mission against anyone who threatens it."[105]

The timing of Lennon's March 14 announcement proved providential. St. Colman Parish annually hosts a large St. Patrick Day Mass attended by thousands of Irish suburbanites who pack the church to celebrate. A St. Colman staff member, Eileen Kelly, quickly created a petition and collected over three thousand signatures asking Lennon to keep St. Colman open. Begin recalled, "I remember saying that the dumbest thing [Lennon] could do would be to close St. Colman's and St. Ignatius and St. James all on the day before St. Patrick's day. And that's what he did."[106]

Begin—who is also a civil attorney—quickly contacted Kate for canonical guidance. She traveled to Cleveland to meet with St. Colman Catholics and other parish groups. Begin found Kate to be "truly competent, confident, and always optimistic." He was especially encouraged by her optimism because "I had listened to Bishop Pilla, who told me privately that Rome never reversed a bishop on something like this."[107] Following Kate's advice, St. Colman formed a ten-member committee to guide its appeal to the Vatican if Lennon denied their appeal letter.[108] As the parish had posted a small deficit in previous fiscal years, finances were believed to have been an issue in the bishop's decision. Renowned for its social outreach, it was not unusual for St. Colman to distribute up to $100,000 to needy families in any given year.[109] For Begin, showing a budget surplus to the diocese was not a priority: "We spend as much as we can on the poor. We don't want to just save money."[110] Even so, he noted, "Last year, we cut our deficit in half. And we're actually going to finish this year in the black."[111] Begin met with Lennon twice to advocate for his people. On May 2, 2009, Lennon reversed himself: "I now have a more complete understanding of the extent of social and community services at the parish and the outreach to the diverse neighborhoods . . . the needs of the church and our Catholic community may better be served with both St. Colman and St. Stephen continuing as parishes."[112]

Richard Lennon's decision to close the stately Saint Ignatius of Antioch Church on the West Side of Cleveland stunned parishioners and politicians alike. Established in 1902 as a multinational parish, St. Ignatius served twelve hundred households and was regarded as perhaps the most diverse congregation in the diocese.[113] The parish—located about two miles from St. Colman on Lorain Avenue—supported numerous social services in the neighborhood as well as a youth athletic league. Its popular parochial school had an enrollment of more than 360 students. Ignoring the recommendation of the cluster committee, Lennon had made the perplexing decision to close the church but keep the school open. This left Rev. James R. McGonegal scratching his head: "The question that remains now is how you run a parish school without a parish?"[114] "St. Ignatius is everything a Cleveland diocese church should be," said Cleveland city councilman Jay Westbrook. "It's like the United Nations here. They have an integrated school and church. This is where the diocese should be taking a stand."[115]

McGonegal received dozens of calls from current or former parishioners asking how they could help. Parish leaders decided to lodge a formal appeal with Lennon. While St. Ignatius had reported a modest budget surplus, it owed $1 million to the diocese and faced expensive roof and foundation repairs. To prove their viability, church leaders quickly organized.[116] In just a few weeks, parishioners and a six-thousand-member alumni association raised more than $1 million to meet the parish's financial obligations.[117]

Terry Gravens, an attorney helping with the parish appeal, named what is perhaps the clearest example of Lennon's lack of familiarity with the Cleveland diocese: "If St. Ignatius is closed, there will be no Catholic presence in the area from West 54th Street to West 136th Street and from Lake to Puritas Avenues," he said. "We're asking the bishop to reconsider his decision."[118] "[Lennon] really didn't know the territory," Begin explained. "He had no idea that there were no churches . . . in an area where most people don't have cars."[119]

At the 5:00 p.m. Mass on May 2, McGonegal told a cheering congregation that Lennon had reversed himself and that St. Ignatius would remain open. The bishop said he granted the reprieves because he had come to a better understanding of the social and community services provided by the parishes and future financial viability.[120] Lennon also said he had "a better understanding of the importance of the Lorain Avenue corridor and its demographics for the work of the church."[121] Both St. Colman and St. Ignatius are historic fixtures along that corridor. The bishop's decisions came with conditions. Both parishes were given four years to become more financially viable, which would include ending deficit spending, completing capital repairs, and creating emergency reserves while growing households and Mass attendance.[122]

Of the twenty-one parishes known to have appealed to Lennon, only St. Colman and St. Ignatius were permitted to remain open. These successes point to Kate's preference for resolving disputes at the local level whenever possible. Lennon denied appeals from the other nineteen parishes. Seven decided against further recourse and were closed: St. Procop, Sacred Heart, Our Lady of Mercy, the Community of St. Malachi, Sacred Heart in Slavic Village (all in Cleveland), and in Lorain, St. Stan's and St. Joseph. Lennon's refusal to consider appeals from Saint Procop in Cleveland and St. Joseph in Lorain was especially heart-wrenching. St. Procop anchored Cleveland's West 41st Street neighborhood. It hosted Alcoholics Anonymous meetings, established affordable neighborhood housing, and provided free groceries and hot food for those in need. Parish life coordinator Sister Annette Amendolia SND told the *Cleveland Plain Dealer*, "I'm in the black, I pay my bills, but that doesn't matter. The whole thing wasn't fair. . . . The part that's been the hardest for me is ending our help for the poor. It's very hard to give that up."[123] In Lorain, parish life coordinator Deacon Lou Maldonado lamented that Lennon ignored the cluster recommendation to merge St. Joseph Church—whose 190 households supported a men's homeless shelter—with nearby Holy Trinity parish. "There's not another parish that has opened its doors to house the hungry and homeless and it seems so unfair to them."[124] To its credit, Catholic Charities assumed management of St. Joseph Homeless Shelter after the church was closed.[125] The diocese also donated St. Procop's Convent to the Community Service Alliance, which had already rehabbed it as a residence for men moving from homelessness to self-sufficiency.[126] Nevertheless, the *Cleveland Plain Dealer* reported at the time that this generosity was "unlikely to be duplicated for the dozens of other nonprofits and churches leasing buildings from the Northeast Ohio diocese. Diocese spokesman Robert Tayek said that church law requires the diocese to sell its properties at market value."[127]

AN UPHILL BATTLE—RECOURSE TO THE CONGREGATION FOR THE CLERGY

While Sister Kate's early anonymous guidance via FutureChurch emails was used by virtually all Cleveland parishes that sought to appeal, a number also contracted with her privately for help preparing their canonical recourse to Rome. In addition to St. Colman, she directly advised parishioners from Historic St. Peter; St. James, Lakewood; St. Patrick West Park; St. Margaret Mary, Euclid; St. Mary, Lorain; St. Wendelin, and St. Emeric. In the end, twelve Cleveland parishes decided to pursue canonical recourse to Rome.[128] Unbeknownst to anyone, Catholics from two other parishes—St. Margaret Mary in South Euclid and St. Martha in Akron—apparently also sent appeals to Rome although these could not later be verified. One of these, St. Mary, Lorain, was not threatened with closure, but appealed to restore its original name after a merger in which it was renamed "Mary Mother of God."[129] In addition to St. Mary in Lorain, the remaining appealing parishes were St. Adalbert, St. Barbara, St. Casimir, St. Emeric, St. James in Lakewood, St. John the Baptist in Akron, St. Mary in Bedford, St. Mary in Akron, St. Patrick in West Park, the Historic St. Peter, and St. Wendelin.

ENDANGERED CATHOLICS

Meanwhile, Catholics from appealing parishes joined together for support and to share strategies, both canonical and political. A group calling itself "Endangered Catholics" regularly spoke to the media, hosted prayer vigils, and participated in public protests. The group's vice chairperson, Bob Kloos, forwarded information from FutureChurch, helped arrange marches, and spearheaded a weekly demonstration in front of St. John's Cathedral. Kloos, a beloved priest who left the active ministry to marry, also consulted with Kate for canonical information to pass along to his group. Kate told him how Cardinal Burke's ruling that a bishop cannot close a church simply "because he can't staff it" would be "front and center" in her work with the Cleveland appeals.[130] "Bishops think they can do whatever they want," she said, "but they don't understand the law. So I'm not surprised they are making mistakes."

On June 27, 2009, Endangered Catholics sponsored a daylong presentation with Boston activist Peter Borré.[131] Borré spoke about Boston's shuttered parishes and strategies that included sit-ins, church occupations, and canonical appeals. In a number of cases vigil/occupation strategies had resulted in the Boston Archdiocese reversing itself and allowing a church to remain open.[132] However, after local efforts failed, the appeals of Boston parishes to Rome were denied. This is probably because they were the first of at least one hundred US appeals that flooded Vatican offices in ensuing years.[133] Kate regularly discouraged demonstrative tactics against dioceses as she knew they were frowned upon in Vatican circles and could diminish the chances of success for any given canonical recourse. Several Cleveland groups, St. Patrick, West Park; St. Casimir in Cleveland; and St. John the Baptist, Akron, among others, chose to work more closely with Borré and hired him as a sort of liaison with Vatican offices. These groups also adopted Borré's demonstrative public strategies. Other parish groupings in Endangered Catholics chose to be more circumspect. Borré himself played a major media role in 2012, when he told the Associated Press that the Congregation for the Clergy had ruled a week earlier that Lennon must reopen twelve Cleveland parishes. In a marked departure from protocol, the Vatican had apparently failed to notify Lennon first.[134]

As Richard Lennon shuttered their churches one by one, individuals from Endangered Catholics attended the closing Masses of its member parishes. Lennon insisted on personally presiding at each parish's final Mass even though most parishioners did not welcome him. He reportedly wore a bulletproof vest, and feelings ran so high that plainclothes Cleveland police personnel were stationed inside the church while their uniformed counterparts patrolled outside.[135]

Parishioners at St. Emeric in Cleveland and St. John the Baptist in Akron staged short-lived sit-ins after their closing Masses rather than voluntarily leave their churches.[136] When Lennon asked congregants at one parish in Akron, "Do you really believe that I like doing this?" parishioners shouted, "Yes!"[137] At the same Akron church, a woman marched up the center aisle, raised her right arm, and said, "Bishop Lennon, in the name of God—in the name of all that is holy—stop closing the churches before it is too late."[138] When Lennon said the final Mass at St. Casimir, many congregants stood, turned their backs, and walked out. For the next three years, forty to fifty Casimir Catholics would gather every Sunday for a prayer service in front of their church.[139] As Clevelanders awaited Rome's ruling in what became a seemingly interminable process, Endangered Catholics worked hard to build solidarity among grieving Catholics who were nonetheless determined to seek recourse against all odds.

Chapter 8

Parishioners Persevere

As the months dragged on, thousands of letters from determined Northeast Ohio parishioners poured into the Vatican. An official Apostolic Visitation of Bishop Lennon was launched, the outcome of which was never made public. Yet in March 2012, thanks in no small part to the faith and canonical skill of Sr. Kate Kuenstler, the perseverance of Catholics would finally pay off. Space considerations preclude an expansive discussion of each of the twelve Cleveland parish communities that endured and won. I will therefore focus on three faith communities in some depth—St. Adalbert and the Black community, St. Emeric, and Historic St. Peter—while providing the occasional cameo treatment of others. Their stories mirror those of many faith communities with whom Kate worked in the United States and abroad who resisted the dissolution of a beloved parish home.

THE BLACK COMMUNITY: ST. CECILIA, EPIPHANY, AND SAINT ADALBERT

Poorer neighborhoods were most affected by the loss of stable church congregations. Cleveland's Black community was especially hard hit. In the Mt. Pleasant neighborhood, Bishop Lennon closed St. Cecilia and Epiphany parishes because of back-due financial assessments. Both parishes were committed to urban evangelization, and both were running in the black, thanks to rental income from the school buildings they owned.[1] But both were also in arrears on diocesan assessments. Ursuline Sister Sheila Marie Tobbe remembers Bishop Pilla being unconcerned about collecting the assessments from either parish because he knew if one or the other eventually closed, proceeds from the sale of church properties would take care of their diocesan debt.

"Don't ever worry about assessments. I'll never pressure you for assessments," Pilla had said to their pastor, the Rev. Dan Begin.[2]

Epiphany and St. Cecilia were engaged in a cluster process with a predominantly white parish that also had a significant endowment. The diocese said the cluster could have just one priest. Three proposals were submitted, one of which named St. Cecilia as the center and Epiphany and the other parish as mission sites. After each cluster meeting, Tobbe and Father Dan would bemoan the culturally insensitive—and largely unconscious—racism displayed at the sessions. Tobbe recalls, "I said to the African Americans, 'I just apologize for what you've had to deal with.' They said, 'Don't worry about us, Sister. We know how to function without buildings.'"[3] When she pointed out that Epiphany and St. Cecilia's ten representatives could vote down the other proposals, her parishioners told her: "We don't want to operate that way. That's not true to who we are as people. Church isn't a win-lose thing. We'll submit our three plans knowing their plan will get accepted."[4] The diocese did accept the proposal put forth by the largely white parish, and both Epiphany and St. Cecilia churches were slated to close. The closure of these two parishes, along with St. Adalbert, left nineteen square miles without any Catholic presence in predominantly Black Cleveland neighborhoods stretching from Shaker Heights in the east to downtown Cleveland.[5] Rev. Dan Begin lamented: "For many Black families, the church is their whole life. Now there's nothing convenient for them to get to. A lot of them are just not going to Mass."[6]

Before Lennon celebrated the closing Mass at St. Cecilia's, Begin "got all kinds of instructions" from the diocese to avoid incorporating traditionally African-American cultural elements into the ritual.[7] "But Dan was allowed to say some words at the end, so he got up and sang an African American spiritual," Tobbe chuckled.[8] Insensitivity to the need for culturally appropriate prayer and ritual was not unusual for Lennon.

After being invited to the first "Faith in Culture" celebration hosted by the Hispanic parish La Sagrada Familia, the new bishop of Cleveland asked, "Faith in culture? What's culture got to do with faith?"[9] Len Calabrese was stunned by his remark. "Did [he] not read anything from Pope John Paul II? John Paul put his emphasis on how faith gets passed down. It's mediated through culture."[10]

Epiphany parish also housed the Thea Bowman Center, a not-for-profit organization that delivered an array of services to poor families, including, among other things, education, computer and GED classes, and food distribution. Sylvia Little-Harris, a program coordinator for the center, was pessimistic about the future: "We are a minority within a minority, and given the rate and recklessness of the bishop's decisions, he has cut off the remnant of African-Americans."[11] But the Thea Bowman Center survived thanks to the initiative of Tobbe, who at the time also served as the center's executive director, and support from her staff and board. After selling Epiphany's school to the daycare center already renting it, the diocese received its back-due assessments. With the support of Catholic Charities director Tom Mullin—who realized the center was well run and fiscally sound—the diocese accepted a proposal from Epiphany staff. It gave the deed to the remaining Epiphany properties to the Thea Bowman Center. Today it continues to serve the Mt. Pleasant neighborhood where 65 percent of families live near or below the poverty level.[12] A demoralized Epiphany-St. Cecilia leadership chose not to pursue a canonical appeal because they believed it was doomed to fail.[13]

Catholics at the predominantly Black Saint Adalbert/Our Lady of Blessed Sacrament (OLBS) parish made a different decision. They chose to pursue a canonical appeal. St. Adalbert/OLBS was the first African-American Catholic parish in Cleveland, and it is the only Catholic parish in the largely Black Fairfax neighborhood. It is also the only Black parish in the Cleveland diocese to pursue a canonical appeal. This is largely due to the faith and diligence of Phillis Clipps, who never wavered in her trust that God would somehow restore her parish to its people.

With 150 households and 381 individuals, St. Adalbert was the smallest parish in their three-parish cluster. Cluster partners offered two proposals to the diocese. One was to merge all three parishes with worship to be held at St. Adalbert. The other was a two-parish scenario in which St. Adalbert would be closed.[14] The diocese elected to close St. Adalbert.[15] Phillis Clipps, her husband Phillip, and several Parish Council members met with Bishop Lennon twice to see if he would change his mind. "We weren't on life support," Phillis recalled.[16] "We had absolutely no debt. We were current with our assessment, our facilities were good, and we even had a little bit of money in the bank." But the bishop was unconvinced. Diocesan media spokesperson Robert Tayek told Phillip Clipps that he needed to accept that St. Adalbert was dying. "Well then you should let us die. You don't euthanize a parish," responded Phillip.

St. Adalbert/OLBS members voted to join the Endangered Catholics group and pursued a canonical appeal. Through Endangered Catholics and with the help of FutureChurch resources, they received the canonical guidance provided anonymously by Kate. "As a group, we would talk about what should be put in our letters and how we should present our arguments to Rome," Phillis recalls. "They stressed the importance of meeting every single deadline. And we worked very diligently to make sure that we met them all. . . ."[17]

Filing recourse in Rome did not stop Bishop Lennon from presiding at St. Adalbert's final Mass and chaining the doors of the church. It would be two long years before Rome would finally rule on their appeal. Meanwhile, led by the dynamic Clipps duo, St. Adalbert's spiritually homeless parishioners formed "Roamin' Catholics"—an itinerant band of about fifty Black Catholics who traveled from church to church each Sunday looking for a new place to worship. In August 2011, Phillis told the *Cleveland Plain Dealer* that she knew of twenty-nine St. Adalbert/OLBS parishioners who no longer attended any church, fourteen members or families who had joined various Protestant churches, and sixty-nine who had joined other Catholic parishes.[18]

SAINT EMERIC—PERSONAL/ETHNIC PARISHES TARGETED

Bishop Lennon ignored the recommendations of the Hungarian community cluster process to preserve all three of its Catholic churches. He ordered St. Margaret in Orange and St. Emeric in Ohio City to close and merge with St. Elizabeth in the old Hungarian neighborhood of Buckeye. Unfortunately, this decision again revealed Lennon's lack of familiarity with the Catholics—and the neighborhoods—of Cleveland. St. Elizabeth on Buckeye Road is in a high-crime area with no nearby freeway access. "You have to go through some really tough territory," said parishioner Eva Szabo. "That's a risk for our elderly."[19]

To understand the passionate efforts of St. Emeric Catholics to keep their church open, one need look no further than the man who spearheaded their appeal, Miklos B. Peller. Peller escaped Hungary on November 9, 1956, after the Soviet Union invaded his country. He was fifteen years old. Most St. Emeric parishioners—or their parents and grandparents—shared similar experiences seeking refuge in the United States. St. Emeric was a personal parish. Personal parishes allow Catholics from anywhere to register as members. In territorial parishes (which are the majority in the United States) only Catholics who live within a certain geographic area are permitted to register as official members of the parish. Personal parishes with financial resources were frequently targeted to merge with indebted territorial parishes, although this does not appear to have been the case at St. Emeric.[20]

Hungarian people came to St. Emeric from all over the Cleveland diocese to pray in their own tongue and to share the faith that strengthened them. Preserving this treasured heritage was extremely important for St. Emeric parishioners who found creative and fun ways to pass that heritage along to their children and grandchildren. Every Friday night 250 boys and girls attended meetings of the Hungarian Scouts where only Hungarian was spoken. The children were also expected to read and write in Hungarian.[21] After Richard Lennon announced the closure of St. Emeric, the largest Hungarian-speaking community in North America was faced with losing a cherished faith and cultural center.[22] Peller was dumbfounded: "We all were taken by surprise. Why should we be closing? We're a very vibrant parish. The three reasons stated were lack of parishioners, lack of priests and lack of funds. And we had all three. So we couldn't figure out why this is."[23]

After emigrating to the United States, Peller studied structural engineering at Case Western Reserve University and founded a world-renowned engineering firm.[24] A music lover, he played the organ every Sunday for Mass at St. Emeric. With the help and advice of the St. Joseph Foundation, he wasted no time in spearheading a canonical appeal on behalf of his Hungarian community. He would later seek the canonical counsel of Sister Kate. In his recourse to the Congregation for the Clergy, Peller said the three factors Bishop Lennon had listed for closing his church "do not exist at St. Emeric parish."[25] The parish had a positive cash flow, with a reported $1.2 million in savings.[26] A Hungarian priest, the Rev. Sandor Siklodi, had led the parish for twenty-five years as resident administrator. He was an "extern priest" whose appointment had been accepted by Bishop Anthony Pilla in 1985. As an extern, Siklodi created no drain on diocesan finances because the parish, not the diocese, paid his stipend. If St. Emeric were to close, argued Peller, the Cleveland diocese would have one less priest available for pastoral work. Peller lamented that if Lennon had visited St. Emeric before making his decision, he would have experienced the "vibrancy and viability" of his parish. By far the greatest concern however was the need for his fellow countrymen to pray in their own language:

[T]he majority of the parishioners, although they can converse in English, need the Celebration of the Eucharist and the prayers in the Hungarian language as a means to the salvation of their souls as that is the language that is closest to their hearts, that is the language they use when praying to or conversing with God, his son Jesus, the Blessed Virgin Mother, and saints.[27]

The St. Emeric community included 350 households and over six hundred individual parishioners.[28,] The average age of parishioners at the time was fifty and above. Most practiced their faith in their native language.[29] As many parishioners were homebound or in extended care facilities, visits from Hungarian speaking Father Sandor were important to their spiritual well-being. Kate described the serious impact closing St. Emeric would have on its people:

Coming over from Hungary, they were a people who had already experienced great pain in their lives. And then to come and have a bishop look them in the face and say, "You're gone. This is over for you." Their heart was ripped out. They thought the one place they could feel safe was the Catholic church. And here in Cleveland with this Bishop, that wasn't the case.[30]

After the closing Mass, without Father Sandor's prior knowledge, at least seven St. Emeric parishioners staged a sit-in with the goal of, as parishioner John Yuhasz put it, "forcing Richard Lennon into a dialogue toward saving their 106-year-old church."[31] The sit-in ended sixteen hours later after police warned protesters they would be arrested if they didn't leave. Some parishioners opposed the vigil, concerned it would harm their Vatican appeal and impede ongoing negotiations with the diocese to allow the ethnic language, cultural, and scouting programs to continue on the property.[32] After the parish closed, determined St. Emeric Catholics hosted prayer outside the church "every Sunday for two and a half years," recalled Peller.[33] A sympathetic Fr. Bob Begin invited St. Emeric Catholics to worship at his parish: "When the people of St. Emeric's were suffering, the people of St. Colman's gladly welcomed them," said Begin, who quickly learned enough Hungarian to celebrate the Mass.[34]

St. Emeric parishioners were ecstatic when Lennon announced in 2012 that he would not appeal a Vatican ruling to reopen their church. Peller and other parishioners hoped to bring back their former pastor, Rev. Sandor Siklodi, who had transferred to Chicago.[35] But Lennon refused to reinstate Siklodi. On May 17, Peller and three other parishioners were summoned to meet with Lennon and other diocesan officials, including the chancellor, Sr. Therese Guerin Sullivan.

After introducing himself as the procurator of the St. Emeric appeal, a churlish Lennon "yelled at me that 'no you are no longer the procurator. The appeals are over.'"[36]

"Ok, I am the organist," Peller nimbly responded.

Lennon informed the group that none of the newly reopened parishes would be restored to what they had been two years ago. Perhaps he would assign a Hungarian-speaking priest for Sunday Mass and an English-speaking priest for daily Mass. But neither would reside at the rectory. In Peller's view this would seriously impair St. Emeric's viability and result in diminishing Mass attendance.[37]

Peller contacted Sister Kate, who helped him prepare a canonical appeal. St. Emeric petitioners asked the Vatican to restore their beloved Father Sandor as pastor to a people he had faithfully served for twenty-five years. Kate well remembers her approach: "[The diocese] was treating them like a territorial parish without making them a territorial parish. And that was how I developed the argument. This is a personal parish, and everything the bishop is doing is invalid and unlawful."

In a last-ditch attempt to try to help Bishop Lennon understand why their Hungarian parish needed Fr. Sandor Siklodi, Peller and his wife Ildiko requested another meeting. On July 27 they met with Lennon at his office. It did not go well.

After asking why Father Siklodi could not be reappointed, it became clear that Lennon blamed Siklodi for the sixteen-hour sit-in after the parish closed.

Peller assured him that "neither Fr. Sandor nor the other parishioners knew anything of this 'sit-in' plan."[38]

Lennon equivocated that the diocese had "personnel issues" with Siklodi but did not elaborate.

Undeterred, the Pellers "in a very nice but determined way" returned to the crucial issue of the Hungarian language.

But Lennon "interrupted, got all red all over again, and said 'don't give me this ethnic stuff.'" The bishop repeated several times, "I am the bishop, I will decide," leading Peller to conclude: "He did not wish to hear what the 'people's needs' were, but sat on the 'throne' of the idea that 'I am the bishop. I make the decision.'"[39]

The Hungarian Lutheran and Hungarian Presbyterian communities in Cleveland were thriving. Both had Hungarian-speaking ministers. For the people of St. Emeric, Lennon's refusal to appoint a Hungarian-speaking pastor would effectively "kill the Catholic presence in the Hungarian community."[40]

After this second futile meeting, Miklos Peller submitted an eight-page recourse to the Congregation for the Clergy on August 11. It included two signed affidavits summarizing the meetings with Lennon as well as other records. "[I]t was a very short document," Kate recalled. "Within weeks, we got the response. All of a sudden, the pastor was reinstated. The building was going to be reopened. And it was just like day and night."[41]

On August 31, Peller received confidential information that a US-based Hungarian prelate with authority over Siklodi had received a call from Lennon who said the Congregation for the Clergy had told Lennon to reopen St. Emeric without delay. Furthermore, Lennon was told, the only acceptable reopening required reinstating the former pastor, Rev. Sandor Siklodi. When Peller met with Lennon to reinstate Father Sandor, he found the bishop "was very kind and friendly."[42] Peller told Kate "A few weeks ago he didn't even wish to hear about Fr. Sandor. Go figure!"

She emailed him: "You and I know how the bishop acted at the two meetings with you. And this new way of acting clearly shows that the bishop has been influenced by the Vatican."[43]

Kate remembers her reaction: "When I got the phone call from Mik that everything was going to happen, I think he and I both did the happy dance."[44] A delighted Kate later traveled to Cleveland for the joyous reopening on November 4, the feast of parish patron, St. Emeric: "I was absolutely thrilled for them because it was just such a blessing. . . . To see this church so packed . . . all the children, all the twenty-somethings, all of the elderly that were involved. The church was there. It was everyone from all walks of life . . ."[45]

Father Sandor presided at the Hungarian language Mass and, for the first time in three years, a deeply touched Miklos Peller played the church's organ.

HISTORIC ST. PETER

In his homily at the final Mass of Historic St. Peter Church, the Rev. Bob Marrone issued a dire warning that the closing of this vibrant, prayerful parish would come to be seen as "one of the most egregious mistakes ever made by this diocese."[46] Marrone did not exaggerate. St. Peter was known nationally and internationally as an excellent Catholic parish whose mission was fed by the reverent celebration of the Sunday Eucharistic liturgy from which the parish's many ministries flowed. In the year 2000, a Lilly Endowment–funded study at the University of North Carolina recognized St. Peter as an Excellent Catholic Parish. It was highlighted in Paul Wilkes's resulting book: *Excellent Catholic Parishes: The Guide to Best Places and Practices* for its outstanding liturgy and engagement of its members.[47] In the year 2000 the Dominican pastoral theologian Rev. Paul J. Philibert O. P. publicly praised the liturgical excellence of Cleveland St. Peter in an article in *Worship Magazine*.[48] While the Cleveland diocese reported an average Sunday Mass attendance of 28 percent, a full 64 percent of St. Peter's seven hundred parishioners—who hailed from five of the eight counties comprising the Cleveland Diocese—attended every Sunday.

Gifted by an uplifting experience of Sunday Eucharist, the people of St. Peter's took part in multiple ministries to impoverished Clevelanders during the week. One of these was to the Marion-Sterling public school which educated 550 pre-kindergarten-to-eighth-graders in one of the city's poorest neighborhoods. In addition to raising thousands of dollars for special education projects, St. Peter volunteers provided reading programs, daylong tutoring, assistance with proficiency tests, guidance toward acceptance into private high schools, and help with grant-writing. The summer Bishop Lennon closed St. Peter Parish, the congregation had raised $250,000 to have a playground and learning garden built at the Marion-Sterling school. Aside from direct service to the poor, St. Peter Parish was widely known for its Adult Religious Education and Arts ministry available to anyone in Northeast Ohio. It included musical performances, displays of visual arts, engagement in community arts projects, and renowned speakers such as the progressive Belgian Cardinal Godfried Daneels and liturgical expert, Bishop Donald Trautman, of Erie, Pennsylvania.[49]

In 2009, the Historic St. Peter Parish celebrated its 150th anniversary as the oldest Catholic church in continuing operation in the diocese. Just thirty years earlier the parish was all but moribund. It was brought back to life after

Fr. Bob Marrone and Humility of Mary Sister Jane Pank arrived. Both were serving as Newman campus ministers at nearby Cleveland State University. Marrone's liturgical giftedness and Pank's inimitable way with students soon attracted people like Mike Griffin and his future wife Vicki. "Bob [Marrone] and Jane Pank were at the Newman center. They sort of pulled a bunch of us into St. Peter's—students—that would've been about 1987," Griffin remembered.[50] "When we began there were like two dozen people. It was pretty dead. Then we all started going there when we got married and had families. Our family kept coming to church there even though we live in Elyria." Griffin and others invested significant sweat equity in restoring their ancient church: "We did a lot of the grunt work, you know, pouring cement for that huge floor in the nave. . . . We were invested there."[51] It is unsurprising that Griffin—whose three children were baptized and confirmed at St. Peter's— led the canonical recourse on behalf of his beloved parish. He did so even though Marrone told him "several times" that he was wasting his time. Griffin describes why he devoted so many hours to the recourse: "My feeling was we can't let people believe that we agreed with this. We have to communicate that it was wrong, and why it was wrong, and all the harm it is doing. . . . And if I'm honest, some of it was to say: 'You [Lennon] may win in the end, but we're going to make sure you pay for it.'"[52]

The Historic St. Peter Parish was financially robust. Several years before Lennon suppressed it, parishioners completed a $2 million restoration funded by grants and parishioner donations.

In 2008, the bishop inexplicably refused a parishioner's offer of an additional $2 million earmarked in part to pay $345,000 in back-due diocesan assessments which—per Bishop Pilla—had been placed on hold until the restoration was completed. $1 million of the gift was designated for St. Peter's outreach ministries, with the remaining funds being used to deconstruct an aging school building.[53] Lennon's intransigence points to a predetermined decision to close St. Peter regardless of the obvious vitality of the parish community and the desperate need of the neighborhood.

Although the diocesan cluster process had given every other parish an opportunity to weigh in on its future, St. Peter's was told at the outset that they would close and "consolidate" with the nearby St. Paul Shrine and St. John's Cathedral, which were both a short walk down the street. Because of ambiguity in the initial May 28, 2007, letter announcing their parish cluster, parish leaders thought they would be discussing coordinating ministries with cluster partners. At a June 2007 meeting the Rev. Ed Estok—who was Lennon's secretary as well as the rector of St. John's Cathedral—told Marrone and St. Paul Shrine pastor Rev. Phillip Bernie that "consolidation" meant only one parish would remain. That parish would be St. John's Cathedral. St. Paul Parish would be suppressed but remain in operation as a shrine. St.

Figure 8.1   Historic Saint Peter Church celebrates the dedication of its refurbished steeple, bells, organ, stained glass windows, and doors on Saturday, September 10, 2005. ©2005 Peggy Turbett

Peter would be suppressed, with its people supposedly being assumed into the Cathedral parish, although no invitation was ever issued to them.[54]

Despite this obviously predetermined outcome, over the next eighteen months St. Peter leaders diligently participated in what can only be considered a charade of a cluster process. Responding to letters from anxious St. Peter parishioners, Lennon flatly denied he planned to close their parish.[55] As the bishop penned his denials, he was simultaneously exploring how to market St. Peter Church and its property. The agenda of a March 19, 2008, diocesan meeting with the Chartwell commercial real estate group lists St. Peter School/Church/Rectory as a "Parish to Market and Sell."[56] Griffin documented the diocesan plan in St. Peter's recourse to Rome: "It is demoralizing to say the least to see our decades of work to rebuild this community and physical plant so cavalierly tossed aside while putting our cluster team through more than a year of painful meetings when the conclusion was predetermined."[57]

After experiencing confusing messaging from the diocese, St. Peter lay leaders began searching for canonical help. It was a difficult search. Two nationally known university-based professors of canon law told them, "You don't have a case, there's no use even talking to us," Griffin remembers.[58] Eventually they contacted Sister Kate, who met with the Parish Council. She was appalled by Lennon's treatment of this vibrant, growing parish, and—as sometimes happened when particularly outraged—she vehemently expressed herself in colorful language that shocked some council members. Griffin remembers with a chuckle: "After the meeting we decided that she knew her canon law and we hired her. But we wouldn't ask her to do PR." Kate worked closely with Griffin and St. Peter leaders as they compiled their recourse: "Her message to us was 'you need to lay out all the facts and the information and why you believe this shouldn't happen. I'll put the canon law piece from there to follow up.'"[59]

A CLOSING MASS AND THE OPENING OF THE COMMUNITY OF ST. PETER

In June 2008, St. Peter was the first diocesan parish to announce publicly that their parish opposed Lennon's reorganization.[60] After Lennon's March 2009 official announcement of closure, they formally appealed to the bishop to reconsider. When he refused, the parish took its recourse to the Vatican.[61] Members also began planning for the future. They wanted to keep their vibrant community together, continue ministering in the neighborhood, and find a new place to worship. "Basically our message to Lennon was 'You may own the building, but you don't own us,'" said Griffin.[62] He remembers "at the beginning it was kind of nebulous. We wanted to continue our ministries but also the education, art, things like that. I don't think there was a full-fledged 'We're going to go rogue and start a parish.'"[63] Parish Council president Leah Gary had extensive experience in nonprofit management, and the Community of St. Peter was soon established as a 501(c)(3) not-for-profit organization. The November before its scheduled April 2010 closing, parishioner Bob Kloos remembers Marrone telling parishioners: "The Finance Committee tells me we have all the money in the bank that we need to pay our bills until we close. So we're not going to take up a collection anymore on Sunday. Instead, if anybody wants, you can donate to the Community of St. Peter."[64] People began donating to the nonprofit to continue their treasured ministries after Lennon closed their parish.

A month before St. Peter's closing Mass, Marrone's mother died. Rick Krivanka, director of the Diocesan Pastoral Planning Office at the time, attended her funeral. Realizing how wrong Lennon's determination to close St. Peter's had been, Krivanka had challenged the decision to close the parish whenever an opportunity arose. Neither the *Vibrant Parish Life* committee nor the Presbyteral Council had supported closing St. Peter.[65] At the funeral, Krivanka remembers, "I was struggling to hold back tears because the experience of the Eucharist there was so sacred. . . . And I realized these are some of the finest people I know. . . . At the deepest level of my being I felt that closing this church was very wrong. This closing was sinful. . . ."[66]

On Easter Sunday 2010, Marrone and St. Peter parishioners celebrated their last Eucharistic liturgy in the exquisite church they had worked so hard to restore. A final Mass with Lennon was scheduled for the following week. It was cancelled after community members told him that while he was welcome to celebrate, they would not be present. Always a powerful preacher, Marrone gave an Easter message that challenged ecclesial leaders and consoled his congregation. The closing of St. Peter, he said, was not because of economics, lack of priests or parishioners. Instead it revealed a "steadfast refusal and/or inability to imagine things in a different way."[67] He gently prodded his tearful flock forward: "This community has always respected and honored its past, but it has steadfastly refused to live in it." He urged his congregation to avoid confusing blind obedience with faithfulness and reminded them that "the power of fear which has caused this injustice is not the last word, must not be the last word and will not be the last word." "I know it seems unbearable," he said, "but we can bear it. Go forth into the world and be living stones. God will tent with us wherever we go." Holding lighted candles, parishioners intoned the hymn "Christ Be Our Light" as they processed out of their beautiful edifice.[68] Before the doors were bolted shut, one last message was left inside. A plastic baggie containing shimmering coins was left at the foot of the altar with a note: "A gift for Bishop Lennon. Thirty pieces of silver for the one who has betrayed us."[69] Mike Griffin was devastated by Lennon's decision. He was devastated not only for himself but for the community of people he had come to love.

> It was like a death in the family. We had worked so hard to physically build up the parish, build up the community. I always described us as the isle of misfit toys. . . . So many members had been hurt by the church, whether it was their sexual orientation or marriage status or some abuse of power they'd experienced previously in the church. Even Bishop Pilla used to send people to St. Peter. And they found refuge in a parish that cared about them. They found a place where they could belong.[70]

Over two hundred exiled St. Peter parishioners soon began meeting regularly in rented space at Cleveland State University. There they celebrated Liturgies of the Word with reflections prepared by various community members, including priests who had left the active ministry to marry, and also a number of women religious.[71] Working with community members who were professional facilitators, the group began a discernment process about their future together. Anticipating that the community would want to continue gathering, the nonprofit Community of St. Peter (CSP) leased space at a former car dealership not far from the church. The Community of St. Peter eventually chose an eleven-member board and established an annual budget of $200,000. They also devised a compensation package for a future pastor, whom they hoped would be Marrone.

Meanwhile Marrone needed a break following the death of his mother and the intensity of church politics. He told the community, "I don't have any more to give right now. . . . I need some time."[72] He was also clear that it was not up to him to decide what came next: "You get a plan, and then I'll talk with you. . . . I don't want to be a pied piper," he told them.[73] About six weeks later, Marrone agreed to pastor the new community. On August 15, 2010, a joyful throng of 350 entered a newly renovated worship space singing "Christ Be Our Light," the same hymn they had sung exiting their beloved former church.[74] After the opening Mass, community leader Bob Zack told the *Cleveland Plain Dealer*, "The Community of St. Peter holds to the fundamental teachings and doctrines of the Roman Catholic Church. We consider ourselves neither a focal point of dissent nor a schismatic organization." Bob Kloos, who was a parishioner at the time, describes the reopening:

There was a little bit of triumph in the air, a little bit of rebellion in the air. . . . But that dissipated pretty quickly. That's a credit to Bob Marrone, because his focus was right back on to the liturgy and to education. And we were soon back to painting houses in a program to rebuild Cleveland, and different things like that. We just picked up right where we left off and the whole ordeal was behind us.[75]

Bishop Lennon was not happy. Having gotten wind that the St. Peter congregation was organizing on its own, Lennon sent letters to each member of the congregation expressing concern "for you and your salvation."[76] He instructed them to register in another parish and warned, "There are consequences which affect one's relationships with the Lord, with His holy Church, as well as with other members of the faithful," should unity be broken.[77] In November 2011, Lennon gave Marrone forty-eight hours to resign from what was now being called a "breakaway church" or face "canonical action."[78] Several days later Marrone read his response to the CSP congregation: "It is my decision to remain in my present position with the Community of St. Peter."[79] At one point he choked up with tears, reflecting that he had served as a priest for thirty-seven years. "This comes to me with great sadness," he said. "There's no joy in this."[80]

Although Kate was extremely concerned that the creation of the Community of St. Peter would impair the parish's chances for a successful canonical appeal, this did not happen. Mike Griffin remembers being completely shocked—and momentarily hopeful—when he learned the Vatican had upheld the St. Peter appeal. "Naively, I'm sure we hoped that maybe the bishop would . . . reappoint Bob as the pastor and we could merrily go back and do our thing."[81] Griffin believed if Lennon made a pastoral overture at this point, the excruciatingly painful situation could possibly be resolved. When it became clear that Lennon would reopen parishes, Griffin decided to reach out. "My view was we've got to at least be willing to talk and say our piece."[82] He contacted a diocesan official to set up a meeting with the bishop.

Before the meeting Griffin called to double check that only himself and representatives from the Parish Council would be present. The official assured him that was the case. When the meeting convened, Griffin was dismayed to discover that disgruntled former members of St. Peter had also been invited. Griffin felt he had been played, and minced no words in telling the bishop: "I specifically asked the question about who was going to be present, and you set this up so there would be contentious argument going on here."[83] He remembers this as "probably one of the most awful meetings of my personal and professional life . . . here you are with the church you've been a member of and committed your life to, and you're being set up in a situation that is just too painful."[84] The meeting deteriorated. Griffin recalls Lennon telling the group, "Father Marrone has said he won't come back as pastor."[85] When Griffin relayed the bishop's statement to Marrone, he categorically denied it, saying Lennon had never spoken to him about another assignment after closing St. Peter.[86]

On May 22, 2012, Lennon called Marrone in and read aloud a document entitled, "Declaration of Loss of Canonical Office." He told Marrone he had seven days to resign as pastor of the Community of St. Peter or be immediately suspended from priestly ministry. Lennon refused to give the priest a copy of the Declaration. A week later, Marrone informed the community of his written reply to the bishop: "I will not comply with your decree to leave the Community of Saint Peter because I must, before all else, follow what my conscience dictates."[87] After the story broke in the media, Lennon denied officially suspending the priest.[88] But for Marrone, Lennon's action had made one thing completely clear: "I now know that I will neither be invited or allowed to return to Historic Saint Peter Church as its pastor. . . ."[89]

In July the Rev. Robert Kropac was appointed pastor for the reopened Historic St. Peter Parish. On September 9, about 145 people attended the opening Mass. "I realize half of these people aren't from St. Peter," Kropac told a local public radio station. "They're people who came to support [and] bring some closure to the whole process of re-opening and all that. . . . It's great to have people here and I hope they come back."[90] Some fifty blocks down the street—as they had done each Sunday for over two years—three hundred members of the Community of St. Peter were celebrating Mass in a remodeled office building. Trustee Frank Titus graciously told the media,

It's not a question of any kind of competition. From the Community of St. Peter's standpoint, we're going to continue to do the work that we do. Move forward in terms of social justice ministries and the presence that we want to have in the City of Cleveland. It's a beautiful place that Father Kropac has to work with, and we certainly wish him the best.[91]

On March 4, 2013—nine days before the election of the pastoral Pope Francis—Bishop Richard G. Lennon excommunicated Rev. Bob Marrone. In a brief statement to members of the community, Marrone said, "I must, as I have stated repeatedly in the past, follow my conscience in this matter" and reaffirmed his commitment as their pastor-administrator: "I will continue to serve the Community of Saint Peter as long as they call me to do so and as long as I am able to fulfill the responsibilities of the work entrusted to me."[92]

When it became clear that Bishop Lennon would not reinstate the Historic St. Peter Church to the community that had rebuilt it, Marrone's path had also became clear. Marrone told *National Catholic Reporter*'s Tom Roberts that in the years since Lennon arrived, he had been forced to reexamine all that he had taken for granted. Despite his ordination promise of obedience to the bishop, he believed the most important promise was the

Figure 8.2   Taize evening prayer becomes an Advent tradition in the new Community of St. Peter worship space, December 15, 2015. ©2015 Peggy Turbett

one he made to himself—to be true to his conscience: "No earthly authority, civil or ecclesial, can force me, by whatever means, to go against that promise," he said.[93]

THE VATICAN SENDS AN APOSTOLIC VISITOR

Bishop Lennon's 2010 letter warning exiled members of Historic St. Peter that their salvation was imperiled outraged both Catholic and Protestant leaders in Cleveland. In a letter to the editor, Methodist minister Kenneth Chalker wrote it was "theological absurdity" to suggest "that a person's immortal soul may be in jeopardy from receiving Communion in episcopally unauthorized spaces."[94] In September 2010, the Rev. Bob Begin enclosed Chalker's statement with his own letter to apostolic nuncio Archbishop Pietro Sambi, asking Rome to investigate. "It is becoming more and more difficult for many parishioners and leaders alike to remain 'Catholic' in our diocese," Begin wrote. "I believe the situation merits an apostolic visitor to conduct an objective inquiry into what is occurring."[95] Chalker asked Rome to make a change. "The marvelous legacy and respect in which the diocese has been held in this community by ALL persons in this city is under assault, not from 'outside forces,' but as a result of its current leadership.[96]

In July 2011, the Vatican responded by sending Trenton bishop John M. Smith to Cleveland to interview local Catholics. Although Lennon announced publicly that he had requested the visitation himself, Nick Cafardi, a canon lawyer and dean emeritus at Duquesne Law School in Pittsburgh, said, "That's like calling an air strike on yourself."[97] FutureChurch's press statement asked that Smith's final report be made public and noted: "The fact that this examination is taking place in response to parishioners' petitions . . . indicates the need for a more systematic, continuing and effective way for bishops and others in positions of authority to be held accountable for their actions, inaction and decisions."[98] In the course of his weeklong visit, Bishop Smith interviewed an estimated twenty-five to thirty people who met him at Cleveland's Jesuit Retreat House. Two Catholics leading the appeal efforts at their parishes spoke publicly. Patricia Schulte-Singleton of St. Patrick's in West Park—another Cleveland parish Kate had assisted in the early stages of its appeal—and Miklos Peller of St. Emeric Parish both found Bishop Smith to be "receptive and concerned."[99] After Peller told Bishop Smith that Lennon had closed five of six Hungarian churches, the bishop shook his head in disbelief. At the end of his hour-long interview Smith asked Peller, "In spite of all that has happened, can you still accept him as your bishop?" Peller answered honestly: "No. There's not much hope for that."[100]

VATICAN AGAIN EXTENDS DEADLINE FOR APPEALS

In September 2011 the Vatican notified Cleveland parishes that their appeal deadlines had, for the fourth time, been extended. This turn of events led some to wonder if the Vatican needed more time to consider the results of Bishop Smith's apostolic visitation to the diocese. "It's kind of disappointing, but it's still a good development," said Patricia Schulte-Singleton, president of Endangered Catholics, the group fighting church closings. "We're still alive. We have to be patient."[101] It would be a full six months before persevering parishioners learned that their patience had been richly rewarded.

Chapter 9

A Landmark Ruling—Rome
Upholds Cleveland Appeals

On Wednesday March 7, 2012, the Associated Press reported the Vatican had upheld thirteen Cleveland appeals on both procedural and substantive grounds.[1] Bishop Lennon was instructed to "enact the implications of this decree." The exact meaning of this statement was unclear at first. After Kate reviewed the Vatican decrees, however, she realized it meant the bishop had three options: reopen the parishes, restart the process and submit new decrees for each parish and each church, or appeal the ruling to the Apostolic Signatura, the church's highest court. Lennon had sixty days to appeal. It was a landmark ruling. Until this time Vatican officials had essentially given split decisions to recourses brought by parishioners. FutureChurch director and this book's author, Sister Christine Schenk, told the *Akron Beacon Journal*:

> We have worked with parishioners in dioceses across the country and this is the first time that Rome has overruled a bishop in [both] suppressing the parishes and closing the churches. In other places, the Vatican has said you can suppress the parish, but you can't sell the church . . . I am just amazed that Rome overturned the [parish] suppressions. The best I had hoped for was that the bishop would be told he could not sell the churches.[2]

Boston activist Peter Borré broke the story about the Cleveland victories with the Associated Press. For a number of years Borré had journeyed to Rome to lobby on behalf of parishioners in Cleveland and elsewhere. In April 2009—in a high-profile media moment—he hand-delivered a request for mediation to the Vatican Secretariat of State on behalf of thirty-one parishioner groups in eight US dioceses.[3] The request asked the secretariat to instruct American bishops to enter promptly into mediation even though in church law the Vatican Secretariat of State has no authority to do so. Several groups of Cleveland parishioners were working closely with Borré. He recruited

137

expensive Rome-based canon lawyers to represent them, even though Rome-based lawyers are only required for appeals to the Apostolic Signatura, not those to the Congregation for the Clergy.[4] This breaking wire story was published in newspapers all over the United States and abroad.

On March 5, 2012, Borré's canon lawyers in Rome sent him a copy of the successful St. James, Lakewood, decree dated March 1. They also emailed copies of decrees to their clients, one of whom—Patricia Schulte-Singleton—had led the appeal process of St. Patrick, West Park, and was president of Endangered Catholics. "I can tell you it's spectacular news," Schulte-Singleton told Religion News Service. "It's a complete reversal of Bishop Lennon's order. Our prayers have been answered."[5] Even non-Catholics were happy to learn of the reversal. Julie Rice told the Associated Press that St. Barbara Parish—which abuts her own home—was an anchor in her neighborhood: "The church does more than services. With the meals and the counseling, especially for marriage and pre-marriage, all that stuff, and youth in trouble—very, very, important in an urban setting like this, with all the negative influences."[6]

A spokesman for the Cleveland diocese, Robert Tayek, told the Associated Press and the *Akron Beacon Journal* that the diocese had received the documents on March 7 but had not reviewed them and could not confirm their contents.[7] Two days later Tayek issued a statement that the diocese was "awaiting official word from the Vatican concerning any decrees. . . ."[8] Finally on March 14, Bishop Lennon announced he had received the decrees from the Congregation for the Clergy.[9] It is unusual for Vatican decisions about controversial issues to appear in the public media before the diocesan bishop is notified. It is also puzzling that parishioners had their decrees more than a week before their bishop did.[10] In retrospect it seems likely that Lennon was caught unawares, or he would have had a media statement ready when the news broke on March 7.

The media lost no time consulting nationally known experts. Fr. John Beal, a canon lawyer at the Catholic University of America, told the *National Catholic Reporter*,

> If the findings of fact in the decrees are correct, Bishop Lennon badly botched the procedure for closing/suppressing the parishes and completely ignored the separate process for reducing parish churches to profane use. In fact, it does not appear that he appreciated the fact that two separate procedures with different criteria are required. In other cases, the Congregation has been extremely demanding on reducing churches to profane use and insisting on demonstrably "grave causes."[11]

The Rev. Patrick Lagges, a canon lawyer at the Archdiocese of Chicago, said, "The Vatican seems to be reminding us that there're people involved here and people's spiritual lives."[12] Michael Dunnigan, who represented parishioners for fourteen years through the St. Joseph Foundation, told Religion News Service, "We've been in the wilderness for ages with cases like this. It's been almost impossible to win, to prevail against a bishop. But now there's hope."[13] Dunnigan, who is also a canon lawyer, elaborated, "I imagine that Vatican officials looking at America must wonder to themselves: 'How can the bishops of such a wealthy country close so many churches, abandon their great cities and exile to the suburbs the great Catholic witness in both flesh and stone?'"[14]

Kate well recalls her initial reaction: "First of all, there was just shock and not just shock on the part of the people, but also me. I had never seen this before. I knew something very special had happened. It was a lifting of the spirit. So it was like somebody has heard us, someone has believed our story."[15] Christine LaSalvia, a civil attorney and parishioner with whom Kate had worked, sent her a copy of the St. James Lakewood decree. Kate lost no time applying her professional expertise. The unprecedented success of the Cleveland appeals became somewhat of a watershed. For the first time in her professional career, Kate decided to jettison her treasured anonymity in order to write a canonical Commentary. She hoped it would help Catholics in the United States and around the world:

> I have decided that the time is right to go public to support the people, in Cleveland and elsewhere. Up until now I have never made a public statement to anyone regarding the over thirty parishes I have consulted with. I am not flashy. I do not seek public media attention. My sole work for the past seven years has been of service to the laity who have suffered so much as a result of decisions by bishops.[16]

SISTER KATE WRITES A COMMENTARY AND CLEVELAND PRIESTS FIND THEIR VOICE

While Bishop Lennon was deciding what to do next, Sister Kate was analyzing the Cleveland decisions. At the request of parishioners whose appeals she had shepherded, and at the request of FutureChurch, she compiled a twenty-three-page canonical Commentary. In a mid-March email she wrote: "I hope to tell the folks what this all means. Some of the information may well help them argue against the bishop if that is needed in the future. . . . There is just so very much that needs to be said."[17] She gave a fuller description of her purpose in a March 29 email to Endangered Catholics co-chair, Bob Kloos:

> I wanted to put into clear language the meaning of the decree so the people would truly understand the scope of the intent of the Congregation for the Clergy. . . . As a canon lawyer I must say what is fact and what is the true

meaning of the law and how it is implemented in the decree. Any personal wish of mine cannot be the impulse of this writing.[18]

Kate's Commentary would help the Cleveland Presbyteral Council, parishioners, and other diocesan leaders understand the canonical implications of what had happened. Only then could they evaluate the various options the bishop might or might not pursue, and what the odds were that any given option would be successful. Judging from the hundreds of downloads from the FutureChurch website, her Commentary eventually influenced diocesan leaders around the country as they reconsidered parish reconfigurations already or soon to be under way in their dioceses.

On Friday March 30, Bishop Lennon was scheduled to meet with priest leaders on the Diocesan Presbyteral Council. Before that meeting, Bob Kloos of Endangered Catholics planned to forward Kate's Commentary to Presbyteral Council priests with whom he was in communication. As a priest who left the active ministry to marry, Kloos still had many contacts in the Cleveland presbyterate. Kate worked feverishly to complete her work, "to help the pastors speak their opinions to the bishop."[19] She consulted other canon lawyers as well as her old friend, Monsignor Lou Marucci, the former pastor of Camden's St. Vincent Pallotti Parish, who agreed to edit her final document. The Pallotti appeal was Kate's first victory and it had marked a turning point in Vatican policy. Marucci's edits were delayed because of a computer crash, so Kate emailed a quick summary to Kloos in the event the final document was not ready in time. Her email hints at her state of mind: "I am so nervous. I am trying to stay patient. My Lenten sacrifice is waiting for this. I want it in your hands so badly, but it is out of my hands. . . . But I am learning to trust in God. When these things happen, I find that to be most difficult."[20]

At 2:00 a.m. on Thursday March 29, Kate finally completed her work and sent the Commentary to Schenk at FutureChurch. Early Thursday morning, Schenk forwarded it—along with the St. James decree upon which it was based—to Kloos and other leaders at Endangered Catholics as well as to appealing Cleveland parishioners known to FutureChurch. While the Commentary included language specific to the St. James decree, a review of decrees for the other eleven parishes revealed that the bishop's canonical errors had been named in those decrees as well. Schenk then sent the Commentary to local and national media outlets, both Catholic and secular.[21] Kloos quickly forwarded Kate's Commentary to waiting Presbyteral Council members who now had over twenty-four hours to study it before their meeting with Bishop Lennon.[22] On the evening of Friday March 30—just after the Presbyteral Council's afternoon meeting—the *Cleveland Plain Dealer* published an article by religion reporter Michael O'Malley that quoted Kate's Commentary in some detail. O'Malley noted Kate had highlighted "how Lennon failed to follow church laws and procedure for dissolving parishes and closing churches" and that the bishop had three options: reopen the churches, appeal the decrees, or start the closing process over, making sure to follow laws and procedures. Furthermore, he noted, Kate's Commentary indicated the bishop:

- Did not demonstrate "grave" reasons for closing the churches.
- Did not thoroughly consult with his Presbyteral Council, a panel of local priests, when he issued his closing orders.
- Did not detail for parishioners his reasons and rationale for closing their churches.
- Did not submit to the Vatican proper legal documents required for closing churches.[23]

So it was that Sr. Kate Kuenstler's treasured anonymity came to an abrupt—if highly fruitful—close.

Kate's work was crucial to Cleveland's Presbyteral Council as priest leaders confronted their bishop and urged him to reopen the twelve long-suffering parishes.[24] Kloos learned what transpired and quickly relayed it to Kate. Her Commentary was a "Godsend," he was told, and every priest at the meeting had read it beforehand.[25] Speaking on behalf of their constituents, Cleveland priest leaders asked the bishop "some very pointed questions."[26] The sentiment was against appealing to Rome. Instead they encouraged the bishop to reopen the parishes in a pastoral manner. Lennon complained that he had sent many documents and that "the [Vatican's] rules changed during the process."[27] A Cleveland pastor who was also past president of the Canon Law Society of America reportedly "nailed the bishop to the wall," telling him there was no basis whatsoever to appeal the Vatican's decision. This respected priest-canonist had found Kate's Commentary "clear, concise and very helpful."[28] After receiving Kloos's summary of the Presbyteral Council gathering, Kate replied,

> I am so very grateful to have been of service to the Presbyteral Council and the pastors of the diocese. Helping them to find their voice is a particular joy. No matter what else transpires, those priests now know what they can and should do. There is no more fear. They are free. What a blessing for all the people whom they serve. God is good.[29]

MORE ABOUT A PIONEERING CANONICAL COMMENTARY

Published in late March 2012, Kate's *Commentary on Vatican Decrees Upholding Cleveland Parishioner Appeals* was the first public explanation of Rome's rapidly changing rules related to parish mergers and church closings.[30]

The Congregation for the Clergy did not publish new official procedures until April 30, 2013, when Cardinal Piacenza sent guidelines to the bishops of the world.[31] Again on July 20, 2020—nearly a year after Kate's untimely death—the Congregation released a twenty-two-page Instruction: "The Pastoral Conversion of the Parish Community in the Service of the Evangelizing Mission of the Church," which reiterated Vatican procedures.[32] Both documents had been set in motion by Kate herself when, in 2009, she intervened with the Apostolic Signatura on behalf of parishioners at St. Mary, Jamesville, in the Diocese of Syracuse and Camden's St. Vincent Pallotti Parish. Two months before the Cleveland victories—in an email to a client—Kate described her catalyzing influence in developing new jurisprudence:

> The Apostolic Signatura made the mandate . . . as a direct result of arguments I developed for other parishes. Also, as a result of the multiple recourses that I developed for about 45 parishes that itemize the numerous mistakes and lack of following canon law that bishops used in closing parishes, Rome is now developing a formal handbook for bishops to follow when merging parishes.[33]

The Cleveland appeals were among the forty-five parishes wherein Kate itemized the "numerous mistakes" of bishops in following canon law. Her Cleveland Commentary analyzed the Vatican ruling and exposed Lennon's ignorance of emerging canonical protocols for modifying a parish and closing a church. She described the bishop's flouting of Vatican authority when he declined to correct his canonical errors once the Dicastery pointed them out. For a bishop who had prided himself for being "self-taught" in canon law, this must have been painfully humiliating. Kate was surprised to find herself writing about the unprecedented Cleveland rulings,

> I never dreamed that I would need to write such a document. When seen unpacked and explained it truly is a volcano. I have never seen such a decree sent by the Congregation for the Clergy to a bishop, let alone 12 of them (and that being every last one of them presented from the same diocese). The bishop used a cookie cutter to reconfigure the parishes and the Congregation for the Clergy also used a cookie cutter to decide the bishop did not act in accordance with law.[34]

The "cookie cutter" decrees issued by the Congregation for the Clergy for Cleveland reflect new canonical procedures which the Vatican would publish the following year.[35] Official procedures issued by the Congregation for the Clergy in 2013 and 2020 clarify distinct canonical processes required for modifying (closing or merging) a parish, closing a church, and selling or alienating church property. For both parish mergers and church closures, the bishop must consult the diocesan Presbyteral Council, although he is not required to follow their recommendations. The bishop must also issue separate decrees for modifying a parish and for closing its church. Each decree must "at least in summary fashion" list the requisite "just cause" for modifying a parish and the "grave cause" for closing a church.[36] The 2013 procedures said a church could not be closed solely because of the "lack of clergy, demographic decline or the grave financial state of the diocese." These criteria do not constitute a "grave cause" to deconsecrate and sell a church building even though all three are usually cited by US bishops to this day. The 2013 document did not name these same criteria as constituting a "just cause" to modify a parish (as opposed to closing a church). Yet in 2020, the Vatican Instruction said all three criteria also applied to parish mergers/modifications.[37] A February 2024 ruling upholding the recourse of a small parish in the Archdiocese of St. Louis suggests the Vatican may be holding bishops to this stricter standard in merging parish communities.[38] Accordingly, Catholics may have additional protections from parish mergers.

In her March 2012 Commentary, Kate carefully explained that Bishop Lennon's original March 29 letter violated other canon laws as well. He had not issued a legitimate canonical decree to suppress St. James Parish, nor did he mention establishing a new territorial parish or new parish boundaries. Neither had the bishop supplied an explicit summary of the required "just cause" (Canon 50) to suppress or merge a parish—in this case, St. James.[39] The Vatican decree, upholding the St. James recourse, explicitly described the parish as "a financially stable territorial parish of some 1,500 families." The significance was not lost on Kate, who raised a number of questions about Lennon's motivations for closing other vibrant parishes in the Diocese of Cleveland:

> [I]t is intriguing that the parish was described in language that depicts an already established vibrant parish. The questions must be asked: What criteria did the Bishop of Cleveland use to suppress and merge parishes and subsequently close the doors of the churches? What was the motivation driving the decision? Further, what rationale did the Bishop of Cleveland provide to reject the appeals sent to him?[40]

Lennon was found to be out of compliance with the law regarding the closing of St. James Church. He had neither demonstrated the "grave cause" required in canon law, nor had he issued a formal decree "relegating the church to secular but not unbecoming use." The bishop's March 12 letter met neither of these canonical requirements. Furthermore, Lennon had not consulted with the Presbyteral Council about closing and relegating the church to secular use. Despite a September 2009 letter sent by the Congregation for the Clergy advising Bishop Lennon of all of these shortfalls, the Congregation for the Clergy decree said the bishop "refused to clarify the matter either by allowing the Church to remain open or by following the procedure for relegation."[41] Therefore, the Vatican ruled that Lennon's decision to close St. James Church was also invalid.

As previously mentioned, Bishop Lennon was given three options: reopen the parishes, start anew to assure that the procedures followed conform to the directives which the Congregation for Clergy had clearly delineated, or appeal the ruling to the Apostolic Signatura.[42] If he chose to start over, the bishop could not simply edit the original documents he submitted, explained Kate. Instead, he must follow the correct procedures, namely:

> Two separate procedures must be accomplished to enact the implications of the DECREE: first, the possible suppression of the parish and second, the possible relegation of the church to secular but not unbecoming use. The Presbyteral Council must be involved from the beginning, in an ongoing way, in any corrective process initiated by the Bishop, as the law intends. The future of each parish is to be addressed separately. Ample time should be extended for serious discussion that involves the rights that a public juridic person holds for perpetual existence. . . . Parish data collected years ago should be revisited by both the Bishop of Cleveland and the Presbyteral Council. Should any data need correction or further clarification; this should be done, and the new data be used in the deliberation. Should any further data be offered by the parishioners or anyone else; it should be welcomed and used in the deliberation.[43]

Bishop Lennon's third option was to appeal to the Apostolic Signatura, the church's highest court. Should the bishop choose this route, Kate's analysis showed that he had virtually no chance of success because he would be required to demonstrate that Congregation for the Clergy had violated canon law in their own decision-making process or procedures, using the articles contained in their Decree. This would be "significantly problematic for the Bishop of Cleveland," Kate explained, "because there is really nothing he can take recourse against."[44]

It is appalling that even though the Vatican's September 2009 letter had advised Lennon that his closures did not follow canon law, the bishop continued the closings anyway. Three years later, every document from the Congregation for the Clergy upholding parishioner appeals cited the Vatican's September 2009 letter. Until then no one knew it even existed. Kate spells out the implications:

> The bishop of Cleveland ignored this correction and closed 43 churches after the date of this letter. Did the Bishop of Cleveland actually follow all of the procedures required in the law for alienation of church property for those other parishes?. . . Why did the bishop of Cleveland proceed with the closure of all of

the Churches of suppressed parishes after he had been warned by the Congregation of the Clergy?[45]

In a poignant statement about the dreadful Cleveland saga, Kate's Commentary also noted,

> Finally, some attention should be [paid] to the more than fifty (50) parishes that were affected by *Vibrant Parish Life—Phase I*. . . . Thirteen (13) parishes [*sic*] took recourse to the Congregation for Clergy. Thirty-seven (37) parishes did not take recourse and they will not benefit from the decisions from the Congregation for Clergy upholding the recourses. Most probably the "closing" or merging of those thirty-seven (37) parishes, and the closing of those many other churches, was also illicit and invalid. Since those decrees, and those procedures, were not challenged, nor could ever be challenged, we will never know.[46]

LEARNINGS

There are significant learnings to be gleaned from reading Kate's Commentary. Here is a summary of two issues that seem especially enlightening not only for the average lay person, but also for the over five hundred Catholics—including canonists and church leaders—who eventually downloaded Kate's Commentary for use in their own dioceses.

The first issue is somewhat of a conundrum: canon law seems more protective of church buildings than of parishioners and parishes. Kate explains this is because canon law does not envision a need to protect a parish since it understands that a parish exists for the salvation of souls and has a fundamental right to perpetual existence (Canon 120.1). Nevertheless canon law does—without exception—uphold the authority of a bishop to suppress a parish. In a devastating critique of US bishops, Kate writes,

> The law understands that the bishop would use his authority in service: with solicitude towards the people he shepherds, and to protect the patrimony and temporal goods of the parish. The law never envisioned a bishop to suppress a parish with the intent or motivation to close and sell its church. In addition, the law did not anticipate that a bishop would implement wholesale suppression of parishes as has occurred in the United States for several years; initially occurring in the Archdiocese of Boston and more recently in the Diocese of Cleveland, with numerous dioceses in between.[47]

An unusually frank March 14, 2012, email reflects Kate's hopes for what the Cleveland rulings might mean for the US church and for her efforts to defend the rights of parishioners:

I am hoping that the singlemindedness of bishops to suppress church property, sell this property for the most money, and pay civil lawyers and pay million-dollar fines relating to sex abusing priests will no longer be allowed to be the norm by Rome. There needs to be other ways to respond to these issues. It is this that Rome still does not understand, and the bishops of the USA do not understand. I wonder at the lack of pastoral, spiritual, and human decency in the bishops of the USA. That absence reflects back on the Cardinals who promoted these men to this office under [Pope] John Paul II.[48]

A second enlightening piece of information about what canon law intends has to do with the requirement that the bishop consult with his Presbyteral Council. This consultation must happen twice, once when modifying a parish and again when closing a church. The nub of the matter has to do with the nature of consultation, which Kate found woefully deficient in Cleveland. It was deficient because Lennon met with the Cleveland Presbyteral Council just once, on February 4, 2009, when he presented plans for the closing and merger of over fifty Cleveland parishes. Just five weeks later he issued letters closing fifty-two parishes. The close timing of these two official acts led Kate to conclude "the Bishop of Cleveland brought finalized plans to the Presbyteral Council," and therefore no true consultation could have taken place.[49]

To fulfill the intent of the law, the bishop must approach the presbyteral council before he has already made his decision. . . . The presbyteral council must first have received detailed and necessary information regarding the parishes being considered for suppression or suppression and merger. . . . The presbyteral council members cannot make well-formed conscience decisions without full and sufficient knowledge of all the facts. There exists no indication in the decree that the Bishop of Cleveland used the presbyteral council, and their required advice, in any meaningful way during the three-year process (2006–2009).[50]

Another important criterion for lawful consultation has to do with the freedom of those consulted. Kate observes, "When the plans presented to the presbyteral council are already finalized, one would question the force, fear, or pressure indirectly imposed upon the council to endorse [the bishop's] intent or decree."[51]

A NEW PRECEDENT—AND NEW ALTERNATIVES TO CLOSING PARISHES

The Cleveland victories set a new precedent. For the first time, a bishop was ordered to restore suppressed parishes as well as reopen their churches. The Vatican rulings in Cleveland and elsewhere clarified that a shortage of priests is not sufficient reason to close churches, even though nearly every US bishop downsizing a diocese had claimed it as a reason (which they continue to do today). According to Kate's Commentary, the following are no longer considered legitimate reasons for closing a church:

1. The shortage of priests.
2. The church is in close proximity to another church.
3. The church is no longer considered necessary for worship when a parish is suppressed or merged.
4. The maintenance for a building no longer needed as a church for Divine worship is a financial burden to the parish.[52]

Realizing that her Cleveland Commentary would receive wide attention, Kate used it as a platform to promote better ways of addressing shortages of priest personnel and other problems facing US bishops. Perhaps the most influential segment is her suggestion to cluster parishes as a canonical alternative to closing them. Noting that Bishop Anthony Pilla's original *Vibrant Parish Life* process was intended to promote parish flourishing through consolidating resources, Kate suggests that Bishop Lennon, in consultation with the Cleveland Presbyteral Council, consider clustering as a possibility in reconfiguring the twelve parishes. Here is her description of the canonical implications involved:

> The parishes that are clustered all remain in existence: they remain independent juridic persons according to the law. As a cluster they share resources. These could include, but are not limited to, the sharing of human resources, such as one priest, one principal, one Parish Administrator, one DRE, one secretary, etc. for overall parish governance. Sometimes, especially in rural areas, there is a lay administrator (religious sister, lay woman, lay man) appointed by the bishop, as the Director for Parish Life, to manage the day-to-day operations and ministries; with one or more priests assigned to supply the sacramental needs for all of the parishes that form the cluster.[53]

As we shall see in the next chapter, after reading Kate's Commentary, leaders in at least one US diocese decided to cluster parishes rather than to close them.

Kate also suggested several parish leadership models permitted in canon law. These included models Lennon had already dismantled in Cleveland such as the appointment of pastoral teams led by one priest, and/or the appointment of parish life coordinators to administer local parish communities under the appointment of one canonical pastor. These models—and clustering—suggested Kate, "provide viable options to the problem of declining numbers of the clergy and the ratio of priests to the Catholic faithful."[54] But most important for Kate was that consideration of these canonically approved options actually promoted and protected existing vibrant parish communities:

> The cluster model for parishes engages the laity to be more involved in the administration of their parishes. Parishes that are clustered all remain in existence: they remain independent juridic persons in the law. In clustered parishes the churches remain open and are used for regular worship and devotional services. The clustering model does not provide a provision for church buildings to be abandoned and sold.[55]

LENNON REOPENS PARISHES—AND CLOSES THE PASTORAL PLANNING OFFICE

On April 17, 2012, thousands of Cleveland Catholics celebrated when Bishop Richard Lennon—citing a need for "peace and unity" in the diocese—announced he would reopen the twelve parishes whose appeals the Vatican had upheld in early March.

FutureChurch characterized his decision as "prudent" and "a final ratification of the courage of Cleveland Catholics whose love for their parish

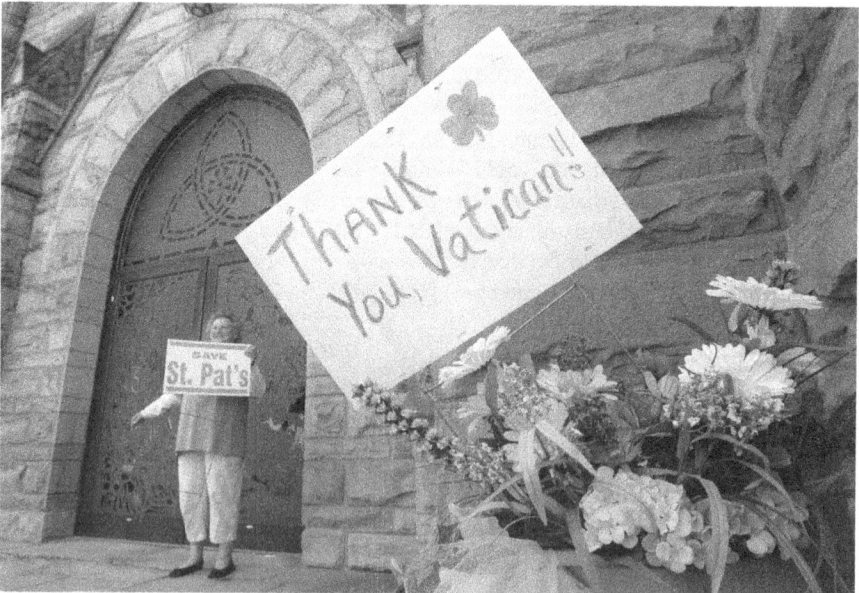

Figure 9.1 A happy parishioner stands outside St. Patrick's Catholic Church, West Park, in April 2012 when Bishop Richard Lennon announced he would reopen twelve Cleveland parishes after the Vatican upheld parishioner appeals. AP Photo/Amy Sancetta

communities led them to appeal."[56] But for some it was a pyrrhic victory. Mary Willett of St. Mary Parish in Akron told the *Akron Beacon Journal*,

> I don't think we're ever going to renew what we had. That's just my opinion, and I hope I'm wrong, but people have settled at other parishes. . . . The parish family has been split up. I have prayed and fought for St. Mary's, and I am grateful that the Vatican heard the petitions of the people. I still pray that St. Mary's will be allowed to open again. It's in the hands of God.[57]

Nine days later—in what is probably the equivalent of kicking the dog—Lennon cited a "budget crunch" and inexplicably closed the Diocesan Pastoral Planning office. With no prior warning the bishop summarily dismissed the two people best equipped to help disoriented parishioners reopen their parishes and strategize for the future. Nationally recognized organizational professionals Rick Krivanka and David DeLambo were abruptly fired.[58] Krivanka had worked at the diocese for thirty-two years and was familiar with every parish in Northeast Ohio. Rev. Bob Begin expressed the dismay of hundreds of Northeast Ohio priests and people:

> I cannot believe that [the bishop's] move was motivated by anything else than a desire to punish the office that helped the parishes through the difficult processes that resulted in resolutions and solutions that were ignored when the final decisions about closings and mergers were made.[59]

Begin testified to the skill of the Pastoral Planning Office in helping his own parish: "It was this office that three years ago helped St. Colman's put together a plan that has helped us double our number of weekend worshipping families, double our collections, more than double the number of outreach workers, and welcome 16 new Catholics into our Parish at Easter time this year."[60] Although the bishop had cited finances, Krivanka didn't buy it.

> I never believed it was financial. I wondered if he just felt very upset and ashamed of the Vatican rejection of his decisions. Perhaps he was angry about things I had said to him during the process, when I questioned the decisions he was forcing on people that would not work. So it felt like now he was just going to punish me and the planning office.[61]

News about the closing of the Pastoral Planning Office spread like wildfire. Although Krivanka remembers that day as "a real shock," he also remembers being inundated with support:

> I was getting so many wonderful calls from Bishop Pilla, from priests and people across the diocese, and—when the *National Catholic Reporter* story got

out—from people across the country. . . . And I realized it was like a funeral—
and I might not have been on earth to hear those things. I have a large file of
pages of letters and emails of people's affirmation of my life's service to the
diocese and the Church nationally.[62]

While Krivanka searched for ways to cope with a crushing injustice,
Cleveland priests were so outraged they wrote to Vatican officials asking
for Lennon's removal. One priest wrote, "Cardinal Piacenza, there is no
joy in Cleveland. Ministry has become a burden for so many of us. We live
in fear of retaliation if we are vocal. Desperation has pushed me to a point
beyond fear. Please help."[63] Another priest expressed a suspicion shared
by many: "In fact there is no plan to supply the professional services that
are necessary to fulfill your decree [to reopen parishes] in any meaningful
way. . . . The perception is that the closing of this office is both punitive and
strategic."[64] At an April 27, 2012, meeting of the Presbyteral Council, priest
leaders openly expressed their frustration at the bishop's failure to consult
them on major decisions and voiced disagreement with his decision to close
the Pastoral Planning Office without any consultation with priests.[65] Hoping
to smooth things over, Lennon sent conciliatory letters to Cleveland priests
and announced a series of nine small group gatherings with diocesan priests
to be held over the summer.[66] At these meetings many priests criticized what
Lennon had done.[67]

FOR THE FIRST TIME IN US HISTORY MULTIPLE
PARISHES REOPEN (BUT IT'S MESSY)

Over the summer and into the fall of 2012 Lennon appointed new pastors and,
to the great delight of dedicated parish activists, he slowly reopened their parishes. On Wednesday July 26, the Feast of St. James the Apostle, over fourteen hundred parishioners—some of whom had to stand outside—celebrated
a joyous reopening Mass at Lakewood's St. James Church. Josephine Hatala
had attended the church for fifty years and had two children who went to St.
James School which was within walking distance of their home. "I was heart-
broken and mad when the bishop closed this church," said Hatala. "I didn't
go to any other church after St. James closed. But today I saw a dream come
true. I didn't want to miss this Mass . . . and I'd say we're back on the job."[68]
  Three months earlier, National Public Radio's Michel Martin interviewed
Christine LaSalvia, the civil attorney who worked with Kate on the St. James
recourse. "[W]e were a vibrant parish," LaSalvia recalled. "We were the
biggest parish with the most people and the most sacraments in our area in
the city of Lakewood. We also believed that some of the procedure wasn't

followed in how the decisions were made for our closing and those are the two main areas that we focused on."[69] When Martin asked if appealing to the Vatican had been intimidating, LaSalvia replied:

> Well, I wasn't worried about that because we have a right to do it under canon law. I think the most intimidating part was figuring out how to do it, and there were a lot of little details that were difficult, like where to send it and how to send this brief and what needs to go in it. . . . But I was shocked—I mean maybe even more than anyone else because it's been so long, and I feel like I really knew a lot about the odds and how bad they were.[70]

As she watched Cleveland parishes reopen one by one, Kate marveled. "This is the first time in the US church for this to take place," she said. "I also think it is the first place anywhere in the world."[71] Ever empathetic about the pain Cleveland Catholics were experiencing, she remarked,

> Hard feelings in the hearts of the parishioners of the closed parishes now to be opened; practical problems involved with opening a parish office again, as well as all other organizational needs; and the hard feelings among the blended parishes that will now be split again; and finally the probable feelings of loss by those laity who lost their parish and church back in 2010 and did not take recourse—all contribute to the pain in the Diocese of Cleveland. I hope for the best for the people who have experienced the most chaotic process in their faith life with their parishes shut down and now reopening. Had the bishop been more pastoral and reasonable in the first place this mess would not have happened. . . . We need to continue to pray for all in the diocese.[72]

On December 28, 2016, Pope Francis granted Bishop Richard Lennon's request for early retirement. He died in Cleveland on October 29, 2019, after a prolonged illness.[73] As providence would have it, Sister Kate died one day earlier on October 28, 2019. While it is risky to speculate, I'm guessing that when Kate met the good bishop inside the pearly gates, she minced no words in giving him a piece of her mind. Then, I like to imagine, both were embraced by the just mercy of a loving God.

Chapter 10

Bringing Forth a Harvest

On Sunday September 30, 2012, FutureChurch gave Sister Kate Kuenstler the organization's highest honor, the Louis J. Trivison Award. Established to honor the memory of FutureChurch's priest cofounder, the award is given "in recognition of outstanding leadership in advancing the FutureChurch mission and vision, in one or more of the areas of teaching, administration, research, publication, advocacy, and pastoral service."[1]

Bob Kloos's spirited introduction delighted over three hundred people gathered in Cleveland for the organization's annual benefit:

> She has degrees in canon law that put her among the elite, but her personal mission has her walking among the poor, those cast out—the victims of bullying in the church. As a result, she has been a very busy lady. Her enormous regard for law drives her headlong, canons blazing, into battles, pitched by bishops. . . . In canon law class you learn that the law of the church is in place to protect the rights of all the baptized. Sister Kate proves that day in and day out. . . . She is eager to help, thorough to a fault, relentless in the fray and the self-proclaimed "mama bear." When it comes to protecting the parish, simply put in her own words, "I am a Poor Handmaid of Jesus Christ. I am happy to be a woman religious. . . ." This is someone Louie would like to have met.[2]

In her acceptance speech, Kate shared fascinating insights about how her pro bono ministry—and her canonical Commentary on the Cleveland decrees—were making a significant difference. "Over the past six years, many milestones have been accomplished. I have worked with many parishes using a computer, a Skype camera, and an iPhone. Thank goodness for technology that allows me to communicate with people all over the world without having to charge high fees."[3] She reprised the "watershed" case of Camden's St. Vincent Pallotti, a precursor to the Cleveland decisions and

Figure 10.1   Sr. Kate Kuenstler graciously accepts FutureChurch's Trivison Award on September 30, 2012. © 2012 James Metrisin

those in Springfield, Allentown, Syracuse, and Buffalo. Her Pallotti intervention "influenced a change in the attitude of the Apostolic Signatura and ultimately the Congregation for the Clergy that resulted in the [Cleveland] decrees issued March first of this year for the twelve parishes in Cleveland."[4] Furthermore, said Kate, "in turn, the people of Cleveland have raised awareness that recourse is possible and can be successful. And this awareness is benefiting many people around the world."

A fascinated audience listened as Kate related that just the previous week, she had received a call from "John" who was involved in the diocese of Peoria's restructuring process. Several months earlier John had sent Kate's Commentary and the Cleveland decrees to his bishop and every member of the diocesan planning commission.[5] The vicar general—who was also a canon lawyer—sent John a written letter of thanks. Kate described the outcome:

This past Sunday the bishop published the decrees for restructuring. In almost every case, the parishes are clustered. The commission and the bishop had used the [Cleveland] Commentary information to restructure the diocese in such a way that prevented unnecessary contention and needless animosity in the faith communities of the laity.[6]

Figure 10.2   Sister Kate with Bob Kloos and his wife Jean at FutureChurch award celebration, September 30, 2012. © 2012 James Metrisin

"Maria," a client in Australia, called Kate immediately after reading the Commentary from the FutureChurch website. After many Skype calls and conversations with Kate, her parish's recourse was soon pending at the Vatican. "What I think is most exciting," said Kate, "is that Maria is now using Facebook to inform other lay people in Australia, that they can challenge a bishop who intends to close their worship sites."[7] Another successful case involved requiring the bishop to issue a decree so parishioners could pursue their right to canonical recourse. Still another involved protecting a personal parish when the bishop wished to "change it to a territorial parish without following procedure and without issuing a legitimate decree."[8]

Kate told the group about cases in which bishops were suspected of fraud and/or misuse of funds. "The laity have informed the Vatican when there is an appearance of fraud perpetuated by a bishop. Fraud invalidates contracts and other legal agreements." She also assisted laity who "challenged bishops whom they suspect are misusing parish money that belongs to the parishioners." Because Catholic laity were holding bishops accountable, Kate reported, "the Vatican [recently] issued a letter informing bishops of the rightful use of parish money. . . . And your honor [the Trivison Award] today also honors these vigilant laity."[9]

FutureChurch folk attending the event especially enjoyed Kate's story about her client "Esther." Just the previous Tuesday, September 25, parishioners from Esther's parish had hired Kate "to help them take recourse against the merger of their parish and subsequent sale of their building and property." Two days later Esther telephoned to report that her parish committee had been "shocked to find out that the proposal for their parish and church had been changed by the regional planning committee. The proposal now being sent to the bishop acknowledged their vital parish and recommended they cluster with the other parish," rather than be closed. Kate explained the implications: "Their parish and church are safe," because "word had gone around the area and the diocese that they were hiring me."[10] The crowd erupted with laughter and prolonged applause. "It seems someone did their homework and realized that clustering was a far better solution," said a grinning Kate.

Kate praised her religious congregation, "[Y]ou also honor the Poor Handmaids of Jesus Christ. . . . It is because of them that I am a canon lawyer today. They continue to support my work as a canon lawyer and advocate for the laity, [because it is] central to the Poor Handmaids charism, to nurture the rightful role of the laity as leaders in the church." She also praised Future-Church, "[I]t's because of this organization and my subsequent collaboration with Sister Chris, that my work with parish and church closings has continued to develop to today. We have common goals to support a healthy future for the church. We love to empower the laity to take their rightful role in the church."[11] And she showered praise on the ordinary Catholics—including the hundreds of FutureChurch members gathered to honor her:

> With this recognition, you also recognize the laity in the church today who use their voice, which was affirmed 50 years ago at the Second Vatican Council and envisioned later in the code of Canon law in Canon 212. And I quote, "The Christian faithful have the right. And even at times the duty to manifest to the sacred pastors, their opinion on matters, which pertain to the good of the church."[12]

News of Kate's Commentary on the successful appeals in the Diocese of Cleveland spread quickly. After ending her anonymity, she was "swamped with new clients," and the Commentary began to significantly impact diocesan policy.[13] In late June 2012, Kate learned it had influenced two successful appeals in Kansas City, Kansas, and Grand Rapids, Michigan, respectively. In Grand Rapids, "the bishop clarified with the people that the church would not be closed. Therefore the church would stay open."[14] In Kansas City, the bishop neither published nor issued a decree to close the church. Therefore, plans to sell the church had to be scrapped and it continued as a sacred worship space. Kate wrote:

Both churches are staying open as a result of the Cleveland decrees and the research and writing of the Commentary. I have used both extensively for clients. . . . These two winners are real indicators of how precedent-setting the Cleveland decrees really are. Those decrees are impacting recourses all over the world.[15]

The cover story of FutureChurch's summer 2012 *Focus* newsletter noted that both canonical documents Kate had prepared for Cleveland—the Commentary and the *Canonical Appeals for Dummies* (now known as *Canonical Appeals Resource Process*)—were "downloaded by hundreds of parishioners in other U.S. dioceses as well as in England, Ireland, Australia and Canada."[16] In fact, Kate's *Canonical Appeals Resource Process*—originally posted in 2009—guided Catholics in other US dioceses through their own successful appeals. As of the summer of 2012, FutureChurch's *SOPC* initiative had helped Catholics from thirty US parishes in six dioceses win their appeals, including thirteen in Cleveland, Ohio; nine in Allentown, Pennsylvania; four in Springfield, Massachusetts; and one each in Camden, New Jersey; Buffalo, New York; Kansas City, Kansas; and Grand Rapids, Michigan. FutureChurch supplied canonical referrals and Kate's resources to parishioners in all of these locales.[17]

On August 12, 2012, Kate received an email from Colleen LaTray of St. Mary Parish in Jamesville, New York. LaTray told Kate that a Mass celebrating the Feast of the Assumption would be held at St. Mary Church on August 15. It was the first Mass since the Vatican upheld the St. Mary appeal in 2011. Kate was beyond thrilled that after five years, dedicated St. Mary parishioners would celebrate liturgy in their beloved church. She emailed LaTray:

> I rejoice with all of you. . . . You were my first attempt at addressing the issue of bishops closing parishes in order to sell churches. I was able to finally get some understanding at the Apostolic Signatura in late 2009. Then the Congregation for the Clergy got on board and also began to uphold the required canonical procedures for closing church buildings. As a result, I have been able to help keep many church buildings open, here in the USA as well as Australia, Canada, and Europe.[18]

Kate praised LaTray's courage: "To stand up against a bishop's decree was an act of heroism. I am delighted to have been a part of the journey that has led to this latest reality: liturgy in your beloved church. I will always remember you." She forwarded the good news to me at FutureChurch. Her long and often lonely canonical ministry was reaping a rich harvest:

> This is a miracle. This is the very first parish/church that I helped way back in 2007. I never thought that they would ever have Mass in their church again. It

seems that this year is the year that all of the long hard days of work are bringing forth a harvest. I am so overwhelmed at all of this. So very many years I
worked and saw no positive results. So many years I was unable to influence the
Vatican. It is an amazing grace for all of this to be happening.[19]

Then, with words I shall not soon forget, Kate shared a personal message:
"Thank you too for your support and encouragement. Without you I would
have been very alone. Your friendship and your walking the path with me was
a blessing beyond telling."[20]

BLACK PARISH REOPENS IN THE ARCHDIOCESE OF MIAMI, FLORIDA

In October 2011 Kate helped Black parishioners at St. Philip Neri Church
successfully convince the archbishop of Miami, Thomas Wenski, to reopen
their church. In 2009 Wenski's predecessor, Archbishop Joseph Favalora,
had closed two of the three predominantly African-American churches in
Miami-Dade County. Thanks to the courage of St. Philip parishioners one
would be restored so there would now be two African-American churches.
Wenski also reversed his predecessor and reopened two other churches closed
by Favalora.[21]

A CHANGE AT THE CONGREGATION FOR THE CLERGY

In November 2013, Kate received a decree from the new prefect of the Congregation for the Clergy, Cardinal Beniamino Stella, who had been appointed
the previous September. She noticed a marked difference in the quality of the
document:

> It was entirely different in tone and professional work . . . a true decree about
> the content of the recourse sent, not about a bishop breaking all the rules. Also,
> it is the first decree that included a formal law section, and it has the best law
> section I have seen. It helps me to see what the thinking is at the Congregation
> for the Clergy.[22]

In addition, the new decree evidenced a greater degree of respect for parishioners. "That is a first," said Kate, who reflected that the previous prefect "was
always heavy-handed. . . . For years I complained to Apostolic Signatura that
the Congregation of the Clergy was not respectful of the laity. Now they seem
to be so. Another win for us." But there was a downside: "There is nothing

I can challenge in such a decree that warrants appeal to the Signatura," lamented Kate, who described previous decrees as "sloppy, rude, incomplete, and containing mistakes." In these instances, "I had grounds to appeal the decree from the Congregation for the Clergy to the Apostolic Signatura. When the decree from the Congregation for the Clergy is written in such a professional way, I have nothing to make an appeal to the Signatura."[23] Nevertheless, Kate would guide many successful recourses in the years ahead.

INDIANAPOLIS: A PARADIGM FOR BISHOPS ON HOW TO DO A MERGER

In 2013, Kate was hired by parishioners from four rural parishes in the Archdiocese of Indianapolis, Indiana. They needed her help to develop recourses against four decrees intending to merge their individual parishes into one large parish. The pastor of the four parishes wanted to close and sell the churches—which were well maintained and about ten miles apart, to build a megachurch and school. This newly merged parish would then have a debt of $20 million, which would likely take more than twenty years to remediate. With Kate's help, parishioners from each parish wrote to the newly appointed archbishop, Joseph Tobin, asking him to rescind the decrees. Trusting the reliability of the original documents from his predecessor, Archbishop Daniel M. Buechlein, Tobin initially denied their request. Kate quickly helped diligent parishioners develop their recourse to Rome even as a consulting firm hired by Tobin's predecessor was holding meetings to implement the flawed decrees. After presenting their intended recourse to Tobin, Kate gratefully remembers,

> He realized the decrees had grave flaws and rescinded the four decrees and the Archbishop said, "Let's leave each campus open." So the church in each of the four towns is open, but we are going to merge the parishes but have four campuses in four different towns. One pastor for the four campuses, but one parish.[24]

Tobin also removed the original pastor and appointed a new one who, according to Kate, "has the skills to heal the people and form a healthy merger with four campuses." In a 2016 interview, Kate provided an update for how the newly merged All Saints Parish was progressing:

> They now have started a capital campaign where each of the campuses is going to be upgrading its building. . . . They have new parishioners moving in. They have resolved the pain that they originally experienced and have become one parish. . . . This is the paradigm of how this can work because in this case, the

bishop realized that it just was not a good decision to shut down four church campuses and sell them and build a multi-million-dollar mega church.[25]

She praised Archbishop Tobin's decision: "It was not for profit. It was not to make money. It was not to sell the buildings. . . . This particular story can be a paradigm for all the bishops of how to do a merger if you're not looking to sell property."[26]

HISPANIC IMMIGRANTS OPPOSE CARDINAL DINARDO AND SAVE ST. STEPHENS

In April 2018, Kate won a hard-fought recourse when the Supreme Tribunal of the Apostolic Signatura upheld the rights of Hispanic Catholics at St. Stephen Parish in Houston, Texas. A parish full of determined blue-collar immigrants opposed Cardinal Daniel DiNardo's plan to merge their parish and sell their church. In 2014, a developer approached the Archdiocese about purchasing St. Stephen's land, which is located in a trendy, rapidly gentrifying Houston neighborhood.[27] St. Stephen's had nine hundred members, most of whom were low-income Hispanic immigrants and their relatives. The parish was financially sound with over $200,000 in reserves.[28] It was also a haven for immigrants from Central America and was proud of an education building that served three hundred children.[29] In May 2016 the Archdiocese merged St. Stephen with the smaller St. Joseph Parish, which was white, German, and historically unwelcoming to immigrants. When her parish was shuttered, Esperanza Fitch, who had been a member of St. Stephen for nine years, compared it to fleeing from Venezuela. "It was like they took my home again," she said.[30] The Archdiocese quickly enclosed St. Stephen property with a chain link fence, locking parishioners out of a church they had built in 1941 with their own funds.

But gutsy St. Stephen Catholics refused to accept DiNardo's ruling and appealed to Rome. Unfortunately, the Congregation for the Clergy overlooked false statements in the decree and denied their appeal. With Kate's help, St. Stephen Catholics prepared a recourse to the Apostolic Signatura.[31] This required significant funding. Undeterred, this low-income Hispanic community sold tamales and chiles rellenos to raise money. They also gathered every Sunday, rain or shine, to pray outside their church.[32] In the Signatura recourse, Kate supplied strong documentary evidence of untruths about reasons to close the parish which parishioners had uncovered in the decree.[33] They had a strong case. In due course the Supreme Tribunal of the Apostolic Signatura reversed the ruling and Cardinal DiNardo was required to reopen the parish and church of St. Stephen.

But it would be eighteen long months before the cardinal finally reopened St. Stephen.[34] The Archdiocese never gave a reason for taking so long to allow Catholics to return to their treasured church.[35] Yet grateful parishioners were beyond magnanimous in victory. "We want to thank Cardinal DiNardo for opening the church, for the opportunity he has given us," Ester Nieto said in Spanish as she cleaned the church sanctuary two days before the reopening Mass. "We want him to know that if there's any dream he wants to achieve here in Texas, he can count on us, on the Hispanic community. This community knows how to work hard."[36] At this writing, St. Stephen is one of only two parish mergers (as opposed to church closings) reversed by Rome outside of the twelve reversals in the Cleveland diocese in March 2012.[37] Their joyous reopening on September 29, 2019, occurred just one month before Kate's death on October 28. It was the last canonical success she would know about. However, she would posthumously win three other appeals which were still pending at the Signatura.

KATE DEFENDS LAITY—AND HOLDS PASTORS AND BISHOPS ACCOUNTABLE

In addition to defending parish rights, Catholics often called on Kate to see what could be done about toxic work situations, abusive pastors, and unfit bishops. On July 17, 2014, she sent me an email describing these cases, always being careful to protect the privacy of those involved. In one case, she praises a bishop for removing an abusive pastor whose behavior had led to the resignations of eight teachers from the parish grade school.

> I have helped a group of women who were former teachers present testimony regarding a hostile work environment. . . . As a result of their documentation, the bishop removed the pastor from the parish and school. The priest was removed from the diocese. . . .What I did too was walk with the women who were shell shocked from the abuse they experienced. When they called me to help, they were in pain and chaos. In four months they were able to focus and tell their story well. It is so good to see a bishop act with compassion.[38]

Kate also spent a substantial amount of time working with priest groupings in two different dioceses who appealed to Rome to have unfit bishops removed. These multi-year cases were in addition to the requests from Cleveland priests to have Bishop Richard Lennon removed. Before her death, I asked Kate to what extent I could or should include this aspect of her work in this book. She requested that no details be included because it is the priests' recourse not hers. Therefore, it would be inappropriate to publicize their testimony. She had many good friends among diocesan clergy who counted on her wise counsel in these delicate and politically fraught situations.[39]

MAJORITY OF SUCCESSFUL US RECOURSES WERE GUIDED BY KUENSTLER

From 2012 until her death in 2019, Kate's canonical counsel helped hundreds of Catholics in at least thirty dioceses file recourse to keep their churches open or otherwise defend their canonical rights. While parishioners often sought recourse against merging their parishes, these rarely succeeded. Recourses against closing and selling churches (relegation) were more likely to succeed. Many beloved churches stayed open for worship even though the parish was merged.

FutureChurch kept a running tally of the status of all church appeals which appeared in the public media, were reported by Kate, or were otherwise reported by involved parishioners (Table 10.1). Owing to parishioner privacy concerns and canon law services that prefer to avoid media coverage, it is possible—indeed probable—that a number of cases went unreported. Nevertheless a quantitative accounting of what can be known may be helpful despite these limitations.

From the first fifteen recourses filed in the Vatican from Boston Catholics in 2005[40] until the onset of Kate's final illness in 2018, a total of one hundred administrative recourses were filed at the Congregation for the Clergy. This includes four international recourses from Melbourne, Australia; Antigonish, Canada; Calgary, Canada; and Liverpool, UK that were guided by Kate. Forty-six of the one hundred recourses filed were successful, and thirty of these—or 65 percent—had been guided by Kate either directly, or through the canonical resources she created for FutureChurch. An additional thirty-eight local appeals were filed at the diocesan or archdiocesan level of which thirty-five were successful. Kate successfully guided seventeen local appeals. The remaining eighteen were granted by Cardinal O'Malley in the wake of widespread opposition to closures from Boston Catholics. At the time of her death, three of Kate's recourse cases were still pending at the Apostolic Signatura and being handled by the requisite special canon lawyers. Two of these were later upheld after her death. St. Patrick Church, Lethbridge, in the diocese of Calgary, Canada, and Most Holy Trinity Church in Mamaroneck, New York, in the Archdiocese of New York, were permitted to remain open. One Signatura case is still pending, St. Elizabeth of Hungary in Manhattan, Archdiocese of New York.[41]

Table 10.1 FutureChurch Tabulation of Parish/Church Merger and Closing Appeals 2005–2018*

Diocese	Diocese only appeal	Rome appeals	Won at diocese	Won in Rome	Kuenstler Rome wins	Kuenstler diocese wins
Boston	18	15	18	9		
Albany		1				
Allentown		17				
Buffalo		3		2	2	
Camden		3		3	2	
Charleston, SC		1		1	1	
Cleveland		12	2	12	12	2
Detroit	2	2		1	1	
Denver		1		1	1	
Galveston-Houston		1		1	1	
Grand Rapids			1			1
Hartford	1					
Indianapolis	5		4			4
Kansas City, KS	4		1			1
Miami	1		3			3
New Orleans	3	2	2			2
AD New York (2007)		2				
AD New York (2014)	4	9	4	8	7	4
Peoria	4	4				
Scranton		8				
Springfield		4		4	1	
St. Paul-Minneapolis		5				
Syracuse		2		2	1	
Toledo		2				
Worcester		1				
Youngstown		1		1		
INTERNATIONAL						
Melbourne, Australia		1				
Antigonish, CA		1				
Calgary, CA		1				
Liverpool, UK		1		1	1	
Totals	**38**	**100**	**35**	**46**	**30**	**17**

*As of March 19, 2024, one Kuenstler recourse—Manhattan's St. Elizabeth of Hungary—is still pending in Rome.

Chapter 11

"Making All Things Revenue"— Archdiocese of New York

On January 26, 2014, Kate and I gave a workshop to Catholics in New York City about "Preserving Parish Communities in a Time of Fewer Priests." We were invited by the Call To Action Metro New York chapter to educate Catholics about their rights and responsibilities when faced with a parish merger or closure. Three years earlier the Archdiocese had announced a pastoral planning initiative, "Making All Things New," which skeptics quickly dubbed "Making All Things Few" or "Making All Things Revenue."[1] Cardinal Timothy Dolan made it clear that he "[might] have to merge, consolidate, and even close" some of the Archdiocese's 368 parishes.[2] In June 2013, the Archdiocese contracted with The Reid Group, a company which specializes in assisting dioceses with pastoral planning processes.[3] In the January presentation Kate told New Yorkers that they could do nothing about the fate of their parishes until the Archdiocese issued decrees. These were not expected until September 2014. Once a decree was issued, they had ten useful days to appeal to the Archbishop.[4]

While making it clear that she did not know the plan for the Archdiocese of New York, Kate told the group that in nearly every diocese where she had assisted laity with appeals thus far, she found vibrant, successful parishes being closed and merged with parishes that were failing: "Even if your parish is solid, your building is in good shape, and you have money in the bank, do not assume you will survive," she told the group. In some cases, the bishop realizes the diocese can benefit financially "by shuttering the moneyed parish and getting funds through [the] indebted parish. When the bishop begins to make those adjustments, he's looking at money," Kate said. "The capital earned from the sale of a good building will be greater than one in disrepair. Though the money from the sale must go into the new, merged parish (and not directly to bishop), the funds will be used to pay down debts, and in many cases, these debts are to the bishop."[5]

Kate also emphasized recent 2013 guidelines from the Congregation for the Clergy that clarified the distinction between the legitimate reasons to merge parishes and legitimate reasons to close a church. For a diocesan bishop to close or merge a parish, a "just cause" is required, and such action must address the unique characteristics of each parish. To relegate a church to profane use, a stricter standard requiring a "grave cause" is required. It was no longer legitimate to relegate a church because of the shortage of priests or because the church is in close proximity to another church, Kate said. Furthermore, a church may not be relegated if it is no longer considered necessary for worship when a parish is suppressed or merged, or if the maintenance for a building no longer needed for worship is a financial burden. The new guidelines were especially pertinent to the New York Archdiocese where Cardinal Dolan had named a shortage of priests, the close proximity of parishes, and changing demographics as justification for the largest reorganization of parishes in the history of the Archdiocese.[6]

Announced in two stages, the larger one on November 2, 2012, and the second grouping on May 5, 2013, the Archdiocese planned a 20 percent reduction of its 368 parishes by merging 150 parishes into 71 new ones which would yield a total of 289 remaining parishes.[7] Forty-two churches from the 71 newly merged parishes would no longer be used for regular services and would effectively close.[8] But savvy New York Catholics weren't buying Cardinal Dolan's rationale. "I believe the real reason for closure was a real estate cash grab," said Kalman Chany, a successful business owner and trustee for the St. Elizabeth of Hungary Parish located on the Upper East Side of Manhattan.

> This is a very tony area of the Archdiocese. Our church property is probably worth $25 to $50 million dollars. Eight of the eleven churches that closed in Manhattan were churches located right next to what would be the new Second Avenue subway. The first phase of the line was slated to open in late 2016. In the year prior to the subway opening, property values less than a city block from the subway station entrance—as is true with St. Elizabeth—went up 30 percent.[9]

Chany wasn't the only one to suspect money was behind the closures. Peggy Noonan, a respected *Wall Street Journal* columnist, wrote an open letter to Cardinal Dolan arguing that the Archdiocese was wrong to consider closing her church. Citing overflow liturgies, a diverse population, solid finances, a successful school, and a legacy of religious vocations, Noonan accused the Archdiocese of wanting cash from the sale of the Church of St. Thomas More, which is located on prime real estate on Manhattan's Upper East Side.[10]

To Kate's amazement, Noonan contacted her for canonical advice. In an email to this author Kate wrote, "I just now received an email from Peggy Noonan who wants to discuss the parish closing with me. OMG!!!! I think this is amazing!"[11] Noonan had a lengthy conversation with Kate via telephone. "She was wonderful. She plans to call again with more questions. . . . She is a real professional. We will now see what comes of this."[12] Thanks in no small part to Noonan's prominence and Kate's solid lawyering, the Archdiocese scrapped plans for closing St. Thomas More—and the church remains open to celebrate weekday and Sunday masses to this day.[13]

After each of the November 2, 2014, and May 8, 2015, announcements, FutureChurch sent Kate's canonical information and a sample appeal letter to its expanding email list of contacts in the New York Archdiocese. Many had already downloaded *Save Our Parish Community* resources as a result of advance organizing beginning the previous January. Two days before Christmas, Kate told the *Wall Street Journal* that she was working with eighteen parishes bringing recourse to the Vatican after Cardinal Dolan refused to reverse his decisions.[14] By early January 2015, Kate had nearly thirty parishes in the New York Archdiocese that were pursuing canonical recourse related to the November round of decisions.[15] After the May 2015 decisions were released, that number increased.

VATICAN ORDERS CARDINAL DOLAN TO RELEASE DECREES

Despite repeated requests from November through February 2015, New York archdiocesan personnel refused to provide copies of the canonical decrees to anyone, even though canon law requires parishioners to include a copy when filing their recourse to Rome. Cardinal Dolan was apparently following Bishop Galante of Camden's playbook by insisting that the original letters sent to their parishes constituted "legitimate notifications" when they were not.[16] After many letters and telephone calls, the New York Archdiocese reluctantly allowed parishioners to view the decrees but only under certain conditions: "There could be no photographs and no transcriptions. Notes could be taken, but sometimes only after the document was out of sight. Viewings were by appointment, monitored by officials."[17] The lengths to which archdiocesan officials went to obstruct Catholics from exercising their rights is remarkable. "I've never seen anything like this before, and I can't imagine its purpose, except to prevent the parishioners from exercising their legitimate appeal rights," said Nicholas P. Cafardi, dean emeritus at Duquesne University in Pittsburgh.[18]

In December, Kate encouraged her clients to document their experience of viewing the decrees. Regardless of whether they had yet seen their decree, she recommended that all her New York Archdiocese clients write to Cardinal Stella at the Congregation for the Clergy and advise him that formal administrative recourse was being brought against the November 2, 2014, decree. She also told them to mention that Cardinal Dolan refused to provide a copy of their decrees. Meanwhile, a steady stream of determined New Yorkers soon began to wear on office staffers for Auxiliary Bishop John O'Hara, who was overseeing the merger process. "I have also heard that Bishop O'Hara's office is not happy with the number of people coming to view the decrees," Kate wrote. "I suspect that the two women in his office who must stand guard are not able to get their other work done. It could be beneficial to have more people make appointments to view their decree," she hinted.[19]

On February 11, 2015, the Archdiocese suddenly published fifty decrees on its website. One day earlier the *New York Times* had sent the Archdiocese a detailed inquiry about withholding the decrees, a fact that reporter Sharon Otterman carefully noted in her February 12 investigative piece.[20] Joseph Zwilling, a spokesman for the Archdiocese, told the *Times* that the failure to post the decrees earlier was an "oversight," and argued "the page-and-a-half letters [sent to the parishes] were equivalent to the three-page formal decrees except 'in presentation.'" He went on to say that in the opinion of the Archdiocese's canon lawyers, the letters provided sufficient notification of the mergers; providing the actual decrees was legally unnecessary.[21] It is important to note that the November letters sent to the parishes—which were read at Sunday Masses that weekend—failed to include the text at the end of the actual decrees which the Archdiocese withheld, stating that those aggrieved are required to "submit a petition in the sense of canon 1734 §1 to [the Archdiocese / Cardinal Dolan] within ten useful days from the legitimate notification of this decree."[22] Kate had a different take on the Archdiocese's sudden release of the decrees.

> The Cardinal is in Rome now and I believe the Congregation for the Clergy called him into their office and ordered the Cardinal to make the decrees available to you. So the letter you sent in December to the Vatican has had the effect hoped for. It does feel good to know the Congregation for the Clergy affirms our argument that paper copies of the decree must be available for the parishioners. What is also an error on the part of the Cardinal is he did not give a copy [of the decree] to the pastors who represent the parish juridic person that was being changed by the Cardinal. Whoever advised the Cardinal was not a canon lawyer who knew the law.[23]

Kate knew the law. She also knew how to get recalcitrant hierarchs to follow the law. Just a year earlier Detroit's Archbishop Allen Vigneron had refused to release paper copies of his decrees, thereby making it impossible for Catholics to appeal his decision to close inner-city parishes. Kate took recourse against the archbishop's action and won. "I successfully argued Vigneron was in error applying canon law. In addition, my clients received a Vatican-forced apology letter from the Detroit auxiliary bishop who manipulated the process against them. I have not seen anything like this before."[24]

IDENTICAL DECREES FOR OVER 125 ARCHDIOCESE OF NEW YORK PARISHES

The ability to view each decree was crucial to understanding the factual basis for the cardinal's decision to close any given parish. Only then could facts be presented to the Congregation for the Clergy to demonstrate why his decision was mistaken. To meet the "just cause" requirement for a merger, canon law requires the decrees to provide specific, individualized evidence for each parish. Cardinal Dolan's decrees all used the same boilerplate language that failed to address the uniqueness of each parish situation. In a 2014 interview, Kate explains:

> I don't want to pick on Cardinal Dolan, but I will just say that the hundred and twenty-eight decrees that were written were identical. Absolutely identical. You cannot tell me a hundred-and-twenty-eight parishes are identical, that have exactly the same reasons on why they're being [merged].[25]

In July 2015, as churches were one by one celebrating their final Masses, she boldly told the *New York Times*, "Canon law requires that when the cardinal merges two parishes, he is to look specifically at the issues involving those two parishes and make a decision involving those two parishes."[26] But, said Kate, the Archdiocese's template-like approach "showed how much the decrees were bogus, did not apply to the individual parishes, and were in complete error to what the cardinal claimed."[27] Nine months later, the Congregation for the Clergy ordered the cardinal to amend five decrees which allowed the churches of appealing parishes to remain open. Kate's April 29, 2016, email to FutureChurch staff explains:

> Dolan signed decrees that were badly written, contained errors, and did not follow procedural law. He did everything wrong. Of course, a year ago he claimed he had followed all procedures perfectly and thus he did not anticipate the Congregation for the Clergy doing anything but uphold the decrees as written. Boy, was he wrong. I knew they were a poor excuse for decrees. They were actually very easy to argue against because of that.[28]

APPEALING TO ROME IS IMPORTANT, EVEN IF IT FAILS

Many New York recourses to the Congregation for the Clergy were not accepted. In late May 2015 a parishioner from a Staten Island parish emailed Kate that their appeal had been denied. They had not written to the cardinal within ten working days of his November 2 letter, even though at the time no one knew the date of the decrees.[29] Thanks to early FutureChurch e-blasts, all those who contacted Kate between November 2 and November 15, the end of the ten working days, were given a letter of petition to the cardinal "to rescind the decree if there was one." This was then sent within ten working days following November 2. Most of these recourses filed within all the requisite timelines were accepted by the Congregation for the Clergy for review. For those who contacted Kate after November 15—such as this Staten Island parish—Kate said she had chosen "to err on the side of a possible recourse for you. It was better for you to try for recourse than to sit by and miss a possible opportunity. I kept saying that this was a long shot. But often in the pain and chaos clients keep up a hope for the best." Unfortunately, the post–November 15 cases were denied. Kate explains,

> I have in the past (2006-2009) been successful in arguing that clients did not know the procedures and thus I was able to get dispensations to the procedural norms. However, for the past three years the Vatican has changed its stance and assumes all laity know the procedures and thus this is no longer possible. They consistently refuse to hear that bishops still keep this secret and laity really do not know the rules.[30]

The Archdiocese's refusal to release decrees made for a chaotic situation which necessitated shrewd canonical decision-making on Kate's part: "The Cardinal, who did not follow the law from November 2 to mid-February, caused me as a canon lawyer to try and out-maneuver his manipulation. This was the most difficult process I have had since 2006. Many parishes did not make the cut at the Congregation for Clergy due to timing issues. All that while, I kept encouraging parishes to attempt to send recourse."[31]

Parish merger recourse cases at the Congregation for the Clergy are notoriously difficult to win based on merit alone. When Kate was able to win, it was always due to procedural errors on the part of the bishop which he could, and did, easily correct. Such cases only succeeded when, as Kate noted with Cleveland, "a stubborn bishop refuses to make procedural corrections." A realistic Kate told her Staten Island client, "I do not expect any of the [merger] cases from New York accepted by the Congregation for the Clergy to be won on any merit of the case."[32] While she didn't expect the parish mergers to win, there was significantly more hope for keeping churches from being relegated to profane use. Nevertheless, she told her distressed client, there are other reasons for pursuing recourse to the Vatican:

> Your sending a recourse document to the Vatican is the only way for the Vatican to be told how the Cardinal is manipulating the law for his own purpose at the cost of the faith communities of the parishes. The Cardinal does not report his administrative decisions and actions to the Vatican. He needs no permission from the Vatican and receives no oversight for what he is doing to the parishes in his Archdiocese. So, it is important for you and others like you to send your recourses against the Cardinals' decisions to shut down your parish and church. . . . I never promise a win for any of my clients. What I do is provide a way for your voice to be heard at the Vatican.[33]

Kate offered this rather grim—although meant to be consoling—picture: "Even those parishes that have won cases at the Vatican are never the same again. The very act of restructuring parishes by a bishop is the most destructive act made by a bishop. A parish seldom recovers from the intense pain and discord and loss of vibrant parishioners."[34] She further consoled her client by candidly offering her own heartfelt reasons for pursuing recourse:

> [A]t this most difficult and most painful time, I can only assure you that your voice has been heard at the Vatican. I wish I had more power and more influence to make the Vatican look at the destruction of the USA Catholic parish life, but I do not . . . I believe that each report, each recourse document, each challenge to restructuring of parishes that destroys vibrant parishes will in time finally cause the Vatican to take a second look at this serious problem in the Catholic Church in the USA.[35]

Yet Kate never hesitated to criticize the Congregation for the Clergy for blindly accepting a bishop's reasons for claiming a "just cause" for closing and merging a vibrant, solvent parish. In a March 15, 2016, email she wrote, "I still have grave criticism of the Congregation for the Clergy's interpretation of the bishop's power to use a 'just' reason. I fail to see how false statements made by a bishop can be just reasons according to the law."[36]

FINANCIALLY SOUND PARISHES AT RISK

As Kate had predicted in January 2014, the Archdiocese of New York merged wealthier parishes with indebted ones. In most, but not all, cases the wealthier entities were personal parishes, that is, a non-geographical parish that serves a unique population, such as an Italian community or a Deaf community. On

December 4, 2015, in an interview for the documentary *Foreclosing on Faith*, Kate told filmmaker Jeff MacIntyre,

> I have fifteen cases—parishes that are at this moment at the Vatican with recourse. There were about five or six other parishes whose recourses were not accepted at the Vatican for various reasons. Not because of the merit of the case, but there were some procedural errors that happened. Almost every one of my clients is a personal parish.[37]

Kate had analyzed the decrees from the first round of Cardinal Dolan's decisions and discovered,

> A hundred and eighteen parishes were being restructured and thirty parishes were going to have their churches locked and closed. Of those thirty parishes, almost every one was a personal parish. In these instances, the personal parish was being merged with a territorial parish. For the most part, all the personal parishes had a pastor who was a religious order priest. The personal parishes had no debt. The personal parishes had buildings that were in good condition. The personal parishes had dynamic, vital activities of their parish. And the personal parishes were in good and very well-placed areas of the Archdiocese that could be used for other purposes and sold in many cases for millions of dollars.[38]

As she had seen in too many other dioceses, the New York Archdiocese was merging indebted territorial parishes with vibrant, financially well-off personal parishes.

> The personal parishes that are being closed and being merged with the territorial parishes, for the most part, these territorial parishes have pastors who are diocesan priests, have severe heavy debt to the Archdiocese, and do not have dynamic parishioners. [They are] parishes, that if you want to call them vital, that would be stretching it. They're not in areas that are conducive for sale. That's just how it is.[39]

Some parishes with which Kate had worked early on—such as Peggy Noonan's well-heeled St. Thomas More—were able to preserve their church, despite being merged with an indebted parish.[40] According to Kalman Chany, it was eventually decided to merge two territorial parishes, St. Thomas More with Our Lady of Good Council, "because Our Lady of Good Council had debt."[41]

THE DEAF COMMUNITY AND ST. ELIZABETH OF HUNGARY

Prior to 2014, the parish of St. Elizabeth of Hungary was a vibrant personal parish that the Archdiocese ordered to merge to the surprise of its pastor, Monsignor Patrick McCahill. Located in the centrally located Upper East Side of Manhattan, St. Elizabeth was a haven for nearly five hundred Deaf Catholics who traveled from the ten counties of the Archdiocese of New York (and beyond) to celebrate Mass with their beloved "Father Pat," the only priest in the Archdiocese who used fluent sign language. "Some of them will get here at 6:00 in the morning, and they'll stay here 'til 4:00 in the afternoon," McCahill told the *New York Times*.[42] As McCahill interpreted, Margaret Arnold, a Deaf actress who was in the parish's Deaf choir, said, "Many of us are from different communities, Staten Island, Brooklyn, Westchester. We come here. This is the only place we can get together. At home, with their families, sometimes they don't feel close to them. Here, they do feel close."[43] McCahill lamented, "I can't understand why it can't stay open and independent. . . . After all, the parish is financially sound, and the church building is in good condition."[44]

A community of Catholic Slovak immigrants established St. Elizabeth of Hungary Parish in April 1891. In July 1980, Cardinal Terence Cooke, the then-archbishop of New York, designated the parish as a church for Deaf Catholics of the Archdiocese. Many hearing Catholics from the local neighborhood were also parishioners who provided most of the financial support for the parish. One member of the hearing community, Kalman Chany, worked closely with Kate. Chany was the principal recurrent in appealing the cardinal's November 2, 2014, decree merging St. Elizabeth with two other parishes and suspending its regular weekday and Sunday masses. At this writing in 2024, that recourse is still pending at the Apostolic Signatura. Chany—who is of Slovak heritage—is the founder-president of Campus Consultants Inc., a Manhattan-based firm that assists families in maximizing their eligibility for financial aid to minimize college costs. Chany grew up just a couple of blocks from St. Elizabeth's. After graduating from college in 1979, he became very active at the parish, serving as a lector and Eucharistic minister. In 2012, he became a lay trustee. He served on St. Elizabeth's core team of both Deaf and hearing parishioners, while also serving as chair of his region's cluster group. For the Archdiocese's reorganization initiative, each parish established a core team consisting of the pastor/administrator as well as four lay members, at least one of whom was to be a current trustee. A number of individual parish core teams, usually from three to five parishes in the same vicinity, were then assigned to a cluster group. "So I was very involved in the *Making All Things New* process, which was not typical for many of the people who brought recourses from other parishes," Chany said. In this capacity, he had few illusions. Despite assurances that "no decisions had been made" when various core teams from the East Side of Manhattan attended their first meeting in the fall of 2013, there was little doubt that the Archdiocese would close many parishes and churches, especially in Manhattan.[45]

As the process unfolded, Chany, who had majored in accounting and finance and worked for several years in corporate finance for a Fortune 500 company, was critical of the financial data the Archdiocese was using to evaluate parishes.

> There was no mention of how much in assets a particular parish had. . . . So the financial statements did not provide an accurate picture of the solvency of the parish. . . . Our church had hundreds of thousands of dollars in the bank with no debt at the time our parish had its last Mass. Our parish's real property, as valued by a top NYC firm, was worth anywhere from $25 to $50 million dollars.[46]

Along with many other parishes on the East Side of Manhattan north of the Midtown business district, St. Elizabeth's is located less than a full city block from an entrance to a station for the new Second Avenue subway line, which was under construction for a number of years before service commenced in December 2016. Not only were property values near the church skyrocketing at the time of the cardinal's decree, but the convenient new subway line was likely to attract more Sunday worshippers for the Deaf community. The new subway also led to plans for many new twenty- to thirty-story high-rise apartment buildings to replace many three- to five-story structures near the church. Therefore, the hearing community would see an increase in parish membership as well. Chany noticed that the Archdiocese's financial data did not follow generally accepted accounting principles:

> Specifically, if you're going to perform major capital improvements to your property, you're supposed to depreciate those improvements over many years. With the Archdiocese of New York, they expensed the entire cost of the improvement in one year. So, because of this flawed accounting method, there were these big deficits that some churches showed on the parish financial statements. [This was] because prior to *Making All Things New*, there was the [Archdiocesan] Bicentennial fundraising campaign and many parishes raised a great deal of money, including St. Elizabeth's. A significant percentage of those funds went back to the parish itself. But then parishes started spending this money for these improvements during the five-year period the Archdiocese looked at for *Making All Things New*. So it appeared as if a number of churches were running large deficits, when they really weren't. They were just spending down the money that they had raised years earlier.[47]

On February 14, 2014, Chany's cluster group, representing five parishes, voted on which of the parishes should or should not close. By a vote of 20 to 0 (with 4 abstentions), they decided against recommending any closures at all. This group of laity and clergy reverenced the uniqueness of each parish even if subsequent archdiocesan decrees did not. According to Chany,

> Each of the parishes had their own unique situation. St. Joseph's for example, was a German national church, where . . . Pope Benedict said Mass when he came to New York. Our Lady Good Council had a big Hispanic community as well as an English-speaking community. Saint Stephen of Hungary had the Hungarian community. We had the Deaf. And then there was also St Monica's, which is a larger church on 79th street, which is a wide main thoroughfare.[48]

As it happened, the vote occurred just one month after Kate and I had given our presentation in New York. Unbeknownst to either of us, our timely information influenced Chany and his parish core team:

> This was after you and sister Kate had already come to New York. So, our lay parish leadership already had an idea of what was going on, as did core team members from other parishes in our cluster. The feeling of our cluster group was: "We are just going to be the fall guys and gals for our parishes. Saying we want to close some parishes down now; we are going to be used." The Archdiocese could then say, "Well, your core teams and your members of your cluster group agreed to close these parishes down." But we took the opinion that if the Archdiocese was going to do it anyway, let them be the bad guys who do it.[49]

Chany said his cluster group felt that despite their recommendation to the archdiocesan advisory group not to close any parishes, at least one would probably be closed. Notably, during the core team and cluster group processes (which lasted roughly ten months), the Archdiocese had only talked about parish *closures*. When the decrees were issued, however, the parishes were to be *merged*. This differed from the Archdiocesan Advisory Group's closure terminology in response to the cluster group's recommendations. Chany recalls that Kate suspected the change in language may have been due to the Vatican's newfound reluctance to close churches. "So the end run around that would be merge parishes and then have the pastor of the merged parish recommend that the new parish doesn't need the other property anymore," noted Chany. "He would tell the Cardinal: 'We should sell it or lease it or do something with it.'" The language change allowed the Archdiocese to circumvent canon law and still close churches.[50]

On Sunday November 2, 2014, Monsignor McCahill at St. Elizabeth of Hungary read a letter from Cardinal Dolan at all Masses, announcing the parish would merge with St. Monica and St. Stephen of Hungary parishes, with St. Monica being the main church of the new parish. Chany immediately gathered with other St. Elizabeth parishioners to collect email contact information "because we feared there was going to be a diaspora with people upset and leaving." He noticed a woman outside the church asking people about the closures. Thinking she was likely a reporter (given the use of her notepad), Chany introduced himself. It was Melanie Grayce West from the *Wall Street Journal*. Chany remembers, "I burst out in tears. I [told her] 'this is the Slovak church. You know, they've closed this church down.' And she asked, 'What's so special about this church?' So I pointed to the billboard outside that has the Mass times listed, and messaging stating: 'This is the church for the deaf.'"[51]

The plight of the Deaf community at St. Elizabeth quickly generated a great deal of coverage by local and national media, galvanized in no small part by Chany himself. In coming months, the *Wall Street Journal*, the *New York Times*, and Reuters ran stories. PBS's *Religion and Ethics Newsweekly* and many local TV stations aired segments as well. For the first time in its history the *New York Times* created a video on a religious topic. It included footage of St. Elizabeth's celebrated Deaf choir which posted simultaneously on social media with a prominently placed feature article in the Sunday *Times*. In the months that followed, foreign newspapers from Brazil, France, and Germany ran articles. In March 2015, a crew from TV 2000—a television station sponsored by the Italian bishops' conference—came to St. Elizabeth's to film segments for a documentary that would air internationally when Pope Francis visited the United States in the fall of 2015.[52] The extensive coverage created what Chany called "a media disaster" for the Archdiocese: "You will never win with public opinion if you do anything against people that are differently-abled. You're never going to win in the media," said Chany. Although the Archdiocese made a point of meeting with members of the Deaf and hearing communities of St. Elizabeth's, Cardinal Dolan never rescinded his decision.

Chany and other St. Elizabeth leaders had been in contact with Kate since the previous July 2014. When the cardinal's letter was read in November, they were already well schooled in the basics of pursuing a canonical recourse. Within ten working days of the November 2 announcement, Chany sent a letter to the cardinal asking him to change his mind. In December the cardinal denied this request. The date on the cardinal's letter of reply was much earlier than the letter's postmark, a fact that did not inspire confidence. Thankfully Kate had instructed everyone to keep postmarked envelopes as proof of when they actually received the cardinal's reply, which was important given the short timeframe in which to file recourse after its receipt. At the end of December, Chany sent a preliminary letter to the Congregation for the Clergy, notifying them of the intent to bring recourse. He further informed the Vatican office that the Archdiocese would not provide a copy of their decree. "We were very careful with the [canonical] timeline," Chany recalls. "Other churches weren't. . . . In some situations, the person who filed left town, so they missed deadlines."[53] Unfortunately, the Congregation for the Clergy quickly denied appeals that missed deadlines on procedural grounds.

Meanwhile Chany and many others visited archdiocesan offices to view their decrees even though no photographs, copies, or notes were permitted. In early February—after the Vatican ordered the Archdiocese to release the decrees—parishes such as St. Elizabeth were able to prepare their recourses for submission to the Congregation for the Clergy. Chany recalls the officials at Clergy "were very accommodating [about the timeline] because they realized that this was a mess up, that we didn't have those decrees." While they waited, he remembers "Sister Kate was wisely telling us to start getting all our documents and exhibits together . . . John Cornell and I put that together. It was about 800 pages long." Meanwhile, on March 19, the *Wall Street Journal* reported that the St. Elizabeth of Hungary recourse would be reviewed further. "It's not game over," Chany told the paper.[54]

In Holy Week 2015, March 29–April 5, Chany filed the St. Elizabeth recourse. Now there was nothing to do but wait. While they waited, Chany's mother, who had been a faithful St. Elizabeth parishioner, passed away. When he cleaned her attic, Chany, who had been trying to track down evidence of the parish's boundaries, discovered an old bulletin from St. Elizabeth that had the boundaries listed. This serendipitous find gave Chany badly needed proof that "our church was not in the boundaries of the territorial parish of St. Monica's. We were in the boundaries of the territorial parish of St. Ignatius. And the maps clearly showed this from the bulletin."[55] This evidence was quickly sent to the Congregation for the Clergy because incorrect parish boundaries would affect the legality of the Archdiocese's decree. Chany explains, "How could you have a personal parish [St. Elizabeth] that's in another church's [St. Ignatius's] territory, be merged with a territorial parish [St. Monica], when that personal parish is not located within that same territorial boundary?"[56]As things presently stood, Chany himself would not be eligible to register as a parishioner of the new parish because he lived in the boundaries of St. Ignatius. Cardinal Dolan's decree specified that only those with domiciles within the boundaries of the new parish would qualify for membership. Even worse, the Deaf community living all over the Archdiocese would not be eligible either.

Almost a full year later, in March 2016, the Congregation for the Clergy ruled on recourses for five personal parishes in the Archdiocese. Although it did not overturn the parish mergers, the Vatican told Cardinal Dolan that he must amend each of his five decrees to say that the churches must remain open for regular worship and that Catholics from each personal parish were to automatically be incorporated into the newly formed parish regardless of whether they lived within territorial boundaries or not.[57] Hoping to remain an independent parish, some Catholics from the five parishes wanted to appeal to the highest Vatican court, the Apostolic Signatura. Kate advised against it. In her opinion there could be more to lose than to gain:

> An appeal to the Apostolic Signatura presents **the entire decree** from the Congregation for the Clergy. **If you appeal the decree, you are also appealing the AMENDMENTS.** You would not want to lose these. I question whether you can get more from Rome by appealing to the Apostolic Signatura. The decision from the Congregation for the Clergy is eight pages long and clearly describes the facts, the law, and the rationale for the decision. This is a carefully written document.[58]

Although the Vatican upheld the Archdiocese's merging of the five parishes, Kate found a good deal of positive news in the rulings. In a letter to FutureChurch staff, she wrote, "The suppression of the personal parishes and abandonment of the church buildings has been halted by the five decrees already received two weeks ago. The new mind of the Congregation for the Clergy will make clustering or linking parishes a better choice."[59]

The St. Elizabeth recourse was not included in the March 2016 rulings from Rome. Kate speculated that the Congregation for the Clergy probably let Cardinal Dolan know that the issue of incorrect boundaries required new decrees. In April 2016, Cardinal Dolan issued three new decrees involving St. Elizabeth's, St. Monica's, and St. Stephen's of Hungary. They first revoked the original merger decree of November 2, 2014. The second decree, said Chany, "was a gerrymandering of the boundaries of St Monica's and St, Ignatius to make St. Elizabeth's campus now fit into the boundaries of St. Monica's."[60] The third decree merged the original three parishes again, this time with language automatically incorporating members of personal parishes into the newly formed parish no matter where they lived.[61] These new April decrees issued by Cardinal Dolan required Chany and St. Elizabeth recurrents to again submit formal recourse against this new merger decree. "So we asked the Congregation for the Clergy to please take all the evidence submitted for the earlier recourse and apply it toward this decree. And then there were some other issues. . . . So we got more time," said Chany. The resourceful Chany and St. Elizabeth collaborators used the time well: "And so then we sent over another 500 pages of new documents," Chany stated.[62]

In December 2016, Chany received a letter and decree from the Congregation for the Clergy upholding the Cardinal's merger of their parish. In January 2017 with Kate's help, Chany filed an appeal to the Apostolic Signatura and began selecting the Rome-based canon lawyers necessary to argue cases at the Signatura. St. Elizabeth parishioners had already formed a 501(c)(3) nonprofit organization to help pay the costs. The following July, in a highly irregular turn of events, Cardinal Dolan issued a decree relegating St. Elizabeth of Hungary Church to profane use. "It made no sense," said Chany. "It was weird because the Apostolic Signatura had not yet made a decision on the original [merger] recourse of St. Elizabeth of Hungary." With Kate's assistance, Chany brought recourse about the relegation decree asking the Congregation for the Clergy (in part), "How can this occur when the other recourse is not yet decided?" In the late summer Chany reports, "The Congregation wrote back and said, 'Given the fact that the Apostolic Signatura has not yet decided [on the merger case], we are not going to address this [church relegation] case until the Signatura makes the decision, because the official status of the parish of St. Elizabeth has not yet been determined.'"[63]

At this writing, some seven years later, the Signatura has still not ruled on the merger case regarding the parish of St. Elizabeth of Hungary. Cardinal Dolan's preemptive decree attempting to relegate the church to profane use is in limbo. The cardinal's puzzling rush to relegate, and other facts that were public knowledge at the time, led Chany to conclude that the cardinal was engaged in a bit of ecclesial sleight-of-hand. Money was at the bottom of it. The usual canonical argument for closing and relegating a church is a financial one. For example, a newly merged parish could argue that it does not have the financial resources to maintain extra church buildings (such as St. Elizabeth) and therefore a canonical case could be made for selling the St. Elizabeth property. But this was not the case here. Before Cardinal Dolan issued his relegation decree, Chany discovered that the Archdiocese had been deep into negotiations for the sale of St. Monica's air rights. These developmental rights are common in New York City with its many high-rise apartments and skyscrapers. City building codes forbid construction companies to build above a certain height unless the company is able to purchase the air rights of adjacent properties. In St. Monica's case, the Archdiocese had negotiated a price of $36 million for sale of their air rights. Chany explains:

So [St. Monica's] didn't have to sell any parish property per se. They just sold the air above the church of St. Monica's and some of the air over some of their other property on their original campus. And that's so [a developer] could construct a higher building on the neighboring property, given higher floors command higher prices than the lower floors. Now, the Archdiocese got a chunk of that money. All the debts St Monica's and St Stephen's owed to the Archdiocese were paid off. (St Elizabeth's had no debt at the time the original merger became effective.) After that, the Archdiocese took 50% of the remainder—so at the end of the day the Archdiocese got close to $20 million dollars.[64]

Chany's sleuthing suggests that the cardinal wrote the relegation decree early because:

> He couldn't relegate the church later on while waiting for a decision [on the merger] because [the newly merged parish] would have all this money. And the Vatican would say, "How do you say the new parish doesn't have money [to maintain the church of St. Elizabeth's] when the parish has all these millions of dollars in the bank?" So it's hard to see how the [St. Elizabeth] relegation decree would've ever held any water if the [St. Monica] air rights were already sold, or it was known that they were sold.[65]

As St. Elizabeth of Hungary Catholics await a decision on their merger appeal from the Apostolic Signatura, Chany is somewhat optimistic:

> We're still hopeful we will prevail. We've been told by sister Kate and others that we have a very strong case for the merger recourse. We've been advised by our attorneys in the Vatican not to disclose some issues regarding the merger. However, there are some grave, systemic irregularities that are not just procedural flaws in the Congregation's December 2016 decision.[66]

Whenever St. Elizabeth parishioners—both Deaf and hearing—are tempted to lose hope, Chany reminds them, "Remember what sister Kate said, 'The longer it takes, the stronger your case.'. . . Don't you realize that if we had no chance in court, they would have sold off our church a long time ago?"[67]

THE REID GROUP

As previously noted, the Archdiocese of New York hired a company known as The Reid Group to assist with its massive downsizing plans. As Chany experienced it, "the Reid Group was this third-party group that came in and sort of acted as an intermediary, even a buffer, between the Archdiocese of New York and the laity, the core team members, and the pastors."[68] In the months leading up to the inevitable parish closings, Chany and other savvy New York Catholics did their homework about what was happening elsewhere.

> We looked at these other dioceses that were ahead of us in the process with their reorganization. And we noticed that there was boiler plate language for the recommendations that came back to us from our advisory group that were very similar, in fact, almost identical to the recommendations that bishops in other diocese sent out to their cluster groups. So this very much gave us the impression that the Reid group supplied a turn-key approach for closing churches that would likely hold up at the Vatican.[69]

Kate was very familiar with The Reid Group, having encountered them in other dioceses. As of the fall of 2013, more than a dozen US dioceses had contracted with the company to help them with parish closures and mergers. A book by the organization's founders, *The Art of Change: Faith, Vision, and Prophetic Planning*, offers a glimpse into the company's philosophy and processes that mimic US corporate business practices. "Corporations have merged at a fast rate during the last two decades, changing their identities and their mission."[70] It lists a boilerplate trifecta of frequently repeated issues which the Vatican ruled in 2013 as insufficient reasons to close churches: "Due to changing demographics, the diminishing number of priests, and limited financial resources many dioceses have entered into comprehensive parish planning processes."[71]

On November 2, 2013, in a presentation at the National Call To Action Conference, Kate shared research her colleagues had gathered about The Reid Group and other strategic planning companies working with US Catholic groups, including dioceses, parishes, and schools.

She warned of a bottom-line, corporate mentality that pervaded some of the diocesan parish reconfigurations facilitated by The Reid Group.

"It is fundamentally a business organization restructuring for the sake of the institute of the diocese, rather than for the faith life of the people of God of the parish," she told a crowd of about 100 activist Catholics. "Typically only 3-4 models for reconfiguring [parishes] are provided to the Diocese as options (ex. linked, partnered, merged) although according to the *Emerging Models of Pastoral Leadership Project* there were 7 main models used with an infinite number of variations possible.[72]

Figure 11.1   Sr. Kate Kuenstler and Sr. Christine Schenk at November 2, 2013, presentation about Kate's pioneering leadership at the National Call To Action conference. Photo courtesy of FutureChurch

Figure 11.2   Sr. Kate Kuenstler with Sister Louise Akers (center) and newly appointed FutureChurch executive director Deb Rose Milavec (on right) at the 2013 National Call To Action conference. Photo courtesy of FutureChurch

Drawing on her extensive experience with clients from dozens of US dioceses, Kate offered these trenchant observations about diocesan planning processes as of fall 2013:

- Misuse—The planning process is used to relieve financial debts or liabilities instead of the pure intent of planning for purpose of promoting faith and better serving the Catholic faith community.
- No Transparency. If diocesan planning is initiated due to financial debts or liabilities, then that reason is not disclosed to the parishioners. Instead there are mission, goals, and objectives of a planning process that do not match the directives implemented when viewed at the parish level.
- The process relies on strong pastors, parish life coordinators, and deanery leaders to communicate and carry out implementations, although most are ineffective.[73]

She then listed the results of these flawed processes:

- Parish suppressions and mergers, when not implemented appropriately, or without just cause, decimate parish communities, disenfranchise parishioners, and alienate their patrimony (property).
- In rural communities the closure of a church directly changes the local community and culture, tearing out the heart of the entire community.
- Parishioners bond together for justice through appeals to the Congregation for the Clergy.[74]

Noting that "the above issues are repeated in diocese after diocese at an aggressive rate," Kate offered a pointed critique:

- The Reid Group book focuses a great deal on conflict management, wilderness zones, and reacting to grief, loss, and sorrow. The Reid Group enables Archbishops with the process and tools to use diocese planning for financial purposes.
- There are no corrections to the process, no different approaches tried, and no relief for the spiritual and emotional pain that is experienced by parishioners who have lost their Catholic home.
- Due to the desire for fast results, there is little consideration given to creative solutions with serious considerations of parishioners' input. According to the *Emerging Models of Pastoral Leadership Project* there were seven main models used with an infinite number of variations.[75]

Just one month later, on November 27, 2013, the Archdiocese of New York sent a letter announcing cluster training sessions for each of the six pastoral areas that would address which parishes would merge or close. The letter lists twelve names of Reid Group consultants—two for each pastoral area.[76] It is revealing that after Pope Francis published *The Joy of the Gospel*, Kate quoted it at the bottom of every email she wrote:

(The Parish reconfiguration process used by Dioceses) . . . can also lead to a business mentality, caught up with management, statistics, plans, and evaluations whose principal beneficiary is not God's people but the church as an institution. The mark of Christ, incarnate, crucified and risen, is not present . . .

The Joy of the Gospel, November 24, 2013.[77]

"I HAVE INFLUENCED THE DEVELOPMENT OF JURISPRUDENCE"

Of the original forty-two archdiocesan churches Cardinal Dolan had planned to close, Kate's canonical expertise helped courageous New Yorkers preserve at least eleven of them for regular worship. Here is a chronological listing from FutureChurch records. 2015: St. Thomas More, Manhattan; Our Lady of Mercy, Port Chester. 2016: Our Lady of Mt. Carmel Church, Mt. Vernon; St. Joseph Church, Poughkeepsie; St. Andrew, Lower Manhattan; plus two unnamed others. 2017: St. Roch's Church, Staten Island; and St. Adalbert, Staten Island; Church of Our Lady of Peace remains available for occasional worship after the Archdiocese sold it to a Coptic orthodox community who agreed to allow Catholic worshippers. Kate did extensive work with this community in the early stages of their recourse. FutureChurch sources in Rome report that the Our Lady of Peace merger recourse was not upheld by the Apostolic Signatura. This led to the formation of the Community of Our Lady of Peace. 2020: Most Holy Trinity, Mamaroneck; St. Veronica, South Manhattan, also won the right to stay open, but this recourse was not handled by Kate. If Rome upholds the St. Elizabeth of Hungary recourse, Kate will have helped to preserve at least twelve churches, 29 percent of those the cardinal had wanted to close. In 2017 FutureChurch received a heartwarming email from a Staten Island parishioner who was grateful for the help two parishes received in working out a solution:

> St. Roch's Church Staten Island, NY, and St Adalbert's also Staten Island, remain open and were merged both with weekly Masses. . . . Thanks to you, Sister Kate, our administrator Fr. Jim, divine miraculous intervention, and great team of parishioners who did everything you advised. It was time consuming, draining, and uncertain but worth it. Thanks again for your professional instruction and guidance. You were the only one who cared. Cardinal Dolan offered nothing, we never heard from him one time. God bless you and Sister Kate for what you do. Keep up the great work.[78]

In April 2016 after Rome required the Archdiocese to amend five decrees so that the parish churches would remain open, Kate sent a rare reflection on the significance of her canonical work:

> I believe this is a seminal time in the US church. I am hopeful we can stop the floodgates that are decimating the faith life of the laity. I think I was able to provide recourse arguments that the Congregation for the Clergy could use to counter the cardinal's plans to make a lot of money by walking over the hearts and souls of the laity. I argued the cases in a new way . . . I have influenced the development of jurisprudence for the first time. Finally my thinking and rationale have been heard. And to my delight, [they] have been used to develop law that has never existed before in the church. Someday, this new jurisprudence may very well become part of the next revision of canon law. I am just amazed . . . I know I am going on and on. But, for the first time since 2005 I have had validation from Rome. It feels good.[79]

Chapter 12

Perseverance, Pain, and the Will of God

Kate's unprecedented success on behalf of the parish rights of her beloved laity came at no small cost. Shepherding the many recourses from the Archdiocese of New York was exhausting. In a February 2015 email from Florida, she wrote: "I realized that I was very near collapse when I got here . . . I am spending long hours in prayer. I am very fragile right now. But [my Florida friend] has given me the most safe and peaceful place to be . . . I worked too hard last year and went right into the NYC parish issues. . . ."[1]

Unlike some diocesan canon lawyers who have relatively limited experience in parishes, Kate had spent years ministering in parishes, training catechists, and organizing diocesan religious education programs. Her earlier studies in theology had left her with a deep love of Vatican II ecclesiology and the giftedness of the People of God. She knew firsthand what was at stake when a parish community was threatened with closure, and it grieved her deeply. After ten years assisting scores of parishes pursuing canonical appeals, she had acquired a deep insight into the destructive reconfiguration practices of too many dioceses, both in the United States and abroad.

In December 2015, she shared what she had learned in a lengthy interview for the 2017 documentary *Foreclosing on Faith*.[2] As Kate saw it, a fundamental problem with the bishops' approach was that two definitions of parish were in play. One definition involved "the theology of parish, the people of God, the faith community who celebrate the sacraments together, who together perform the spiritual and corporal works of mercy. They are the visible face of God, of Jesus Christ," she said.[3] This understanding is very different from most bishops making parish reconfiguration decisions: "When the bishops talk about a parish in these mergers, they are not talking about the faith community. . . . They're looking at the corporation of the diocese and they're looking at all the little franchises within that corporation and each

185

parish is a franchise." In diocesan reconfigurations, "Now, we're looking at the needs of this mega-corporation of the diocese [rather than the parish] and seeing how we can rearrange these franchises. . . ."[4]

The people in parishes whom Kate accompanied had a very different understanding of their parish: "It's a faith life. The parish as the people of God doesn't merge the same way as a corporation document does. That's where the bishops keep running into a brick wall. The people are not documents and the people are lost. . . . They hurt because it's their faith life that is rearranged, not just the document."[5]

Diocesan reconfiguration plans invariably failed to distinguish between the parish as a family of faith and the parish as a corporate juridical entity in canon—as well as civil—law. This had disastrous consequences. "It is so demoralizing to the laity," Kate lamented.

> They do their homework, they go through all these procedures, they write up all these reports telling everything that's going on in their parish, how successful it is, how they like it, and how it's good for the church. But no matter what they write it is never going to keep the corporation from being shut down. The bishop is using a whole other set of criteria for the corporation and just not telling the people.[6]

In Kate's experience, the companies a diocese hires to implement its reconfiguration plan also fail to make this distinction. Instead they exacerbate the pain by using spiritualized language about "the Paschal Mystery," for example, to justify the wholesale destruction of vibrant faith communities.[7]

Kate spent much time consoling hundreds of people when their canonical recourses were denied.

> When we get the negative decisions from the Vatican—which are more likely than not to take place—I am then on the phone with these people I have worked with for, sometimes, a year. I sometimes spend two to three hours with them on the phone, crying together with what happened, mourning the fact that it's over, going through this pain. I don't let them hang up until we come to some form of peace. . . . They can't accept it, and they shouldn't, but just a peacefulness, a calmness, comes. . . . The [original] agony is not there.[8]

Unsurprisingly, this compassionate canon lawyer at times experienced bone-weary exhaustion. While she understood a bishop's "need to balance the budget," she fiercely rejected doing so "on the backs of people's faith." Instead she believed Catholics would respond generously if a bishop would just admit up front his unprecedented need for financial help: "I know in my heart that the people would respond appropriately. There would be money coming out of the coffers that the bishop wouldn't know what to do with, and he would still have dynamic parishes that exist today." She bemoaned the fact that bishops rarely met with the people themselves. "For the most part, I do not believe the bishops have ever really gone and visited these parishes," she said. "They do not know who these people are. . . . Unfortunately, it makes it easier for a corporate model decision to be made when you do not see the faces of the people who are in great pain."[9]

Having spent hours consoling despondent Catholics led Kate to realize, "This is what the bishop should be doing. I am taking the place of this bishop—not that I claim that—I just wonder why these men are bishops if they cannot walk with the pain that they themselves have created for the people." Eventually, she found great meaning in sharing the wounds of the people she served: "I find that, as important as it is to do what I do as a canon lawyer, as a Christian, as a woman of faith, this walking with the people and their pain is the most important thing I do."[10] Kate also accompanied mourning parishioners whose parishes did need to close:

> I have received phone calls from parishioners of parishes where there are 80 people. . . . I spend maybe 2, 3 hours on the phone with them mourning . . . I ask, "How can I argue to keep your parish open under these circumstances?" They admit, "No, Sister Kate you can't do that." But I spent time with them through the pain of the loss of their parish. It is not viable.[11]

MOST PARISHES ARE VIABLE

After working with scores of faith communities, Kate discovered that very few of her clients were from non-viable parishes. "My experience of [working in] 30 dioceses of the United States and a few other countries is that, for the most part, the parishes are fine. They're doing just fine. . . ." She staunchly defended the centrality of the faith community: "I find it very difficult to support a bishop who uses temporal realities . . . to argue against the faith community. How small is small? Why is a mega parish more important?" She could not understand why a bishop would shut down a smaller, somewhat average parish that nevertheless had "a beautiful faith life together," and was functioning well, paying its bills, and doing the corporate and spiritual works of mercy. She also helped many dynamic parish communities:

> Then there are those parishes that are the most vibrant, vital parishes. They have money in the bank (if you're going to just talk about money). They are in the people's wills. . . . They are serving the poor in their neighborhoods. They are sponsoring a parish in Haiti. They're doing all these things and yet they are the ones being shut down.[12]

IMPLICATIONS FOR CANON LAW

Kate's experience working with so many vibrant—and threatened—parishes led her to consider more deeply how canon law should be brought to bear in their defense.

> There's a canon [515.2] that says a bishop has the authority and the power to alter parishes, to erect a parish, suppress a parish, merge a parish. . . . He does not need permission from anyone. . . . Canon law [c. 1752] goes on to say that the bishop can do that as long as the salvation of souls is not damaged in a negative way.[13]

Canon 1752 is the very last canon listed in the 1983 Code. It deals with the removal of an unfit pastor, and references "the salvation of souls, which must always be the Supreme law of the church." Canonical experts note that the text and its context (as the very last word—literally—in canon law) "suggest that this reminder is meant to apply to all areas of canonical jurisprudence."[14] Other canons addressing the responsibilities of bishops also point to the primacy of spiritual care for the People of God.[15]

Kate viewed Canon 1752 as central to her advocacy: "The very last sentence says fundamentally that the power and authority of the bishop cannot go against the salvation of souls of the people in the faith community. And that sentence is the sentence that has been ignored and abused by bishops in merging parishes and selling church buildings."[16] Shepherding a grieving people who felt abandoned by their bishops gave Kate a new awareness of certain ambiguities—and omissions—in canon law:

> [I]t is only recently that I've been asking a new question. How can a corporation have a soul? . . . The bishops argue to the Vatican that as long as we provide for Mass, the sacraments, and we have a functional organization—that we just move into this new merged parish—everything's fine. I question if that is the case because we see so much fallout. We see so much pain, anger, confusion, and chaos. [People] are abandoning their faith, abandoning the Catholic religion, abandoning life as a Christian. [All] as a result of these very easy paper adjustments called corporation mergers.[17]

Witnessing these devastating outcomes led Kate to conclude: "I say when the bishops do this, they in fact damage the salvation of souls. You cannot use the excuse that 'We still provide Mass. We still provide a priest. We still provide a church building.' That's not what we're talking about. We're talking about the salvation of souls."[18]

A DARK NIGHT OF THE SOUL

During the summer preceding her death, I visited Kate three times at the Poor Handmaids center in Donaldson, Indiana. Although physically weak, her mind remained clear. She was determined to continue our interviews for this book which we had originally planned to write together. In mid-October 2019—at what would be our last visit—I asked how she had managed to persevere despite the Vatican's frequent rejection of her appeals. Wasn't it dispiriting to see bishops deliberately deceiving and obstructing the rights of parishioners? Even though I had worked with her for over ten years, I had no notion of the closely guarded personal struggle Kate endured in fidelity to her mission. "Yeah well, I actually spent seven years in a dark night of the soul," she reluctantly confessed. Yet she continued her canonical work, even though she had "no affective attitude or energy for it" at all. She became "more and more seriously depressed." At times "I would curl up in a ball and cry," she remembered. At other times she found solace from a "little circle of women" who supported her, including myself, Deb Rose from FutureChurch, and Lena Woltering from the Fellowship of Southern Illinois Laity.

Kate finally chose to embrace her situation: "I didn't fight the depression. I know it sounds strange, but I did not fight it. I kind of held it in my arms and walked around with it. . . . I was like Quasimodo with this extra appendage on my back that I was lugging around with me." Kate did not seek spiritual direction or counseling at this time. "I just don't do well talking to other people about my spiritual life," she said. Instead, she persevered alone:

No one knew. I continued to work in my own religious community, but I was not active in my parish. . . . I didn't have the energy. I didn't want to look at a parish. I actually walked away from the Church for a while. But all the time I'm writing this [recourse], doing studies on what I could, should do. . . . I was too stubborn to give up.[19]

While Kate's self-described "stubbornness" helped, three other foundational elements guided her through this painful time. The first was a wise practicality that tempered her expansive compassion:

I would keep in mind the look on the faces of the people I've been with. I can hear in their voices all the pain that they were experiencing and all the other feelings they were going through. And I finally said to myself, "Look Kate, this is not your parish. These people are having a far more difficult time doing this than you are. So grow up. . . . I can sit here and cry in my room but that doesn't get anybody anywhere."[20]

Kate's love for her foundress, Mother Katharina Kasper, was the second, and probably most central, element that guided her. She realized she needed to set aside her ego. "What was important were the people from the parishes who were doing this for the right reasons . . . I realized I had to start following what my foundress said about not following my ego and always asking is this in the will of God? . . . That's where I redirected a lot of my energy. Am I doing the will of God?" She began noticing people—"priests, sisters, lay people"—who were acting more from their egos than from a higher purpose. This deep-seated insight rearranged Kate's inner landscape and led to a new set of priorities. "It wasn't easy, but it was the only thing I knew how to do. . . . But in the end, I had to stay very faithful to the mission. I had to stay faithful to the will of God and to what the needs of the people were, not my needs. That was a real learning experience for me."[21]

The third source of guidance for Kate was her love for canon law. Kate especially appreciated Book II in the 1983 Code—"The People of God"—which describes what it means to be a disciple of Christ. "I went back to Canon Law, Book II which is a wonderful chapter to set the parameters for a person desiring to be a disciple. It describes how that person can get there. The first several canons are real mind benders." A brief review of these canons illuminates how they may have reminded Kate not only of her own dignity and mission, but also that of the Catholics she served.[22] Canon 204.1 reads:

> The Christian faithful are those who, inasmuch as they have been incorporated in Christ through baptism, have been constituted as the people of God. For this

Figure 12.1   Despite her "dark night of the soul," Sr. Kate Kuenstler renews her vows on the Feast of the Annunciation at the Church of Annunciation during a 2016 pilgrimage to Israel. Courtesy of Poor Handmaids of Jesus Christ

reason, made sharers in their own way in Christ's priestly, prophetic, and royal function, they are called to exercise the mission which God has entrusted to the Church to fulfill in the world, in accord with the condition proper to each.

Canon 205 reminds us that being joined with Christ is the first reality for those in full communion in the Church: "Those baptized are fully in the communion of the Catholic Church on this earth who are joined with Christ in its visible structure by the bonds of the profession of faith, the sacraments, and ecclesiastical governance." Canon 207 reminded Kate that as a lay person and a vowed religious, she too belonged to the "life and holiness" of the church and contributes to its "salvific mission" even though she was not part of the "hierarchical structure."[23] Canon 208 is perhaps the ultimate ratification of the full equality—including ministerial equality—of all the baptized in the Church. "From their rebirth in Christ, there exists among all the Christian faithful a true equality regarding dignity and action by which they all cooperate in the building up of the Body of Christ according to each one's own condition and function." It is touching to reflect that that canon law itself provided comfort and guidance to a struggling woman who had dedicated her life to its service.

The Vatican II–inspired *Code of Canon Law* greatly fueled Kate's mission to ordinary Catholics: "I realized that the laity have a voice and that it had been stifled. It had been scared off by the hierarchy. And so my goal was to empower the laity to know they had a right to a voice, that they had a voice, and [I would show them] how to use it."[24] Despite the depths of her "dark night," Kate never considered abandoning the institutional Church to its own demons. She knew the importance of her work in fulfilling the Vatican II vision:

> I decided to fight from within and there is no way I am leaving this Church. And if somebody wants to leave, go for it. But I'm not going with you. I have also been so blessed, especially for the last 12 years, that I'm one of the few people in the world that's been able to influence Roman Canon law. And why would I want to give that up? It's a surprise to me that I have. I had hoped I could. I wanted to. But then to see that I really am affecting church, jurisprudence is such a blessing.[25]

SUPPORT FROM THE PHJC SISTERHOOD

Kate received significant support from several Poor Handmaids sisters with whom she was close. Sisters Pat Peters and Cathy Schwemer were longtime friends and members of Clare House, an intentional community located on the motherhouse grounds in Donaldson, Indiana. Kate and Peters had both mentored Schwemer when she first entered the order. Post–Vatican II changes were unsettling to some sisters, and this often led to confusing experiences for newer members like Schwemer. She describes Kate's support:

> I was the sole person [who entered] and with everybody's eyes focused on you, it was not always easy. But Kate was a safe sounding board. She and Pat were saying, "No, you're not nuts. This is kind of nutty what you're going through, but you're not nuts. . . . What you're feeling, what you're seeing is correct. We don't have it all together yet as a community, we're changing."[26]

When Kate returned to Donaldson for meetings and community events, she always stayed at Clare House. The Poor Handmaids sisters value community and work hard to accommodate the needs of sisters like Kate, whose ministries take them far from home. Schwemer explained: "We searched for ways of still being community-based. [So] with a realization that our ministry took us to places [where sisters were alone], we built contact houses."[27] Kate was a diaspora member of Clare House. This was very important to her, especially after she moved to the East Coast. Clare House sisters devised innovative ways of staying in each other's lives including Zoom faith sharing and connecting on birthdays and anniversaries. "Kate often told me how much those meant to her," said Schwemer. "We called ourselves "ever faithful" because [when we first began] the internet was still a little shaky, but we always connected. It was very intentional. That's the key word here."[28] When she came home for community meetings, Kate loved to talk—at length—about canon law and about her work. Schwemer recalls, "It was not always easy for Kate within the community because of her colorful way of saying things. Sometimes she had people within our own community that just wanted to back away from her. They were kind of scared of her that she dared to question a bishop."[29]

Kate served on the Poor Handmaids' directory committee for many years, only ending her participation six months before her death. The directory provides guidance about how to live the Poor Handmaids charism. "Kate could always help us with things that were in canon law about religious life," recalled Sr. Carol Langhauser. She was a methodical thinker who "could always say things very succinctly and clearly."[30] Sr. Judith Diltz, who was in PHJC leadership, especially appreciated Kate's gift for explaining canon law:

> She didn't just give us interpretations of canon law, but she helped us understand that if it wasn't written in canon law, then, we were free. And if it was written—if there was statement in canon law—[she helped us] capture the spirit of it rather than a legalistic interpretation. I've heard several people say we learned how to read canon law because of Kate.[31]

As provincial superior, Diltz remembers consulting Kate several times, especially when communicating with church officials: "Kate was very good about the language to use in an official approach for whatever reason we were approaching them."[32]

Although Kate loved telling stories about her canonical adventures, she was also discreet about risky high-profile situations with various bishops. She never spoke of these until after any given case had been resolved. "She was concerned that if certain people found out that she was behind some of the things that were going on, there could be repercussions for the community. . . . That's why she kept herself in the background," said Schwemer.[33] Kate's discretion was not always easy to maintain, but she did it. "She was trying to protect the community," said Schwemer. "Once our community leadership understood the depth of what Kate was doing, they fully supported her, but she carried that a long time before she shared it with leadership."[34]

As a provincial leader Diltz had occasion to observe Kate's discretion, especially Kate's professional encounters with episcopal leadership.

> She was a good judge of character, but she was very discreet. She would not talk names, but it was clear that there were certain bishops that she knew were not themselves of very noble character. And she had insight into what was motivating them that was far beyond anything you would pick up through canon law. . . . She would not talk publicly about it. She didn't brag about her own insider information in that way.[35]

While Kate deplored the bad behavior of certain bishops, she also rather enjoyed watching the politics unfold:

> We would have conversations and she would say, "I love the politics of it."
> I would say, "Okay, I hate the politics."
> But she just really enjoyed observing the power plays and [then] find a way to interpret what was going on . . .[36]

Kate's discretion on behalf of her Poor Handmaids community paid off. Community leaders did not experience repercussions from Kate's canonical advocacy. Furthermore, Diltz doubts the PHJC leadership would have pressured Kate to stop had any bishop complained to them.[37] She does recall asking Kate to seek donations for her canonical work. To their everlasting credit, the PHJC community financially supported Kate throughout her years of advocacy. Diltz explains: "It was very much in keeping with our support of the common person to really be behind [Kate] because the laity had so little income. Parishes had very little income, but they were up against the diocese that had the money for the court fights. And so we supported Kate. . . ."[38]

When Kate came home to Clare House, Schwemer and Peters provided a safe space for her to talk about the more painful aspects of her ministry: "She often came home, and she would share [her struggles] and cry. And we cried with her because she deeply loved the Church. And she was in pain for the Church. . . . When she saw what the institutional Church was doing to these people it really crushed her heart."[39] Schwemer and Peters worked hard to provide a sense of normalcy for their friend: "When she would come home to be with us, we tried to give her some sense that this [community life] was the norm for her, not all that crap she had to deal with out on the East Coast."[40]

Kate was human enough to enjoy telling stories about how she had won cases in certain dioceses. "Kate has a wicked sense of humor," chuckled Schwemer: "When she's very passionate, she can be very, um, shall I say colorful? There are parts of her that just loved nailing a bishop to the wall. At the same time she realized he came from the background he had been taught. So she struggled between compassion and [that instinct]."[41]

KATE'S ILL HEALTH AND MOTHER KASPER'S CANONIZATION

Kate visited me in Cleveland October 4–7, 2018, to attend a screening of *Foreclosing on Faith*, a documentary which prominently featured Kate, myself, and other Cleveland leaders. While thrilled about the documentary, Kate was even more excited to be flying to Rome for the October 14 canonization of her Poor Handmaids foundress, Mother Katharine Kasper. Despite her obviously good spirits, I was concerned about her health. She became lightheaded after our celebratory meal and tripped and fell en route to our seats in the dimly lit theatre. Thankfully nothing was broken. She dismissed her symptoms, saying her doctors were adjusting her medications. Still, I was uneasy about her well-being. Much later Kate admitted that she had already begun experiencing symptoms of the colon cancer that would take her life. She decided to attend the canonization even if it meant delaying critical medical care. At the time I was shocked by her choice. Yet I now understand how much she needed to honor Mother Katharine, her lifelong patron and guide.

Kate's friend, Sr. Cathy Schwemer, was also concerned about Kate's Rome trip: "Even though I was one of those saying, 'Kate, you shouldn't be going to Rome, you're not strong enough,' I'm glad in hindsight that she did go. To be at the canonization was kind of like full circle in her devotion to Katharine [Kasper]."

I think the trip to Rome was really a catalyst. It just brought everything together for her. In many ways it was a completion. . . . And that trip was the pinnacle of her life. Afterwards she never talked about loneliness. During that year of being ill, I saw her do things I never thought I'd see her do. She lived so graciously with the sisters in the retirement community and at the nursing home. I saw her compassion and love for them. Her patience grew. So I saw a growth in her, a softness in her.[42]

Kate's other friend, Sr. Pat Peters, recognized another possible reason for Kate's devotion: "Kate drew strength from the fact that Mother Mary Katharine also stood her ground with the bishop," she said. "There are several [historical] places where [Mother Kasper] says [to the bishop,] 'No, this is what's going to happen.'"[43]

While she was in Rome—and even before she embarked—Kate's community and other friends began to see that "something was drastically wrong." They chose to support her physically and "saw to her needs so she could participate," recalled Schwemer.[44] One such person was Kate's lifelong friend, Linda Rozycki, whom she had met when she was director of religious education at St. Cecilia's Parish in Glen Carbon, Illinois. Rozycki had always loved Kate's stories about Mother Kasper. She joined a special "canonization tour" arranged by the Poor Handmaids community for themselves, as well as their families and friends.

When she first saw Kate in Rome, Rozycki noticed that her color was not good, and she was walking with a cane. "There's something wrong with Kate. She's sick," Rozycki told her husband. The two friends met for occasional meals. "We just talked as fast as we could about things and catching up. But I just knew that she wasn't doing well."[45] Rozycki stayed in telephone touch with Kate during her final illness but never again saw her before she died.

Sr. Carole Langhauser spent a good deal of time with Kate on the canonization tour because neither could walk very far. While others toured various sites, Kate and Langhauser spent time reminiscing. When the Canon Law Society met in Orlando, Kate had engineered an expedition to Disney World and, in light of special "two for one" pricing, she invited Langhauser to join her. "We had a great time together and I still have a wonderful red t-shirt 20 years later that we both bought." In Assisi, a concerned Langhauser noticed that Kate "just didn't have it [energy]. In fact she almost passed out. That was really the first time we realized that maybe something was going on."[46]

Before the canonization Kate stayed for a week with her Italian friend, Divina Melotti, whose family had pretty much adopted her when she studied in Rome. Melotti sensed that Kate wasn't well. She remembers Kate went out only twice that week. Once was to record an interview about her work, and a second time to meet with Federika Boldini, a lawyer and legal historian who worked at the Apostolic Signatura.[47] As luck would have it—this being Rome—there was a transportation strike the day of Kate's scheduled recorded interview. Melotti arranged for a taxi and reassured a nervous Kate, "Stay calm because you have enough time." Kate did not tell Melotti how serious her illness was until well after her return to the United States. Today Melotti takes comfort remembering that her dear friend found a refuge at her home. "Here she was good . . . here she rested a lot."[48]

"DANGEROUS NUN" MAKES "HUGE SYMBOLIC IMPACT"

Melotti remembers Kate being very proud of her friendship with Boldini, who was an assistant to Andrea Errera, the procurator shepherding Kate's recourses at the Apostolic Signatura.[49] Boldini was passionate about the administrative recourse possibilities in canon law. She also helped Errera with a number of parish appeals from the United States. While reviewing recourse documents from Catholics who lived in a poor US mining town, Boldini had discovered an unusual document from the local bishop. The prelate warned about an unnamed "dangerous nun" and canon lawyer from outside the diocese who was "causing problems."[50] Boldini was impressed: "Wow. A dangerous canon lawyer. I never met a female doing canon law before." She was so surprised and excited that she told a friend. "Oh, there is a nun lawyer—incredible!"[51] Two days after Boldini read the local bishop's letter, Errera asked her to translate an email he had received from the United States. It was from the "dangerous nun" herself, Sr. Kate Kuenstler. Boldini quickly corresponded with Kate about some of the US cases she was working on: "I am a young lawyer working on this [US] case. . . . So thank you for all that you do," she wrote. "And I explained my doubts and she very gracefully answered them." Kate promised to meet with Boldini for lunch during her visit to Rome for Mother Kasper's canonization. Boldini soon learned that Kate was working with many other clients and that "many of the people we were representing [at the Signatura] had been represented by Sister Kate before at the Congregation for the Clergy and with the local bishop."[52] Boldini concluded that she "had plenty of things to talk about" when Sister Kate arrived.

When the two met, Boldini remembers, "We spoke a lot about all the cases. We took pictures together and sent them to our clients. It was a very nice moment." Although Kate was "not in good shape" physically, the young

lawyer remembers she "was so very happy being there for the canonization. . . . She was very merry."[53] As the duo shared stories about how they
became interested in canon law, Boldini remembers, "Kate stood out as a role
model for me—especially being a woman which is not so usual. Finding a
religious woman working as a lawyer and representing lay people was great
for us."

Kate's broad canonical experience negotiating for her clients was helpful
to her young protégé: "She told me, 'I lost more cases than I won, but I saved
some churches. And sometimes, [I saved them] even at the last moment. . . .'
She said at times she felt like she was running into the party to stop a sale
at the very last moment." When asked if Kate had made a difference in the
institutional Church or in Church law, Boldini replied:

> [I]t is possible that she was part of a movement to let [Rome] know that we
> were speaking about a huge tragedy for Catholics in the U.S. . . . a big, big
> tragedy. And they [Rome] can't go on simply accepting what [local bishops]
> are doing. . . . It is more complicated. At least now the Signatura considers each
> case. And it [the Signatura] doesn't just say, "Okay, they are in economic dif-
> ficulty. So we have to sell this church." Sister Kate was part of the movement
> that let them understand that big tragedy.[54]

Whether or not Kate significantly changed the institutional Church is
perhaps for history to decide, although, as may now be readily apparent, I
believe she did. At least as important is the effect Kate had on Catholics like
Boldini: "She has had a huge, symbolic impact for people like me—knowing
that there was someone like Sister Kate. A nun, a female, a religious woman,
but lay, not a cleric, not part of the clergy, fighting for other laity. That was
so powerful—really, really powerful. So in this way, I'm sure she had an
impact."[55]

THE JOURNEY HOME

A week after Kate returned to her home in Providence, Rhode Island, Langhauser emailed to see how she was doing. Kate told her she had not been
out of bed for a week. She was evaluated by specialists who told her they
suspected a serious cancer. Kate's provincial, Judith Diltz, made "probably
one of the hardest phone calls I've ever had to make as a provincial." She
called on a Sunday afternoon in December to say, "Kate, I'm going to ask you
something really difficult. We want you to come home, we want you to come
back to Indiana."[56] Diltz understood how much Kate loved and respected her
Rhode Island physicians. Yet, aside from her landlady with whom she was

fast friends, Kate had few other supports in Providence. "It was obvious that she was going to need a lot of follow up care," remembers Diltz. Kate was gracious and told her provincial: "Yes, I will come." The PHJC community quickly lined up specialists in Indiana whom Kate came to trust as well.

When she moved to Donaldson, Kate asked to live at Catherine's Cottage, a community of senior sisters located on the motherhouse grounds. Her good friend, Sr. Michelle Dermody, also lived there. Dermody narrates this segment of Kate's journey:

> She held on to her independence until she couldn't. And that was such a maturity of hers—teaching all of us how to die. . . . And her spirituality became her top priority. Her health became her second, and her job—and she did it well—it would become the third. And we laughed. We hugged. We cried. She just was such a good woman. And even now [after her death] I've heard sisters say, "Well, let's talk to Kate about it." I believe she's way up there, wherever there is.[57]

In January 2019 Kate's new oncologist at St. Joseph Hospital in Mishawaka wanted her to begin a regimen of chemotherapy. Mishawaka is about forty-five minutes northeast of Donaldson. Kate's first chemo treatment was scheduled over two days. As there was a snowstorm in progress, Kate stayed with her friend Sr. Carole Langhauser, a retired oncology nurse who worked in mission advancement at the hospital and lived across the street. Langhauser—who had herself served in PHJC leadership—became Kate's hospital liaison. She remembers Kate's many friends, and more than a few clients, seeking her out:

> Many people from all over the country and all over the world were calling. She didn't have the energy to talk to them on the telephone. . . . I wanted to take her phone away and just say to the person, "Look, she just can't do this," but Kate wouldn't do that. . . . She struggled with both wanting and not wanting her friends to know what was happening in her life. She couldn't tell them how sick she really was.[58]

On Holy Saturday (April 20) Kate was admitted to St. Joseph Hospital for surgery. She stayed nineteen days in several different care units. Langhauser visited each day. Every time she moved to a new unit Kate would tell the nurse: "This is Sister Carole. She is not my friend. She is my advocate." Carole thought this was "a bit weird," so after Kate introduced her this way a third time, she objected: "I thought we were friends." Kate replied: "We are friends, Carole. But if you're my friend, they'll kick you out. If you're my advocate, they won't touch you. You can stay. And so you're my advocate."[59] Kate—the canonical advocate—understood the need to have someone in her corner to negotiate the inevitable hospital bureaucracy. From then on,

Langhauser became Kate's communicator in chief, especially since she was at times "so sick that she could hardly talk."

Kate was very private. "She had a very clear delineation of who she wanted to talk to, who she wanted to know about anything. And Sister Judith [Diltz] was top of her list," said Langhauser. Diltz and the provincial team were in Germany for meetings at the time. Langhauser kept the provincial informed of how things were going via Skype or text.

Things were not going well. After Kate's operation, the surgeon—a religious man himself—told Langhauser that Kate's tumor was large, and it was not curable. The next day he visited Kate and gently explained everything at length. He suggested hospice: "Sister, I really think you need to go home to your sisters who love you. Let them take care of you. Be with them and share the last part of your life with them. And then you'll be an angel watching over them."[60] Later, at Kate's request, her oncologist began a regimen of lower-dose oral chemotherapy.

Although Kate told Langhauser that she did not fear death, it was clear that she was also determined to focus on living, which led this experienced oncology nurse to observe, "She could know that [she had a terminal illness], process it, and say, 'Okay, but I'm not ready yet.' And so she put it in the back of her head and lived her life until she was ready to answer to God."[61]

Kate's provincial, Sr. Judith Diltz, also noticed Kate's fierce will to live: "She always believed that she was going to get better. When I was elected General Superior, I had to move to Germany, and I went over to say goodbye. My hunch was that it was going be a final goodbye. But [Kate] wouldn't go with that. She never gave up the hope that she was going to get over this."[62]

Over the summer Kate and I also spent hours recording interviews for this book. Although I checked several times to make sure she truly wanted to use her waning energy for this project, she was determined to complete it. She hoped the story of her struggle for canonical justice would serve the Church. She especially wanted everyone to learn about the brave parishioner clients who had persevered in defending their parish homes. During our interviews it became clear to me that while Kate was not afraid of dying, she also hoped to live.

As it happened, God gave Kate quite a bit more time, five more months to be exact. Her sister, Agnes, her brother, Matt, and his wife, Deb, came several times to visit. She also visited many far-flung friends by telephone. One friend, Lena Woltering, came in person. Woltering found her bishop-challenging friend as undaunted, colorful, and spirited as ever. "I'll never forget walking into that hospice room. . . . And she shakes her head and says, 'Lena, they're all [expletives].' I just howled because she was always trying to be supportive of bishops—telling me there's a few of them that are good—but now they're all [expletives]. She was just phenomenal."[63]

Kate finally told her Roman friend, Divina Melotti, about her cancer. The two spoke several times via an internet app. "Kate sent me a photo of herself without hair," her friend recalled somewhat wistfully.[64] Kate's good friend Linda Rozycki—a volunteer with hospice in her hometown—also visited by telephone. "I knew she was in good hands at the Kasper home. She wasn't left alone for a minute." Kate sent Rozycki photos via telephone until "she really got to that last stage. And that was hard. . . . [Kate] knew what was happening and what was going to happen, but she was very brave."[65]

Kate also shared powerful moments with her PHJC sisters. Not long before her death, a group of sisters in her age cohort (dubbed the "Kate and under" group) decided to celebrate a special Mass in her room in honor of her seventieth birthday and her Fiftieth Jubilee. The former had gone unheralded the previous January and the latter would not occur until the following year. It was apparent that Kate would not be attending her Fiftieth Jubilee except from heaven. Sr. Cathy Schwemer describes this powerful, bittersweet event:

> It was like a sacred moment. At the end of Mass Father asked Kate, "Do you have anything to say?" By then she was too tired really to speak much, but she held her hand up in blessing and blessed all her sisters in that room. I think back on it now and I still get kind of weepy. It was so powerful. She could barely talk but said: "I bless you. I bless you. You've been a blessing to me, and I bless you." It was her final gift.[66]

In succeeding days Kate spoke only rarely and was content to "just have people sit with her." Schwemer was asked to help with Kate's wake and funeral. She visited Kate not long before her death hoping to find out how she wanted "people to talk about you at your funeral." Deciding to reframe the awkward question, Schwemer asked a barely conscious Kate, "How would you like people to remember you in the future?" Kate didn't respond at once. Thinking she had not heard her, Schwemer started to repeat the question. "I heard you the first time," said a surprisingly emphatic Kate. There was more silence. Then she said, "I want them to remember me as God wills." This was the last time Kate spoke to her friend. Following in the footsteps of her much-loved Saint Katharine Kasper, Kate's desire in death, as in life, was to be faithful to what God wanted before all else.

CANON LAWYER FOR THE PEOPLE OF GOD

The Gospel passage chosen by Kate's PHJC sisters for her funeral well describes her unobtrusive yet formidable leadership: "Jesus went on to say, 'What is the kingdom of God like? To what shall I compare it? It is like yeast a woman took and mixed in with three measures of flour till it was leavened all through'" (Luke 13:18, 20-21). Kate's pastoral service was powerful leaven to the thousands of Catholics she served, first as an educator and then as a canonical advocate for laity in the Church. Bob Kloos, who helped lead Cleveland's parish appeals from 2009 to 2012, wrote a reflection about working with baker-woman Kate as she gently kneaded in the yeast so necessary for the rising of the People of God. I shared his reflection at her funeral and reprint it here in part:

> Kate was there for the little people. For all the baptized. She was a servant first and foremost. What else could a professed Poor Handmaid be? She listened to their heart and she understood. She was accustomed to their disillusionment when they wrote, called or showed up at her door. She would help. She would hope. She would heal. And often, she would win.
>
> Bishops she tangled with should have known better than to try to go around the law. She was patient with them, but firm. They should have known that bold is never a substitute for love, and she hoped that every decision rendered on behalf of the lowly would teach a valuable lesson to those who needed to learn.
>
> Even when the bishop lost, the church was served.
>
> A great woman has earned her eternal rest. Others will have to step up now. But they will have to do so with precision, perseverance and perfect clarity if Kate's legacy is to endure. The poor will still need and deserve what Kate provided, willingly and without reserve. There is no better way to honor Kate than to imitate her commitment to her calling—you to yours. There is still much work to be done.[67]

Epilogue

A Change in Diocesan
Reconfiguration Practices

One could ask if Kate's pioneering canonical work—subsequently validated by Vatican procedural norms—has made any difference. After Kate's
untimely death in 2019, a number of US dioceses engaged in large-scale
reconfigurations involving parish mergers and church closings. Do recent
parish reconfiguration processes and decrees show a greater respect for the
canonical rights of parishes and of the laity? A review of reconfiguration
processes undertaken in five dioceses between 2019 and 2024 (Chicago,[1] Cincinnati,[2] Columbus,[3] Joliet,[4] and St. Louis[5]) suggests substantial progress has
been made. The table below contains specific criteria I identified that reveal
greater respect for the canonical rights of parishes and the laity. I analyzed
canonical decrees, website information, and relevant media to determine the
presence or absence of any given criterion in the three archdioceses and two
dioceses named above.

With one exception (Columbus) current arch/diocesan practices have
improved significantly. No longer are decrees being withheld from Catholics
seeking recourse, as was the case in Camden, Detroit, and the Archdiocese of
New York. No longer—as in Cleveland and the Archdiocese of New York—
are arch/dioceses writing boilerplate decrees that fail to include individualized data showing a "just cause" for parish mergers or a "grave cause" for
church relegations. No longer do parishioners have to guess when a decree
may have been promulgated, as was the case in Syracuse, Camden, and the
Archdiocese of New York. Except for Columbus, all diocesan and archdiocesan decrees clearly state the laity have a right to hierarchical recourse, and
then they provide the canonical timeframe. In nearly all cases diocesan and
archdiocesan resources provide at least a modicum of education in canon
law. In two instances (Cincinnati and St. Louis) that education could be said
to be substantial. It is remarkable that the Archdiocese of St. Louis allowed

parishes pursuing recourse in Rome to remain open until a decision was made. Until now virtually no bishop has ever permitted this even though it is implied in canon law.[6]

Respect for the Canonical Rights of Parishes and Laity

Does the arch/diocesan website or decree process include education about canon law and parish/church closures?
o Yes: explicit on website—Cincinnati, St. Louis
o Somewhat:
  • Chicago (website explains mergers and relegations)
  • Joliet (decree says education happened during parish consultation)
o No: Columbus

Once promulgated, is the decree readily available to anyone seeking recourse?
o Readily visible on website: Chicago, St. Louis
o Available but website search function required: Cincinnati, Joliet
o Available but difficult access (diocesan paper): Columbus

Do the decrees
o provide individualized data (sacramental, attendance, and financial) for each parish and/or church, identifying a "just cause" for parish merger or a "grave cause" for parish closure?
  • Yes: Chicago, Cincinnati, St. Louis
  • In part (no financial data): Joliet
  • No individualized data whatsoever: Columbus

o explicitly name a parishioner's right to seek canonical recourse within the appropriate time frame?
  • Yes, with date supplied: St. Louis
  • Yes, "within ten useful days": Chicago, Cincinnati, Joliet
  • No: Columbus

o include explicit information about the faithful's "right of entry" to the church of a merged parish?
  • Yes: St. Louis
  • No: Chicago, Cincinnati, Columbus, Joliet. (Disposition of churches not identified as worship sites are the responsibility of newly merged entity.)

When parishioners seek recourse in Rome, does the arch/diocese "suspend the effects" of the decree, allowing the parish to remain open until Rome makes a decision?
o Yes: St. Louis*
o No evidence to date: Chicago, Cincinnati, Columbus, Joliet

*Jennifer Brinker, "Archbishop Rozanski Suspends Effects of Decrees for Seven Parishes," *St. Louis Review*, July 31, 2023.

CATHOLICS ARE STILL ORGANIZING TO APPEAL
MERGERS AND CLOSURES

And what of Catholics who disagree with decisions to merge their parish home and close its church? Are Catholic laity still exercising their canonical rights? Currently, there are organized networks of Catholics resisting wide-scale reconfigurations in the archdioceses of Chicago, Cincinnati, and St. Louis. The dioceses of Columbus and Joliet also have parishioner appeals under way.[7] Other canon lawyers and some civil attorneys have picked up where Sister Kate left off in guiding those appeals.

As of July 2022, a multi-year reconfiguration process in the Archdiocese of Chicago reduced the number of parishes from 344 to 221. The plan involved consolidating resources into "one, unified parish" that could have several churches as worship sites. While theoretically 123 churches could have been closed, the Archdiocese projected that under half that number, fifty-seven, would actually be relegated.[8] As of February 2024, the Archdiocesan website listed fifty-one relegation decrees. In September 2020, Brody Hale, a practicing civil attorney who works as an unpaid volunteer for a group called *Saving Our Catholic Churches*, told Chicago media that he was associated with nine Chicago church closure appeals pending at the Vatican.[9] Hale's particular interest is preserving historic churches, and he has helped win many relegation appeals.[10]

In 2021, in light of fewer priests and declining Mass attendance, the Archdiocese of Cincinnati launched a multi-year "Beacons of Light" process that subsequently assigned 208 Catholic parishes to fifty-seven "parish families." The process could eliminate more than 70 percent of active parishes.[11] In 2023, as parish mergers and church closures got underway, Mark Pettus founded Save Our Parishes, an advocacy group that supplies information for how to appeal church restructuring decisions. Kate's 2012 commentary on the successful Cleveland appeals is prominently featured on the organization's website.[12] Parishioners throughout the nineteen-county Cincinnati archdiocese signed petitions naming him as their representative, and petitioned for the "cessation of the Beacons of Light initiative."[13] Pettus works with canon lawyer Philip Gray, of the nonprofit St. Joseph Foundation, who created a "parish packet" explaining how parishioners can organize. As of February 2024, the Vatican had agreed to consider Gray's appeal contesting a merger of four archdiocesan parishes. Gray is also helping Catholics in St. Louis take recourse against their mergers.[14]

In May 2023, after an eighteen-month "All Things New" planning process, the Archdiocese of St. Louis announced it would reduce the number of parishes from 178 to 135.[15] Catholics opposed to restructuring had begun organizing months earlier. Early feedback from laity apparently convinced the

Archdiocese to decrease the number of planned closures from eighty to one hundred parishes to forty-three.[16] In January 2023, after perusing information on the FutureChurch website, Joseph Young, an enterprising businessman who resides in the Archdiocese of St. Louis, spoke with staff in the Pastoral Planning Office in the Archdiocese of Boston. He then submitted a collaborative plan similar to Boston's to the St. Louis Archdiocese. Young learned that archdiocesan staffers had then spoken directly to Boston staffers. While hesitant to say his input was influential, Young believes that along with direct feedback from over eighty-eight thousand Catholics elicited by the Archdiocese, his advocacy did make a difference.[17] Many more St. Louis parishes remained intact than would have otherwise been the case.

In April 2023, Save Our St. Louis Parishes also sent a petition with three thousand signatures asking Archbishop Mitchell Rozanski to halt restructuring plans altogether.[18] The group worked closely with canon lawyer Phillip Gray in submitting "at least" six or seven appeals to Rome. Seven other parishes with Vatican appeals pending were permitted to remain open until a decision was rendered.[19] As of February 2024, at least sixteen parish merger recourses were submitted to Rome, including three being shepherded by canon lawyer Robert Flummerfelt, two of which were not publicly named.[20] In an unprecedented February 5, 2024, decision, the Vatican reversed the Archdiocese's decision to close St. Richard Parish in Creve Coeur. It disputed demographic projections and said St. Richard is "large enough to be a viable community," including 374 registered parishioners under forty-nine years old "in their prime earning years."[21] Again on May 14, 2024, the Vatican upheld two more St. Louis parish recourses opposing the archbishop's decision to close and merge their parishes.[22] The Dicastery for the Clergy did not find just cause for St. Angela Merici Parish to be merged with St. Norbert and Holy Name of Jesus parishes. Neither did the Dicastery find just cause to merge St. Martin of Tours Parish in Lemay, Missouri, with St. Mark Parish. Until now it has been exceedingly rare for the Vatican to reverse a bishop on a parish merger. It is rarer still to see the Dicastery for the Clergy defend the viability of one smaller parish, let alone three. These rulings could bode well for smaller—yet viable and vibrant—parishes that pursue recourses in the future.

STATUS OF OTHER RECOURSES

After Kate's death in 2019, FutureChurch suggested other canon lawyers, including Robert Flummerfelt and canon lawyers at the St. Joseph Foundation, to Catholics who downloaded resources from its website. At this writing, Flummerfelt is working or has worked with about fourteen parishes. Four parishes convinced their bishops to reverse his original decision, thereby winning at the diocesan level. One parish is in the process of appealing to the bishop. Six parishes currently have active appeals at the Dicastery for the Clergy and at the Signatura where "some have languished for some time, which in our experience is FAVORABLE to the parishes," said Flummerfelt.[23] Three other appeals did not succeed. It is likely that many other canonical appeals are currently being shepherded by canon lawyers unknown to me.

CONCLUSION

This review provides abundant evidence that Sister Kate Kuenstler's pioneering canonical work continues to bear rich fruit into the present day. Her unwavering love for an admittedly flawed and damaged church paved the way for ordinary Catholics to exercise leverage in church decisions that affect them directly. Today's parishioners are still standing up to defend their parish homes, and now they have the canonical tools to succeed. Kate's passion for empowering the laity helped prepare the way for synodality to become a Catholic reality in the twenty-first-century church. Because of her faith in God and in the People of God, the arc of Catholic history may at last be bending toward justice.

Notes

CHAPTER 1

1. Center for Applied Research in the Apostolate (CARA), "Frequently Requested Church Statistics."

2. CARA, "Frequently Requested Church Statistics."

3. CARA, "Frequently Requested Church Statistics."

4. Michael Paulson, "Vatican Ruling Bad News for Parish Closing Opponents," *Boston Globe*, February 27, 2008. See also "Statement from Boston's Council of Parishes," May 17, 2010.

5. Jerry Filteau, "Appeals to Reopen Closed US Parishes See Partial Victories," *National Catholic Reporter*, March 14, 2011; Maureen Nolan, "Holy Trinity Parishioners Appeal to Vatican High Court to Reopen Church," *Syracuse Post-Standard*, April 9, 2011.

6. Congregation for the Clergy, "Procedural Guidelines for the Modification of Parishes, the Closure or Relegation of Churches to Profane but Not Sordid Use, and the Alienation of the Same," Vatican City, April 30, 2013; Congregation for the Clergy, "Instruction, 'The Pastoral Conversion of the Parish Community in the Service of the Evangelizing Mission of the Church,'" July 20, 2020. See also Mark Nacinovich, "Vatican Instructions Give Parishioners More Hope in Face of Closings," *National Catholic Reporter*, August 6, 2020, and Christine Schenk, "Let's Use the Title 'Coworker' for Lay People Who Exercise Parish Leadership," *National Catholic Reporter*, August 15, 2020.

7. Kevin Cullin and Stephen Kurkjian, "Church in an $85 Million Accord," *Boston Globe*, September 10, 2003. See also Michael Paulson, "Diocese Gives Abuse Data," *Boston Globe*, February 27, 2004.

8. Cullen and Kurkjian, "Church in an $85 Million Accord."

9. Karen Hensel, "Priest Sex Abuse Scandal Accelerated Declining Catholic Church Attendance in Boston," NBC Boston, December 20, 2017.

10. Jason Berry, *Render Unto Rome: The Secret Life of Money in the Catholic Church* (New York: Crown Publishers, 2011), 82, 85.

11. Stephanie Kirchgaessne and Amanda Holpuch, "How Cardinal Disgraced in Boston Child Abuse Scandal Found a Vatican Haven," *Guardian*, November 7, 2015. See also Robert D. McFadden, "Bernard Law, Powerful Cardinal Disgraced by Priest Abuse Scandal, Dies at 86," *New York Times*, December 19, 2017.

12. Today this office is known as known as the Dicastery for the Clergy after Pope Francis issued *Praedicate Evangelium* on March 19, 2022. As the canonical recourses described in this book occurred before 2022, the term Congregation for the Clergy will be used throughout.

13. Tom Roberts, "Parish Groups Seek Mediation on Church Closings," *National Catholic Reporter*, April 8, 2009.

14. Berry, *Render Unto Rome*, 136.

15. Sixty-five decrees were issued in May with another eighteen to follow later in the year.

16. Berry, *Render Unto Rome*, 86, 91.

17. Michael O'Malley, "Cleveland Catholic Diocese Announces Church Closures," *Cleveland Plain Dealer*, March 14, 2009. See also, "Complete List of Churches Impacted in Diocese Reorganization; Bishop's News Conference," bishop-accountability.org, and Jessica Ravitz, "Catholic Faithful Face Church Closures," CNN, March 25, 2009.

18. Berry, *Render Unto Rome*, 134.

19. Berry, *Render Unto Rome*, 106.

20. Associated Press, "Scituate Catholic Church That Held 12-Year Vigil Is Sold by Archdiocese," April 4, 2018.

21. Berry, *Render Unto Rome*, 93.

22. John C. Seitz, *No Closure: Catholic Practice and Boston's Parish Shutdowns* (Cambridge, MA: Harvard University Press, 2011), 12.

23. Seitz, *No Closure*, 13.

24. Seitz, *No Closure*, 13. See Seitz's Endnote 43 on page 257 for a complete listing of Boston parish outcomes.

25. Seitz, *No Closure*, 13.

26. Seitz, *No Closure*, 153.

27. Dennis Sadowski, "Vatican Denies Boston Parishioners' Final Appeal to Keep Churches Open," *Catholic News Service*, June 14, 2014.

28. Paulson, "Vatican Ruling Bad News."

29. Michael Paulson, "65 Parishes to Be Closed," *Boston Globe*, May 26, 2004.

30. CARA, "Frequently Requested Church Statistics."

31. CARA, "Frequently Requested Church Statistics."

32. CARA, "Statistical Overview of Catholic Priests Formation in the United States for 2022–2023."

33. CARA, "Frequently Requested Church Statistics."

34. Stephen Huba, "Catholic Priest Ordinations Not Keeping Pace with Retirements," *TribLive* (Pennsylvania), August 23, 2017.

35. O'Malley, "Cleveland Catholic Diocese Announces Church Closures," and David Briggs, "Diocesan Reorganization Hits Ethnic, Minority Parishes," *Cleveland Plain Dealer*, July 13, 2008.

36. Ravitz, "Catholic Faithful Face Church Closures."

37. Mark M. Gray, ed., CARA, 1964 Research Blog.

38. Gray, 1964 Research Blog.

39. Michelle Boorstein, "Scandals, Compensation Programs Lead Clergy Sex Abuse Complaints to Quadruple in 2019," *Washington Post*, June 26, 2020.

40. Associated Press, "New Wave of Sexual Abuse Lawsuits Could Cost Catholic Church More Than $4 Billion," December 2, 2019; Boorstein, "Scandals, Compensation Programs Lead Clergy."

41. Boorstein, "Scandals, Compensation Programs Lead Clergy."

42. Boorstein, "Scandals, Compensation Programs Lead Clergy."

43. Bishop Accountability (bishop-accountability.org).

44. Bishop Accountability, list of settlements; Associated Press, "New Wave of Sexual Abuse Lawsuits Could Cost Catholic Church More Than $4 Billion," December 2, 2019.

45. Brian Fraga, "Parishes, Dioceses Feeling the Financial Pinch," *Our Sunday Visitor*, January 30, 2019.

46. CARA, "Frequently Requested Church Statistics." Those who self-reported attending Mass at least monthly (rather than weekly) registered a smaller decline.

47. CARA, "Frequently Requested Church Statistics."

CHAPTER 2

1. Unless otherwise indicated, all Kuenstler quotations in this book are taken from a series of interviews conducted by the author in July, August, and October 2019. Transcripts available at the Kuenstler Collection.

2. Harcourt Religion Publishers acquired Brown-ROA in 1999. In 2009 *Our Sunday Visitor* acquired Harcourt Religion Publishers.

CHAPTER 3

1. Kate Kuenstler, author interviews, August 2, 3, 2019. Unless otherwise noted, all quotes in this chapter come from these interviews.

2. Kate Kuenstler PHJC, "Canon Law and the Rights of the Lay Christian Faithful," May 17, 2007, FutureChurch website.

3. Divina Melotti, author interview, December 16, 2020.

4. Pope John Paul II, *Pastores Dabo Vobis*, 60, March 25, 1992.

5. Also Mark 15:40-41, 47; 16:1; Matthew 27:55-56, 61; 28:1; John 19:25; 20:1-2. For a comprehensive review of the women who accompanied Jesus, see Raymond E. Brown, *The Death of the Messiah*, vol. 2 (New York: Doubleday, 1994), 1013–25.

6. *Pastores Dabo Vobis*, 66.

7. *Pastores Dabo Vobis*, 50, 67.

8. See Code of Canon Law c. 246 §4.

9. Donald B. Cozzens, *The Changing Face of the Priesthood* (Collegeville, MN: Liturgical Press, 2000).

10. Seth Doane, "Catholic Institute Accused of Failing to Act on McCarrick Allegations," *CBS Evening News*, September 29, 2018; see also the Vatican's "Report on the Holy See's Institutional Knowledge and Decision-Making Related to Former Cardinal Theodore Edgar McCarrick (1930–2017)," November 10, 2020.

11. These reports have been confirmed in the present day by Frédéric Martel's exhaustive exposé, *In the Closet of the Vatican: Power, Homosexuality, Hypocrisy* (London: Bloomsbury Continuum, 2019).

12. While Kate never identified her English friend to me, the acknowledgments section of her published dissertation names "Langdon S. Smith who was instrumental in the discovery of this topic." See Mary Kathleen Kuenstler PHJC, "Post-Conciliar Renewal of the Legislative Texts for the Order of the Discalced Carmelite Nuns of the Blessed Virgin Mary of Mount Carmel," *Dissertatio ad Lauream in Facultate Iuris Canonici apud Pontificum Universitatem S. Thomae in Urbe*, Rome, 1995.

13. Technically the word *discalced* means shoeless, but the sisters typically wear sandals.

14. Opus Dei is a conservative international group of Catholic laity who share a core ideal about the sanctification of work. It has been criticized by former members and others for having cult-like characteristics and a right-wing agenda. See Terry Gross, "A Glimpse Inside a Catholic 'Force': Opus Dei," National Public Radio, November 28, 2005.

15. Kate Kuenstler, "The Fractured Face of Carmel," *The Way Supplement* (Summer 1997-98), 48–63.

16. Constance FitzGerald, OCD, author interview, October 26, 2020.

17. FitzGerald, author interview, October 26, 2020. The word *charism* typically means a particular spiritual gift given to a community or an individual to help them bring God's goodness to the world.

18. FitzGerald, author interview, October 26, 2020.

CHAPTER 4

1. Robert McClory, "Background: Wisniewski v. Diocese of Belleville," *National Catholic Reporter*, July 25, 2011.

2. Alan Cooperman, "The Bishop, the Scandal and His Plan," *Washington Post*, September 28, 2002.

3. Wisniewski v. Diocese of Belleville, January 13, 2011.

4. McClory, "Background."

5. Wisniewski v. Diocese of Belleville.

6. "Questions and Answers Regarding the Canonical Process for the Resolution of Allegations of Sexual Abuse of Minors by Priests and Deacons," US Conference of Catholic Bishops.

7. Associated Press, "Priests' Group Wants Diocese to Pay Up in Abuse Case," February 24, 2011; Robert McClory, "Braxton Battles On in Abuse Suit," *National Catholic Reporter*, July 25, 2011.

8. Jess Bogan, "Diocese Pays $6.3 million After Failed Appeal of Sex-Abuse Case," *St. Louis Post-Dispatch*, August 10, 2011.

9. Today the "Faithful of Southern Illinois"; Lena Woltering, FOSIL leader, author interview, October 12, 2020. Subsequent quotes in this chapter are from this interview.

10. "History of FOSIL," Faithful of Southern Illinois website.

11. "History of FOSIL."

12. "History of FOSIL."

13. Lena Woltering, remembrance at Sr. Kuenstler's wake, November 1, 2019.

14. Woltering, remembrance.

15. Kate Kuenstler's resumé, Kuenstler Collection.

16. Woltering, author interview, October 12, 2020.

17. The 1983 Code is available at the Holy See website.

18. John Paul II, *Sacrae Disciplinae Leges*, January 25, 1983, *Acta Apostolicae Sedis* (AAS) 75 (1983). As translated in John Beal, "Toward a Democratic Church: The Canonical Heritage," in *A Democratic Catholic Church*, Eugene C. Bianchi and Rosemary R. Reuther, eds. (New York: Crossroad, 1992), 60.

19. James H. Provost, *The Code of Canon Law* (New York: Paulist Press, 1985), 134.

20. Provost, *Code of Canon Law*, 136.

21. James A. Coriden, "The CLSA and the Protection of Rights: Legacy and Vision," Canon Law Society of America conference, October 10–13, 2011, 19.

22. John P. Beal, "Rights in the Church: Great Expectations, Meager Results," Canon Law Society of America conference, October 10–13, 2011.

23. Beal, "Rights in the Church," 49. Beal quotes Charles Wackenheim, "L'influence des modèles juridique sur la théologie catholique," *Revue de Droit Canonique* 39 (1989), 41.

24. Canon 223 §1, §2.

25. Daniel J. Ward. "The Rights of Christians within the Code of Canon Law," in *Readings, Cases, Materials in Canon Law* (Collegeville, MN: Liturgical Press: 1990), 184.

26. Ward, "Rights of Christians," 184.

27. John P. McIntyre, "The Acquired Right: A New Context," *Studia Canonica* 26, 1992, 31.

28. John P. Beal, "The Protection of the Rights of Persons in the Church" (Washington, DC: Canon Law Society of America, 1991), 8–9.

29. Ricardo E. Bass, "Due Process. Conciliation and Arbitration," Proceedings of the 53rd Annual Conventions of the Canon Law Society of America, 1991, 70.

30. James H. Provost, ed. *Due Process in the Dioceses of the United States 1970–1985* (Washington, DC: Canon Law Society of America, 1987), 28.

31. "A Synodal Church in Mission: Synthesis Report," available at the Synod 2021–2024 website.

32. Christine Schenk, "Synod Report Has Wide-Ranging Implications for Church Governance, Ministry," *National Catholic Reporter*, January 29, 2024.

33. James A. Coriden, *The Parish in Catholic Tradition, History, Theology and Canon Law* (New York: Paulist Press, 1997).

34. Coriden is one of three general editors of the *Code of Canon Law* and was a renowned professor on the faculty of the Washington Theological Union.

35. Coriden, *Parish in Catholic Tradition.*

36. Coriden, *Parish in Catholic Tradition*, 80.

37. Sr. Kate Kuenstler, "Canon Law and the Rights of the Lay Christian Faithful," FutureChurch recording May 17, 2007. Except where indicated, all quotes are from this presentation.

38. 1983 *Code of Canon Law*, Book II, Part 1, "The Christian Faithful."

39. 1983 *Code of Canon Law*, "Christian Faithful."

40. For Canon 212, paragraph 2, the Vatican translation reads: "The Christian faithful are free to make known to the pastors of the Church their needs, especially spiritual ones, and their desires."

41. This is the actual Vatican translation.

42. Bruening Foundation, Tuohy Family Foundation. Female officials at both agencies were parishioners of FutureChurch's cofounder, the Rev. Louis J. Trivison.

43. "Bishop Apologizes for Misuse of Funds," *National Catholic Reporter*, February 8, 2008.

44. "Belleville Priests Call for Bishop to Resign, Braxton Says No," *Catholic News Service*, April 4, 2008.

45. Website of CLP, Canon Law Professionals.

CHAPTER 5

1. Elizabeth Doran, "St. Mary's Appeal to Be Heard by Vatican in February," *Syracuse Post-Standard*, December 24, 2010; Jerry Filteau, "Appeals to Reopen Closed US Parishes See Partial Victories," *National Catholic Reporter*, March 14, 2011.

2. Doran, "St. Mary's Appeal to Be Heard." See also J. Sawchuk, "Diocese's Merger Reversal Spares St. Vincent Pallotti," *Camden Courier-Post*, October 13, 2010.

3. Renée K. Gadua, "CNY Congregations Appeal to Vatican to Save Churches," *Syracuse Post-Standard*, June 25, 2007.

4. FutureChurch tabulation, Kuenstler Collection.

5. Elizabeth Doran, "St. Mary Parishioners' Prayers Answered," *Syracuse Post-Standard*, May 24, 2011.

6. Filteau, "Appeals to Reopen Closed US Parishes"; Maureen Nolan, "Holy Trinity Parishioners Appeal to Vatican High Court to Reopen Church," *Syracuse Post-Standard*, April 9, 2011.

7. Nolan, "Holy Trinity Parishioners Appeal."

8. Sawchuk, "Diocese's Merger Reversal Spares St. Vincent Pallotti."

9. Now known as the Dicastery for the Clergy following Pope Francis's reform of the Roman Curia in 2022.

10. Christopher Lamb, "North-East Faces Steep Fall in Numbers of Priests," *Tablet*, January 22, 2011.

11. Leslie Richardson, "Mahanoy City Church Not Closed?" *Allentown Republican Herald*, January 11, 2011.

12. Renee K. Gadoua, "How Will 100 Priests Serve 350,000 People?" *Syracuse Post-Standard*, November 19, 2006; James M. Moynihan, Bishop of Syracuse, "Equipping the Saints for the Work of Ministry, a Pastoral Letter," Diocese of Syracuse, November 1, 2001.

13. Renee Gadoua, "Diocese: Changes Are in the Works," *Syracuse Post-Standard*, February 27, 2007.

14. Gadoua, "Diocese: Changes Are in the Works."

15. Moynihan, "Equipping the Saints."

16. Cleveland's bishop, Richard Lennon, also instituted this model.

17. Moynihan, "Equipping the Saints."

18. Renee K. Gadoua, "Despite Church Closings, Diocese Still Likely to Face Priest Shortage," *Syracuse Post-Standard*, May 14, 2007.

19. Colleen Kenney (LaTray), email with author, May 23, 2021. Unless otherwise indicated, all author interviews in this chapter may be found at Kuenstler Collection.

20. Colleen Kenney (LaTray), email with author, September 1, 2021.

21. Kate Kuenstler, author interview, July 20, 2019.

22. Kuenstler, author interview, July 20, 2019.

23. Colleen Kenney (LaTray), email with author, May 23 and 24, 2021.

24. John P. Clinton, Affidavit, State of New York, County of Onondaga, February 4, 2008, Attachment #4, Administrative Hierarchical Recourse, February 5, 2008. Unless otherwise indicated, all correspondence and canonical recourse information related to St. Mary Jamesville can be found in the Kuenstler Collection.

25. "Hierarchical Recourse in Response to Decree of Suppression and Confiscation," submitted by Jamesville St. Mary parishioners to Bishop James Moynihan, Apostolic Nuncio Cardinal Pietro Sambi, and Cardinal Claudio Hummes at the Congregation for the Clergy on May 26, 2007.

26. "Hierarchical Recourse."

27. Ngoc Huynh, "Family Must Find Another Church," *Syracuse Post-Standard*, April 30, 2007.

28. LaTray email to author, August 31, 2021.

29. Except where otherwise cited, information about the parish is taken from St. Mary's Faithful archival files documenting their canonical recourse to Rome supplied by LaTray, specifically "Response to Advocate Gullo's Ten Questions," December 17, 2008, Kuenstler Collection.

30. Doran, "St. Mary's Appeal to Be Heard by Vatican in February."

31. St. Mary's Letter to Hummes, February 5, 2008.

32. St. Mary's Letter to Hummes, February 5, 2008.

33. St. Mary's Letter to Hummes, February 5, 2008.

34. St. Mary's Letter to Hummes, February 5, 2008.

35. Mauro Piacenza, Titular Archbishop of Vittoriana, Secretary of the Congregation for the Clergy, *Congregatio Pro Clericis*, August 5, 2008, Prot. n. 20082142.

36. Piacenza, *Congregatio Pro Clericis*.

37. Most Rev. James M. Moynihan, Bishop of Syracuse, Letter to Mark A. Donnelly and Colleen K. LaTray, September 9, 2008.

38. Bishop Frans Daneels, O. Praem, Letter to Colleen K. LaTray and Mark A Donnelly, November 4, 2008.

39. Vatican, Apostolic Signatura, *Contentious Administrative Recourse to the Supreme Tribunal of the Apostolic Signatura.* Available at https://tinyurl.com /4nwsr85u.

40. LaTray, "Response to Advocate Gullo's Ten Questions."

41. Kuenstler, author interview, July 20, 2019.

42. Carlo Gullo, Protest 41.719/08 CA, Syracuse, Suppression of a Parish, *Brief for the Appellants*, C. LaTray, M. Donnelly and others, parishioners of St. Mary in the locality known as Jamesville, January 27, 2009.

43. Carlo Gullo, Protest 41.719/08 CA, Syracuse, Suppression of a Parish, *Brief for the Appellants*, C. LaTray, M. Donnelly and others, January 27, 2009.

44. Mark Donnelly, Minutes of the [St. Mary Appeals Committee] Meeting of February 8, 2009.

45. Colleen K. LaTray, Mark A. Donnelly, and Robert C. Hopkins Sr., Letter to Bishop Robert J. Cunningham, September 12, 2009.

46. LaTray, Donnelly, and Hopkins Sr., Letter to Cunningham, September 12, 2009.

47. Letter from Bishop Robert J. Cunningham to Colleen LaTray, Mark A. Donnelly, and Robert C. Hopkins Sr., September 25, 2009.

48. Doran, "St. Mary's Appeal to Be Heard."

49. Doran, "St. Mary's Appeal to Be Heard."

50. Filteau, "Appeals to Reopen Closed US Parishes."

51. Meghan Rubado, "Syracuse Trying to Tax Closed Catholic Churches for the First Time," *Syracuse Post-Standard*, February 23, 2010.

52. "Is Vatican Policy Shifting to Keep Churches Open?" *Focus on Future-Church*, Winter 2011, FutureChurch archives.

53. "Vatican Ruling Favors Parishioners of Closed Syracuse Church," CNY Central, March 28, 2011.

54. "Ruling Upholds NY Church Merger; Appeal Is Mulled," *Wall Street Journal*, March 28, 2011.

55. Supreme Tribunal Apostolic Signatura, Protocol no. 41719/08 CA, SYRA-CUSEN, *Suppressionis parroeciae et missionis BMV "Jamesville" et reductionis ecclesiae ad usum prfanum*, die 21 mai 2011.

56. "Definitive Sentence of the College of Judges of the Supreme Tribunal of the Apostolic Signatura: Protocol no. 4171908/CA Suppression of the Parish of St. Mary in 'Jamesville' and Reduction of the Church to Profane Use," August 11, 2011.

57. "Definitive Sentence."

58. "Definitive Sentence."

59. Can. 1222 §1, §2.

60. "Definitive Sentence."

61. Elizabeth Doran, "St. Mary Parishioners' Prayers Answered: Vatican Says Jamesville Church Must Remain a Worship Site," *Syracuse Post-Standard*, May 24, 2011.

62. LaTray email with author, May 23, 2021.

63. LaTray email with author, May 23, 2021.

64. Maureen Nolan, "Mass Will Be Held at Shuttered St. Mary's Church in Jamesville," *Syracuse Post-Standard*, August 13, 2012.

65. Associated Press, "Vatican: No Reason to Close Thriving NY Church," *Wall Street Journal*, December 19, 2011; Letter from Bishop Robert J. Cunningham to Ms. Colleen LaTray, September 21, 2011.

66. St. Mary's Appeals Committee, Letter to Bishop Robert J. Cunningham re: "Reopening for divine worship of the church of St. Mary's in Jamesville, New York," September 12, 2011.

67. Letter from Cunningham to LaTray, September 21, 2011.

68. Associated Press, "Vatican: No Reason to Close."

69. Letter from Bishop Frans Daneels, O. Praem., secretary at the Apostolic Signatura, to Ms. Colleen LaTray, December 21, 2011.

70. Letter from Daneels to LaTray, December 21, 2011.

71. Email from Colleen LaTray to Carlo and Alessia Gullo, January 22, 2012.

72. The Most Rev. Robert J. Cunningham, Bishop of Syracuse, "Revised Statement Regarding St. Mary's Church, Jamesville," January 10, 2012.

73. Meeting notes, "Meeting with Fr. Yeazel, Pastor of Holy Cross Church," January 20, 2012.

74. This is inaccurate at best. In January 2011 Cardinal Burke told a group of British canon law judges that it is better for a church to be left open for monthly Masses than to be closed—see Lamb, "North-East Faces Steep Fall." The decision about Sunday Masses is ordinarily left to the discretion of the local pastor or bishop.

75. Meeting notes, "Meeting with Fr. Yeazel."

76. Email from Colleen LaTray to Christopher Wiles, attorney general of the State of New York, March 29, 2012.

77. Email from LaTray to Carlo and Alessia Gullo, January 22, 2012.

78. Letter from St. Mary Appeals Committee to Most Rev. Robert J. Cunningham, Bishop of Syracuse, *Remonstratio ad Cautelam* regarding the reopening of the church of St. Mary in Jamesville, January 24, 2012.

79. Letter from Appeals Committee to Cunningham, January 24, 2012.

80. Letter from Most Rev. Robert J. Cunningham, Bishop of Syracuse, to Mrs. Colleen LaTray, January 31, 2012.

81. Letter from Cunningham to LaTray, January 31, 2012.

82. Letter from Cunningham to LaTray, January 31, 2012; The Most Rev. Robert J. Cunningham, Bishop of Syracuse, "Revised Statement Regarding St. Mary's Church, Jamesville," January 10, 2012.

83. "In its most recent correspondence the Sacred Signatura indicates the solution to be followed. It is time for all concerned to acknowledge that this matter is resolved." Letter from Most Rev. Robert J. Cunningham, Bishop of Syracuse to Mrs. Colleen LaTray, January 31, 2012.

84. Monsignor Antonio Neri, Undersecretary, Congregation for the Clergy, Letter to Colleen K. LaTray et al. Prot. N. 20120191, February 3, 2012.

85. Neri letter to LaTray, February 3, 2012.

86. Gerald Aloe, email correspondence to committee, February 5, 2012.

87. Letter from Christopher Prosak to Msgr. J. Robert Yeazel, February 19, 2012.

88. Letter from Msgr. J. Robert Yeazel to Mr. Christopher Prosak, February 24, 2012.

89. Letter to Rev. Msgr. J. Robert Yeazel from V. William Doran, Claims Manager, Roman Catholic Diocese of Syracuse, August 21, 2013; Carlo Gullo and Alesia Gullo, "Brief for the Appellants, C. LaTray, M. Donnelly and Others, Parishioners of St. Mary in the Locality Known as Jamesville Congregation for the Clergy," Protest 41.719/08 CA, January 27, 2009; "Definitive Sentence."

90. Letter from the Appeals Committee of St. Mary Church to Most Rev. Robert J. Cunningham, April 24, 2012.

91. Email from Colleen LaTray with scanned documentation to Carlo and Alessia Gullo, May 8, 2012.

92. Email from LaTray to Carlo and Alessia Gullo, May 8, 2012.

93. Email from Colleen LaTray to David Castronovo, and Advocate Carlo Gullo, July 23, 2012.

94. Maureen Nolan, "Mass Will Be Held at Shuttered St. Mary's Church in Jamesville," *Syracuse Post-Standard*, August 13, 2012.

95. Colleen K. LaTray, emailed interview with author, May 23, 2021.

96. LaTray emailed interview, May 23, 2021.

97. Letter from John. P. Clinton and Christopher J. Prosek to Msgr. J. Robert Yeazel, August 29, 2012.

98. Email from Colleen K. LaTray to Advocate Carlo Gullo, September 7, 2012.

99. Letter to Colleen LaTray from Frans Daneels, O.Praem, Secretary of the Apostolic Signatura, r: Prot. N. 48568/13 CA (cf. prot. n. 41719/08/CA) SYRACUSEN, February 12, 2014. Also Advocate Carlo Gullo and Advocate Alessia Gullo, Protocol no: 20082142, Congregation for the Clergy C. LaTray and others, parishioners of St. Mary in the Locale of Jamesville, the Bishop of Syracuse. The third Motion for the execution of the sentence of May 21, 2011, of the Apostolic Signatura, March 29, 2012.

100. Letter from "Representatives of the St. Mary's Faithful" to Most. Rev. Robert J. Cunningham, November 30, 2014.

101. Letter from "Representatives" to Cunningham, November 30, 2014.

102. In 2021—after LaTray again wrote the Gullos—the new bishop, Douglas J. Lucia, authorized a monthly Mass to be celebrated on Mondays over the succeeding

five months. Per emailed information to author from Colleen Kenney (LaTray) on August 31, 2021.

103. Time Warner Cable web staff, Onondaga County, "Jamesville Church Continues to Pack the Pews since Reopening," Spectrum News NY1, September 8, 2016.

104. Time Warner Cable staff, "Jamesville Church Continues to Pack."

105. LaTray emailed interview with author, May 23, 2021.

106. LaTray emailed interview with author, May 23, 2021.

CHAPTER 6

1. FOSVP, Haddon Township, New Jersey, USA Administrative Recourse to the Congregation for the Clergy, Prot. N. 20082827, December 12, 2008, Book 2, Exhibit 15, 1. Unless otherwise indicated, all correspondence and recourse files may be found in the Kuenstler Collection.

2. FOSVP, Administrative Recourse.

3. Monsignor Louis Marucci, author interview, August 14, 2020, Kuenstler Collection.

4. FOSVP Prot. N. 20082827, Book 2, Exhibit 15.

5. Daniel Rubin, "Excuse Me for Not Getting Up," *Philadelphia Inquirer*, May 16, 2008.

6. Marucci, author interview, August 20, 2020.

7. Marucci, author interview, August 20, 2020, and see website of the Church of St. Andrew the Apostle.

8. Marucci, author interview, August 14, 2020.

9. Marucci, author interview, August 14, 2020.

10. Bishop Joseph Galante, remarks from video posted by diocese at 1:30 p.m. April 3, 2008, announcing a drastic reduction of Camden parishes from 124 to 66. For text, see Parish of SVP, Administrative Recourse, Prot. N. 20082827. Book 1, Exhibit 1.

11. Parish of SVP, Administrative Recourse, Prot. N. 20082827, Book 1, Exhibit 4.

12. Kim Mulford and Jim Walsh, "Bishop Announces Massive Diocese Shakeup," *Courier-Post*, April 3, 2008; Jim Walsh, "Parishioners Demand Churches Be Kept Open," *Courier-Post*, May 28, 2008.

13. Process described in Parish of SVP, Administrative Recourse, Prot. N. 20082827, Book 1.

14. FOSVP, Administrative Recourse, Prot. N. 20082827, December 12, 2008, Book 1, Exhibit 9.

15. FOSVP, Administrative Recourse, 20082827, Book 1, Exhibit 8.

16. FOSVP Recourse, Book 1, Exhibit 8.

17. FOSVP Recourse, Book 1, Exhibit 8.

18. FOSVP Recourse, Book 1, Exhibit 8.

19. FOSVP Recourse, Book 1, Exhibit 8.

20. FOSVP, Administrative Recourse, 20082827. Book 1, Exhibit 9.

21. FOSVP Recourse, Book 1, Exhibit 9.

22. FOSVP Recourse, Book 1, Exhibit 9.

23. FOSVP Recourse, Book 1, Exhibit 12.

24. FOSVP Recourse, Book 1, Exhibit 15.

25. FOSVP Recourse, Book 1, Exhibit 16.

26. FOSVP Recourse, Book 1, Exhibit 16.

27. FOSVP Recourse, Book 1, Exhibits 18–19.

28. FOSVP Recourse, Book 1, Exhibit 19.

29. FOSVP Recourse, Book 1, Exhibit 19.

30. David O'Reilly, "Bishop: Answers Lie within the Laity," *Philadelphia Inquirer*, April 6, 2008.

31. David O'Reilly, "Catholics Challenge Bishop's Decision to Merge Parishes During Meeting at Malaga Church," *Philadelphia Inquirer*, May 28, 2008.

32. Kim Mulford and Jim Walsh, "Bishop Announces Massive Diocese Shakeup," *Courier-Post* online, April 3, 2008.

33. FOSVP, Administrative Recourse, Book 1, 20.

34. Marucci, author interview, August 14, 2020.

35. Julie Dengler, "Pallotti Parish Appeals Church Closure," *Retrospect*, April 18, 2008.

36. Kristen A. Graham, "Congregants Fight Their Church's Closing," *Philadelphia Inquirer*, April 27, 2008.

37. Lavinia DeCastro, "Decision a Shocker for Parish, Pastor," *Courier-Post*, week of April 10, 2008.

38. Dengler, "Palotti Parish."

39. Marucci, author interview, August 20, 2020.

40. Marucci letter to Galante, April 4, 2008, FOSVP, Administrative Recourse, Prot. N. 20082827, Book II, Exhibit 6, attachment 2.

41. Galante letter to Marucci, April 4, 2008, FOSVP, Administrative Recourse, Prot. N. 20082827, Book II, Exhibit 6, attachment 3.

42. Galante letter to Marucci, April 4, 2008.

43. Property Evaluations Co. Inc. See FOSVP, Administrative Recourse, Prot. N. 20082827, Book II, Exhibit 2, attachment 7 and attachment 9; see also Juliet Fletcher, "Mergers Leave Parishes with Prime Real Estate," *Press of Atlantic City*, August 17, 2008.

44. Jan Hefler, "Camden Diocese Plans for New High School," *Philadelphia Inquirer*, June 18, 2008.

45. FOSVP, Prot. N. 20082827, Book 3, Exhibit 28, 4.

46. Stephen M. Silverman, "Raffaello Follieri Sentenced to 4½ Years," *People*, October 23, 2008.

47. George Mast, "Bishop Sold Home to Man Now Charged with Fraud," *Courier-Post*, July 16, 2008.

48. Jeane MacIntosh and Kati Cornell, "A Deal with the Devil," *New York Post*, July 15, 2008.

49. Fletcher, "Mergers Leave Parishes with Prime Real Estate."

50. Geoff Mulvihill, "Diocese: Vatican Recommended Indicted Developer," Associated Press, July 16, 2008.

51. Stephanie Brown, "Accused Developer in Galante Sale," *Gloucester County Times* (Woodbury, NJ), July 16, 2008.

52. Jason Berry, "The Last Bull: Cardinal Sodano Goes Out," *National Catholic Reporter*, December 27, 2019.

53. Joe Feuerherd, "Catholic Real Estate Bonanza," *National Catholic Reporter*, March 3, 2006.

54. Feuerherd, "Catholic Real Estate Bonanza."

55. Feuerherd, "Catholic Real Estate Bonanza."

56. Jason Berry, "Vatican Monsignor Pressured to Return Church Valuables That Went Missing on His Watch," *National Catholic Reporter*, October 25, 2014.

57. Berry, "Vatican Monsignor Pressured."

58. Berry, "Vatican Monsignor Pressured."

59. Berry, "Vatican Monsignor Pressured."

60. Berry, "Vatican Monsignor Pressured."

61. For a comprehensive treatment of the saga, see Jason Berry, *Render Unto Rome: The Secret Life of Money in the Catholic Church* (New York: Crown Publishers, 2011), 119–32.

62. Berry, "Vatican Monsignor Pressured."

63. John B. Canuso, Trustee, FOSVP Report to Bishop Joseph A. Galante on April 15, 2008, Pallotti correspondence file, Kuenstler Collection.

64. John B. Canuso to Msgr. Lou Marucci, August 19, 2008. Unless otherwise indicated, all letters may be found in the Pallotti correspondence file, Kuenstler Collection.

65. Canuso to Marucci, August 19, 2008.

66. Canuso to Marucci, August 19, 2008.

67. Letters dated April 4, April 7, June 3, June 23, and July 9, 2008, and summarized in letter to Hummes, August 18, 2008.

68. Williams letter to Galante, April 15, 2008, and FOSVP, Prot. N. 20082827, Book 3, Exhibit 1, 1.

69. Letter from Galante to SVP, Prot. N. 20082827. Book 2, Exhibit 6, no. 12, May 9, 2008.

70. Marucci, author interview, August 14, 2020.

71. Marucci, author interview, August 14, 2020.

72. Marucci, author interview, August 14, 2020.

73. Marucci, author interview, August 14, 2020.

74. Marucci, author interview, August 14, 2020.

75. Galante letter to Marucci, June 11, 2008.

76. FOSVP, Prot. N. 20082827, Book 3, Exhibit 14.

77. Marucci, author interview, August 20, 2020.

78. Marucci, author interview, August 20, 2020.

79. Marucci, author interview, August 20, 2020.

80. Ginny Hargrave, interview with author, July 1, 2021.

81. Marucci, author interview, August 20, 2020.

82. Letter from SVP to Hummes, August 18, 2008.

83. Jim Walsh, "Parish Appeals Merger to Vatican," *Courier-Post*, August 20, 2008.

84. FOSVP, Prot. N. 20082827, Book 2, Exhibit 8, "Lack of Due Diligence to Persons with Disabilities," 7.

85. Julie Dengler, "Pallotti Donors Seek Diocese Refunds in Court," *Retrospect*, February 5, 2010.

86. Adam Smeltz, "A Few Stay Independent, Others Will Continue as Worship Sites," *Courier-Post*, August 27, 2008.

87. Letter from SVP pastoral and finance councils to Galante, August 27, 2008.

88. Galante to Marucci re: August 27, 2008, letter from SVP parish leadership.

89. Jessica Beym, "Parishioners Protest," *Gloucester County Times* (Woodbury, NJ), April 9, 2008.

90. Marucci, author interview, August 20, 2020.

91. Marucci, author interview, August 20, 2020.

92. Marucci, author interview, August 20, 2020.

93. Marucci, author interview, August 20, 2020.

94. Marucci, author interview, August 20, 2020.

95. Marucci, author interview, August 20, 2020.

96. Canon 8.2.

97. SVP to Hummes, September 20, 2008.

98. SVP to Hummes, September 20, 2008.

99. SVP to Hummes, September 20, 2008.

100. Carrú to Marucci, September 30, 2008.

101. Marucci, author interview, August 20, 2020.

102. Marucci, author interview, August 20, 2020.

103. Marucci, author interview, August 20, 2020.

104. Marucci, author interview, August 20, 2020.

105. Letter, FOSVP to Hummes, December 12, 2008.

106. See Cindy Wooden, "Official Looks at Meaning, Role of Metropolitan Archbishop," *Catholic News Service*, June 1, 2019.

107. Letter, FOSVP to Sambi, December 12, 2008.

108. Marucci, author interview, August 20, 2020.

109. Marucci, author interview, August 20, 2020.

110. Marucci, author interview, August 20, 2020.

111. Carru to Wilson, June 12, 2009, FOSVP, Prot. N. 20082827.

112. Marucci, author interview, August 20, 2020.

113. Beym, "Parishioners Protest."

114. Beym, "Parishioners Protest."

115. Joseph Gidjunis, "Malaga Parishioners Protest," *Courier-Post*, May 3, 2008.

116. Mark Swanson, "Protest Crosses Make Next Move the Bishop's," *Retrospect*, July 4, 2008.

117. Paula H. Carlton, "The Merging and Closing of Camden Diocese's Parishes," Part 1 of a series, CNB News–Gloucester City, May 13, 2009.

118. Carlton, "Merging and Closing."

119. Carlton, "Merging and Closing."

120. Carlton, "The Merging and Closing of Camden Diocese's Parishes," Part 2 of a series, CNB News–Gloucester City, May 28, 2009.

121. SVP letter to Hummes, November 4, 2009.

122. Letter from Piacenza to Wilson et al., November 10, 2009.

123. Letter from Piacenza to Wilson et al., November 10, 2009.

124. Diocese of Camden, "Vatican Affirms Bishop's Parish Reconfiguration Process," website blog, December 3, 2009.

125. Marucci, author interview, August 14, 2020.

126. Marucci, author interview, August 14, 2020.

127. Marucci, author interview, August 14, 2020.

128. Confirmation Letter of Sambi to John D. Wilson, SVP Parish Council President, affirming that both letters were sent, December 5, 2009.

129. FOSVP press release, made public around December 7, 2009.

130. Marucci letter to Sambi, December 6, 2009.

131. Marucci letter to Sambi, December 6, 2009.

132. Jaclyn Peiser, "A Conservative Cardinal Who Criticized the Vaccine Caught Covid. Days Later He Was Put on a Ventilator," *Washington Post*, August 16, 2021.

133. Letter, FOSVP to Burke, March 10, 2010.

134. Letter, FOSVP to Burke, March 10, 2010.

135. Letter, Daneels to Hatch et al., April 10, 2010.

136. Letter, SVP to Burke, April 19, 2010.

137. Unless otherwise indicated, all information in preceding section is taken from the letter of SVP to Burke, April 19, 2012.

138. Letter, Daneels to Hatch et al., Prot. N. 43940/10 CA, May 27, 2010.

139. Letter, Hatch to Daneels, 43940/10 CA, June 23, 2010.

140. Letter, Daneels to Hatch, Prot. N. 43940/10 CA, July 10, 2010.

141. 1983 *Code of Canon Law*, Part V, Section I, Recourse Against Administrative Decrees (Canons 1732–1739).

142. Marucci, author interview, August 20, 2020.

143. Kuenstler, author interview, October 14, 2019

144. Kuenstler, author interviews, July 20, 2019, and October 14, 2019.

145. Kuenstler, author interviews, July 20, 2019, and October 14, 2019.

146. Kuenstler, author interview, October 14, 2019.

147. Kate Kuenstler acceptance speech upon receiving the Louis J. Trivison Award from FutureChurch, September 30, 2012.

148. J. Sawchuk, "Diocese's Merger Reversal Spares St. Vincent Pallotti," *Courier-Post*, October 13, 2010.

149. Diocese of Camden, *Catholic Star Herald*, September 8, 2011.

150. Carly Q. Romalino, "Franklin Township's St. Mary's Avoids Long-Term Closure of Malaga Church," *South Jersey Times*, September 15, 2011.

151. "As Parishes Close, Mass Attendance in Camden Plunges," *Philadelphia Inquirer*, April 11, 2011.

152. Hargrave, author interview, July 1, 2021.

153. Hargrave, author interview, July 1, 2021.

154. Marucci, author interview, August 20, 2020.
155. Marucci, author interview, August 20, 2020.
156. Marucci email to author, October 21, 2022, Kuenstler Collection.
157. Marucci, author interview, July 10, 2020.

CHAPTER 7

1. Rocco Palmo, "Lennon, Had -- Vatican Orders Reopening of 13 Cleveland Churches," *Whispers in the Loggia*, March 7, 2012, https://tinyurl.com/4ejy737a.

2. Sr. Kate Kuenstler, *Commentary on Vatican Decrees Upholding Cleveland Parishioner Appeals*, FutureChurch *Save Our Parish Community* Packet, free download.

3. "Who We Are," website for Diocese of Cleveland.

4. David Briggs, "Era of Change for the Church," *Cleveland Plain Dealer*, November 25, 2006.

5. "Who We Are."

6. Andrew DePietro, "U.S. Poverty Rate by City in 2021," *Forbes*, November 25, 2021.

7. Alan Achkar, "Symposium Marks Fifth Anniversary of Pilla Appeal," *Cleveland Plain Dealer*, April 19, 1998.

8. Anthony M. Pilla, "The Moral Implications of Regional Sprawl: The Cleveland Catholic Diocese's *The Church in the City* Vision Process," City Club of Cleveland, June 17, 1996.

9. Pilla, "Moral Implications of Regional Sprawl."

10. Alan Achkar, "Symposium Marks Fifth Anniversary of Pilla Appeal," *Cleveland Plain Dealer*, April 19, 1998. See also Karen Long and Darrell Holland, "Pilla's Initiative Gains Interest—Protestants Look at 'Church in the City,'" *Cleveland Plain Dealer*, October 25, 1996.

11. Rev. Kenneth Chalker, "Bishop Anthony Pilla, a Bishop for Us All," *Cleveland Plain Dealer*, September 24, 2021.

12. Rick Krivanka, author interview, October 1, 2021. All author interviews in this chapter may be found in the Kuenstler Collection.

13. Krivanka, author interview, October 1, 2021.

14. James F. McCarty and David Briggs, "Diocese Suspends 9 More Priests," *Cleveland Plain Dealer*, April 9, 2002.

15. James F. McCarty and David Briggs, "Diocese Uses Tough Tactics in Sex Suits Facing Steep Liability, Church Plays 'Hardball' with Accusers, Critics Say," *Cleveland Plain Dealer*, March 10, 2002.

16. Jason Berry, "Immunity: A Haven for Sensitive Files, Too?" *Cleveland Plain Dealer*, June 17, 1990. See also Jason Berry, *Render Unto Rome: The Secret Life of Money in the Catholic Church* (New York: Crown Publishers, 2011), 215.

17. James F. McCarty, "Bishop Pilla Walks Tightrope in Priest Sex Abuse Scandal," *Cleveland Plain Dealer*, May 5, 2002.

18. For an exhaustive treatment of Cleveland's financial scandal and clergy sex abuse cover-up, see Berry, *Render Unto Rome*.

19. Frank Bentayou, "Local Diocese Tries to Build Confidence with Clearer Budget," *Cleveland Plain Dealer*, July 23, 2005, bishopaccountability.org.

20. Estok eulogy for Pilla, September 28, 2021, http://tinyurl.com/388s5cv5.

21. Virgildee Daniel, "The Volunteer Ministry Institute," Unpublished MA thesis, Saint Mary-of-the-Woods College, Indiana, April 1994, 4.

22. "Lay Ecclesial Ministry," Diocese of Cleveland website.

23. Anthony Pilla, "Steps Toward Collaboration Among Parishes," *Origins* 30:39 (March 15, 2001), 621–28.

24. Lisa Frey, "Laity as Leaders and Ministers in Guiding the Future of the Church," Synod on Synodality session for FutureChurch, March 23, 2022, FutureChurch collection, Women and Leadership Archives, Loyola University, Chicago.

25. Anthony M. Pilla, *Vibrant Parish Life*, Diocese of Cleveland, February 2001.

26. Pilla, *Vibrant Parish Life*.

27. John Maimone, Chief Financial Officer of the Diocese of Cleveland, with Rick Krivanka and Fr. Lawrence Jurcak, presentation at Cleveland's Central West District, March 12, 2007, and at the Cleveland City Club, April 5, 2007. See also Briggs, "Era of Change for the Church."

28. Pilla, *Vibrant Parish Life*.

29. Pilla, *Vibrant Parish Life*.

30. Pilla, *Vibrant Parish Life*.

31. Pilla, *Vibrant Parish Life*.

32. Dennis Sadowski, "Bishop Pilla, Who Led Church in Cleveland for 25 Years, Dies," *National Catholic Reporter*, September 21, 2021, and David Briggs, "Bishop Anthony M. Pilla, Cleveland Native Who Guided Northeast Ohio Catholics for Quarter-Century, Dies at 88," *Cleveland Plain Dealer*, September 21, 2021.

33. Rocco Palmo, "Lennon Bound for Cleveland—Boston Free at Last," *Whispers in the Loggia*, April 4, 2006.

34. Colette M. Jenkins, "Bostonian Who's to Fill Pilla's Shoes Unfamiliar with Ohio but Versed in Abuse Scandal," *Akron Beacon Journal*, April 5, 2006.

35. Jenkins, "Bostonian Who's to Fill Pilla's Shoes."

36. Berry, *Render Unto Rome*, 86. See also Robert M. O'Grady, "Obituary: Bishop Richard Lennon Dies at 72," *Boston Pilot*, November 1, 2019.

37. O'Grady, "Obituary."

38. As reported by Michael O'Malley, "Cleveland Catholic Bishop Richard Lennon: A Profile," *Cleveland Plain Dealer*, December 5, 2010.

39. Denise LaVoie, "Victims' Group Leader Criticizes Interim Leader of Boston Archdiocese," bishop-accountability.org, January 27, 2003.

40. Staff, "Boston Archdiocesan Documents Showing the Involvement of Bishop Richard G. Lennon in Abuse Cases," bishop-accountability.org.

41. Staff, "Boston Archdiocesan Documents."

42. John C. Seitz, *No Closure: Catholic Practice and Boston's Parish Shutdowns* (Cambridge, MA: Harvard University Press, 2011), 153.

43. Archdiocese of Boston, Parish Reconfiguration Fund Oversight Committee, Final Report, November 1, 2007.

44. Berry, *Render Unto Rome*, 154–55.

45. O'Malley, Lennon profile.

46. Leonard Calabrese, author interview, February 18, 2022. Unless otherwise indicated, transcripts of all author interviews may be found in the Kuenstler Collection.

47. O'Malley, Lennon profile.

48. Begin, author interview, January 5, 2022.

49. Calabrese, author interview, February 18, 2022.

50. Krivanka, author interview, October 1, 2021.

51. Anonymity granted to interviewees by the author, February 2022.

52. David Briggs, "Local Catholic Finances 'Stretched,'" *Cleveland Plain Dealer*, February 6, 2007.

53. Berry, *Render Unto Rome*, 388, footnote 52.

54. Berry, *Render Unto Rome*, 225, 388, footnote 52; Begin, author interview; Michael Griffin, author interview, February 28, 2022; Sr. Sheila Tobbe, author interview, February 5, 2022.

55. Calabrese, author interview, February 18, 2022.

56. Begin, author interview, January 5, 2022.

57. Begin, author interview, January 5, 2022.

58. Berry, *Render Unto Rome*, 270.

59. Introduction, *Vibrant Parish Life—Phase II: Purpose, Steps and Values*, Diocese of Cleveland, February 27, 2006.

60. Introduction, *Vibrant Parish Life—Phase II*.

61. Briggs, "Local Catholic Finances."

62. Diocese of Cleveland, "Detailed Timeline for *Vibrant Parish Life*—Phase II," Lent 2006–April 2007, February 27, 2006.

63. Introduction, *Vibrant Parish Life—Phase II*.

64. Colette M. Jenkins, "Catholic Diocese of Cleveland May Release Proposals," *Akron Beacon Journal*, October 13, 2006.

65. Jenkins, "Catholic Diocese of Cleveland."

66. Colette M. Jenkins, "Catholic Parishes Will Be Partners," *Akron Beacon Journal*, February 9, 2007.

67. Joe Milicia, "Cleveland Diocese Asks Parishes to Help Determine Church Closings," Associated Press, May 30, 2007; "Diocese Downsizing Could Involve 23 Churches," Associated Press, June 6, 2007.

68. Staff, "Confirmed Closings by Diocesan Cluster," *Cleveland Plain Dealer*, June 1, 2007; Dennis Sadowski, "Bishop Asks One-Third of Clusters to 'Downsize,'" *Catholic Universe Bulletin*, June 1, 2007.

69. Sadowski, "Bishop Asks One-Third of Clusters."

70. Author interview with a priest member of the *Vibrant Parish Life* committee.

71. Seitz, *No Closure*, 7.

72. Krivanka, author interview, October 1, 2021.

73. Krivanka, author interview, October 1, 2021.

74. Krivanka, author interview, October 1, 2021.

75. William A. Clark, *A Voice of Their Own: The Authority of the Local Parish* (Collegeville, MN: Liturgical Press, 2005).

76. FutureChurch letter to Cleveland supporters, December 2007.

77. William A. Clark, podcast for FutureChurch on "A Voice of Their Own," February 27, 2007.

78. Clark podcast.

79. In attendance from FutureChurch were Schenk, Trivison, and FutureChurch program coordinator Emily Holtel Hoag.

80. Conference for Pastoral Planning and Council Development, "2003 National Study of Parish Reorganization" (2004: by Loras College Press, Archdiocese of Dubuque), and the Conference for Pastoral Planning and Council Development, https://tinyurl.com/4u3pu4p3.

81. Christine Schenk, "FutureChurch Notes of January 30, 2007, Meeting with Bishop Lennon." See FutureChurch collection, Loyola University, Chicago.

82. "FutureChurch Supports Parishioners," *Focus on FutureChurch*, Winter 2007, and Schenk, "FutureChurch Notes of January 30, 2007."

83. Sister Kate Kuenstler, "Canon Law and the Rights of the Christian Faithful," FutureChurch, May 17, 2007, https://futurechurch.org/save-our-parish/.

84. Kuenstler, "Canon Law and the Rights."

85. David Briggs, "Landmark Churches, Minority, Ethnic Parishes Recommended for Closing," *Cleveland Plain Dealer*, November 7, 2008; John Kroll, "Akron, Barberton Churches Added to List of Catholic Closings," *Cleveland Plain Dealer*, December 16, 2008; Cliff Pinckard, "Diocese Plans for Church Closings Opens Up Emotions Among Catholics," *Cleveland Plain Dealer*, February 23, 2009.

86. David Briggs, "In Cleveland, St. Peter Hope to Avoid a Proposed Merger with St. John Cathedral," *Cleveland Plain Dealer*, June 9, 2008.

87. Briggs, "In Cleveland, St. Peter Hopes to Avoid"; Briggs, "Landmark Churches, Minority, Ethnic Parishes"; Briggs, "Three More Catholic Churches Oppose Diocesan Reorganization," *Cleveland Plain Dealer*, September 12, 2008; Pinckard, "Diocese Plans"; Colette Jenkins, "Parishioners Brace for News of Church Closings," *Akron Beacon Journal*, March 13, 2009.

88. David Briggs, "Historic St. Peter to Close," *Cleveland Plain Dealer*, October 11, 2007.

89. Michael O'Malley, "Cleveland Council Members Prepare to Fight Over Catholic Diocese's Plans to Demolish Some Churches," *Cleveland Plain Dealer*, March 2, 2009.

90. Robert L. Smith, "Bishop Lennon's Decisions on Cleveland Catholic Church Closings Leave Parishes Wondering: Why Us?" *Cleveland Plain Dealer*, March 22, 2009.

91. Michael O'Malley, "Cleveland Catholic Diocese Announces Church Closures," *Cleveland Plain Dealer*, March 14, 2009.

92. FutureChurch Media Release, "FutureChurch Laments Loss of Parishes, Asks Diocese to Reconsider," March 14, 2009. See FutureChurch collection, Women and Church Leadership archive at Loyola University, Chicago.

93. In Catholic parlance, *discernment* is more than simply making a prudential judgement. It also entails prayerful attention to how the Holy Spirit may or may not be leading any given person or community.

94. Sister Kate Kuenstler acceptance speech as she received FutureChurch's Trivison Award, September 30, 2012, https://vimeo.com/54625186.

95. Sister X (pseudonym), "Cross Examination: Why Is Rome Investigating U.S. Nuns?" *Commonweal*, October 21, 2009.

96. Generally speaking, "useful days" corresponds to the days the chancery office is open, although sending a letter within ten calendar days is encouraged.

97. Michael O'Malley, "Cleveland Catholic Diocese Parishes Slated for Closing Plan to Appeal," *Cleveland Plain Dealer*, March 28, 2009.

98. Kate Kuenstler, "Sample Appeal Letter to Bishop Lennon," published by FutureChurch, March 2009. Unless otherwise indicated, all materials related to the Cleveland canonical appeals are available from the Kuenstler Collection.

99. Richard G. Lennon, letters dated March 9, 2012, to Rev. Joseph Fortuna, Rev. James McGonegal, and Rev. Anthony Schuerger announcing decisions to merge or close (respectively) Annunciation and St. Patrick West Park, St. Ignatius and St. Phillip and James, and St. Wendelin.

100. Sharon Otterman, "New York Archdiocese Parishioners See System of Secrets as They Fight Church Closings," *New York Times*, February 12, 2015.

101. See "Save Our Parish Community" at FutureChurch.

102. "Parish Initiative Catalyzes Far-Reaching Change in Vatican Policy," *Focus on FutureChurch*, Summer 2012, FutureChurch archive, Loyola University, Chicago.

103. John Kroll, "Cleveland Catholic Churches Plan to Appeal Bishop's Order to Close," *Cleveland Plain Dealer*, March 21, 2009.

104. Kroll, "Cleveland Catholic Churches Plan to Appeal."

105. Jessica Ravitz, "Catholic Faithful Face Church Closures," CNN, March 25, 2009.

106. Begin, author interview.

107. Begin, author interview.

108. O'Malley, "Cleveland Catholic Diocese Parishes Plan to Appeal."

109. Begin, author interview.

110. Begin, author interview.

111. Smith, "Bishop Lennon's Decisions."

112. Michael O'Malley, "Bishop Lennon Reconsiders; St. Colman Catholic Church to Remain Open," *Cleveland Plain Dealer*, May 2, 2009.

113. Smith, "Bishop Lennon's Decisions."

114. Joseph Noga, "St. Ignatius of Antioch Parishioners, Leaders Stunned by News of Church Closing," *Cleveland Plain Dealer*, March 18, 2009.

115. O'Malley, "Cleveland Catholic Diocese Announces Church Closures."

116. Smith, "Bishop Lennon's Decisions."

117. Amanda Garrett, "St. Ignatius of Antioch Will Remain Open," *Cleveland Plain Dealer*, May 2, 2009.

118. Smith, "Bishop Lennon's Decisions."

119. Begin, author interview.

120. *Focus on FutureChurch*, Winter 2009, FutureChurch archive, Loyola University, Chicago.

121. Tom Roberts, "Cleveland Diocese Shaken by Seismic Shifts," *National Catholic Reporter*, May 7, 2009.

122. Roberts, "Cleveland Diocese Shaken."

123. Bill Benedict, "Threatened Catholic Churches Seek Suburban Support," *Cleveland Plain Dealer*, August 26, 2009.

124. Ron Vidika, "Cause for Concern: Many Critical of Decision to Close, Merge Churches," *Lorain Morning Journal*, March 17, 2009.

125. Ron Vidika, "St. Joseph Shelter to Reopen for Homeless in Lorain," *Lorain Morning Journal*, November 1, 2010.

126. Margaret Bernstein, "Cleveland Diocese Gives Away Convent at St. Procop," *Cleveland Plain Dealer*, November 5, 2009.

127. Bernstein, "Cleveland Diocese Gives Away Convent."

128. Michael O'Malley, "Bishop Richard Lennon Clears the Way for Reopening 12 Catholic Churches, Timeline Unclear," *Cleveland Plain Dealer*, April 18, 2012.

129. Michael O'Malley, "Closed Catholic Churches in Cleveland Area Could Begin Reopening Next Month, Bishop Lennon Says," *Cleveland Plain Dealer*, March 23, 2012.

130. Bob Kloos, author interview, January 3, 2022.

131. Kathy Antoniotti, "Parishioners Protest Closing of Akron Church," *Akron Beacon Journal*, June 24, 2009.

132. Seitz, *No Closure*.

133. FutureChurch tabulation by author as of March 5, 2024, Kuenstler Collection.

134. The Associated Press mistakenly identified Borré as an attorney. See "Cleveland Catholic Church Closings Overturned by Vatican," *Cleveland Plain Dealer*, March 7, 2012, and Colette M. Jenkins, "Lawyer: Vatican Overrules 13 Cleveland Closings," *Akron Beacon Journal*, March 8, 2012.

135. Calabrese, author interview, February 18, 2022; Ralph Vartabedian, "Cleveland's Catholic Church Closures Leave Ethnic Enclaves Dispirited," *Los Angeles Times*, June 14, 2010.

136. Thomas J. Sheeran, "Faithful End Sit-In at Closed Cleveland Church," Associated Press, July 1, 2010 (two stories)

137. Viktoria Somogyi and Jeff MacIntyre, *Foreclosing on Faith: America's Church Closing Crisis*, documentary, 2017, https://www.foreclosingonfaith.org.

138. Somogyi and MacIntyre, *Foreclosing on Faith*.

139. Bill Sheil, "Church Closing Spurs Walkout on Bishop," WJW Fox8.com, November 20, 2009; Michael O'Malley, "St. Casimir Church Advocates Protest, Call for It to Reopen," *Cleveland Plain Dealer*, November 29, 2009.

CHAPTER 8

1. Sister Sheila Marie Tobbe SND, author interview, February 5, 2022. Unless otherwise indicated, all author interviews are available at the Kuenstler Collection.

2. Tobbe interview, February 5, 2022.

3. Tobbe interview, February 5, 2022.

4. Tobbe interview, February 5, 2022.

5. Michael O'Malley, "In Wake of Church Closings 'Roamin' Catholics Look for Home," *Cleveland Plain Dealer*, August 21, 2011; Phillis Fuller Clipps, documentation supplied personally to Bishop Richard Lennon on May 22, 2009, Kuenstler Collection.

6. O'Malley, "In Wake of Church Closings."

7. Tobbe author interview, February 5, 2022.

8. Tobbe interview, February 5, 2022.

9. Leonard Calabrese, author interview, February 18, 2022.

10. Calabrese, author interview, February 18, 2022.

11. Tom Roberts, "Among Black Catholics, a Deep Loss," *National Catholic Reporter*, May 8, 2009.

12. "About," Website of Thea Bowman Center, Cleveland, Ohio.

13. Tobbe interview, February 5, 2022.

14. Cluster proposal presented to Rome as documentation of due diligence, St. Adalbert/Clipps file, Cleveland, Kuenstler Collection.

15. Robert L. Smith, "Cleveland Catholic Church Closings Leave Parishes Wondering: Why Us?" *Cleveland Plain Dealer*, March 22, 2009.

16. All quotations in this paragraph are from author's interview with Phillis and Phillip Clipps, February 17, 2022.

17. Clipps interview, February 17, 2022.

18. O'Malley, "In Wake of Church Closings."

19. Michael O'Malley, "Displaced St. Emeric Parishioners Find New Home at St. Colman in Cleveland," *Cleveland Plain Dealer*, October 8, 2010.

20. Kuenstler interview with Jeff MacIntyre for *Foreclosing on Faith* documentary, December 4, 2015.

21. Robert L. Smith, "Members of Old Ethnic Parishes in Cleveland Fear the Worst," *Cleveland Plain Dealer*, March 9, 2009.

22. Michael O'Malley, "Closing of St. Emeric Marks End of Cleveland Catholic Downsizing," *Cleveland Plain Dealer*, June 30, 2010.

23. Viktoria Somogyi and Jeff MacIntyre, *Foreclosing on Faith*, 2017 documentary.

24. Berry-McGreevey-Martens and Zeis Funeral Home, obituary of Miklos B. Peller, March 13, 2021.

25. St. Emeric Parish, "Recourse Against Administrative Decree Suppressing St. Emeric Parish," May 5, 2009. Unless otherwise noted, all documentation of the St. Emeric's recourse is located at the Kuenstler Collection.

26. Ralph Vartabedian, "Cleveland's Catholic Church Closures Leave Ethnic Enclaves Dispirited," *Los Angeles Times*, June 14, 2010.

27. St. Emeric Parish, "Recourse Against Administrative Decree."

28. St. Emeric Parish, "Recourse Against Administrative Decree." See also O'Malley, "Displaced St. Emeric Parishioners Find New Home."

29. Miklos B. Peller, Procurator for St. Emeric Parish, "Recourse Against Administrative Decree Suppressing St. Emeric Parish," Attachment A, May 5, 2009.

30. Somogyi and MacIntyre, *Foreclosing on Faith*, 09:27.

31. Thomas J. Sheeran, "Faithful End Sit-In at Closed Cleveland Church," Associated Press, July 1, 2010.

32. Sheeran, "Faithful End Sit-In."

33. Somogyi and MacIntyre, *Foreclosing on Faith*, 25:24.

34. Somogyi and MacIntyre, *Foreclosing on Faith*, 25:28.

35. Michael O'Malley, "Bishop Richard Lennon Clears the Way for Reopening 12 Catholic Churches, Timeline Unclear," *Cleveland Plain Dealer*, April 18, 2012.

36. Miklos B. Peller, "Report on the Meeting with Bishop Richard G. Lennon," May 17, 2022, affidavit signed August 7, 2022, and submitted to Congregation for the Clergy.

37. Peller, "Report on the Meeting."

38. Ildiko C. Peller and Miklos B. Peller, "Report on the Meeting with Bishop Richard G. Lennon, July 27, 2012," affidavit notarized August 5, 2012.

39. Peller and Peller, "Report on the Meeting."

40. Peller and Peller, "Report on the Meeting."

41. Somogyi and MacIntyre, *Foreclosing on Faith*, 43:59.

42. Miklos B. Peller, "The Latest on St. Emeric's Reopening," email to Sr. Kate Kuenstler September 16, 2012. Unless otherwise noted, all email correspondence is located at the Kuenstler Collection.

43. Kate Kuenstler PHJC, "Re: the Latest on St. Emeric's Reopening," email response to Miklos Peller, September 16, 2012.

44. Kate Kuenstler PHJC, as quoted in Somogyi and MacIntyre, *Foreclosing on Faith*.

45. Kate Kuenstler PHJC, Jeff MacIntyre interview for *Foreclosing on Faith* documentary, December 4, 2015.

46. Rachel Dissell, "Final Mass at Downtown St. Peter Catholic Church Leaves 'An Empty Tomb,'" *Cleveland Plain Dealer*, April 4, 2010.

47. Paul Wilkes, *Excellent Catholic Parishes: The Guide to Best Places and Practices* (Mahwah, NJ: Paulist Press, 2001).

48. Paul J. Philibert, "Is There Still a Canticum Perenne? Where Can it Be Found?" *Worship Magazine* 3:3, May 2000.

49. Philibert, "Is There Still a Canticum Perenne?"

50. Michael Griffin, author interview, February 28, 2022.

51. Griffin, author interview, February 28, 2022.

52. Griffin, author interview, February 28, 2022.

53. St. Peter Parish, Hierarchical Recourse to the Congregation for the Clergy, appendix "Waste of Resources," July 16, 2009; David Briggs, "St. Peter Church Opposes Diocesan Reorganization," *Cleveland Plain Dealer*, June 10, 2008.

54. St. Peter Parish, Recourse to Clergy, "Faulty Process" Exhibit B, Verbatim I affidavit from Rev. Robert J. Marrone, April 25, 2009.

55. St. Peter Parish, Recourse to Clergy, "Faulty Process" Exhibit F, Letter from Richard Lennon to Thomas F. Nimberger, November 5, 2008.

56. St. Peter Parish, Recourse to Clergy, "Faulty Process," Exhibit O.

57. St. Peter Parish, Recourse to Clergy, "Faulty Process," Exhibit O.

58. Griffin, author interview, February 28, 2022.

59. Griffin, author interview, February 28, 2022.

60. Briggs, "St. Peter Church Opposes Diocesan Reorganization."

61. Gabriel Baird, "St. Peter Catholic Church Parishioners Say Bishop Lennon Denied Appeal of Closing," *Cleveland Plain Dealer*, April 25, 2009.

62. Griffin, author interview, February 28, 2022.

63. Griffin, author interview, February 28, 2022.

64. Bob Kloos, author interview, January 3, 2022.

65. Rick Krivanka, author interview, October 1, 2021; St. Peter Parish, "Faulty Process," 32, and see Exhibit Q: Comment Form to Accompany the Proposed Cluster Plan *Hierarchical Recourse to the Congregation for the Clergy*.

66. Krivanka, author interview, October 1, 2021.

67. Dissell, "Final Mass at Downtown St. Peter."

68. Bernadette Farrell, "Christ Be Our Light," Oregon Catholic Press, 1994.

69. Dissell, "Final Mass at Downtown St. Peter."

70. Griffin, author interview, February 28, 2022.

71. These celebrations involve reflecting on and praying with Scripture readings and do not require an ordained priest to preside.

72. Tom Roberts, "Cleveland Parish Remains a Community of a Different Sort," *National Catholic Reporter*, March 5, 2012.

73. Roberts, "Cleveland Parish Remains a Community."

74. Michael O'Malley, "Parishioners, Priest from Closed St. Peter Catholic Church Defy Bishop, Celebrate Mass in New Home," *Cleveland Plain Dealer*, August 16, 2010.

75. Kloos, author interview, January 3, 2022.

76. Roberts, "Cleveland Parish Remains a Community."

77. Roberts, "Cleveland Parish Remains a Community."

78. Michael O'Malley, "Bishop Warns the Rev. Robert Marrone to Stop Breakaway Church Masses," *Cleveland Plain Dealer*, January 23, 2011.

79. O'Malley, "Bishop Warns Marrone."

80. O'Malley, "Bishop Warns Marrone."

81. Griffin, author interview, February 28, 2022.

82. Griffin, author interview, February 28, 2022.

83. Griffin, author interview, February 28, 2022.

84. Griffin, author interview, February 28, 2022.

85. Griffin, author interview, February 28, 2022.

86. Griffin, author interview, February 28, 2022.

87. Michael O'Malley, "The Rev. Robert Marrone, Priest Who Leads Breakaway Cleveland Catholic Congregation, Suspended from 'Priestly Ministry,'" *Cleveland Plain Dealer*, May 31, 2012; Tom Roberts, "Priest Heading Controversial Cleveland Community Threatened with Suspension," *National Catholic Reporter*, May 31, 2012.

88. Michael O'Malley, "Bishop Richard Lennon Says He Has Not Suspended Priest Who Leads Breakaway Congregation," *Cleveland Plain Dealer*, June 1, 2012.

89. Roberts, "Priest Heading Controversial Cleveland Community."

90. Kabir Bhatia, "St. Peter's Church Reopens and What It Means for the Future," WKSU, September 10, 2012.

91. Bhatia, "St. Peter's Church Reopens."

92. Brian Roewe, "Cleveland Priest Excommunicated for Role in Breakaway Worship Community," *National Catholic Reporter*, March 6, 2012.

93. Roewe, "Cleveland Priest Excommunicated for Role."

94. Michael O'Malley, "Two Pastors Calling on the Vatican to Stop Cleveland Church Closings," *Cleveland Plain Dealer*, September 25, 2010.

95. O'Malley, "Two Pastors Calling on Vatican."

96. O'Malley, "Two Pastors Calling on Vatican."

97. Michael O'Malley, "Cleveland Catholics Abuzz Over Investigation of Bishop Richard Lennon," *Cleveland Plain Dealer*, July 23, 2011.

98. Dennis Coday, "More on Cleveland's Apostolic Investigation," *National Catholic Reporter*, July 13, 2011. See also Coday, "Apostolic Visitator in Cleveland This Week," *National Catholic Reporter*, July 11, 2011.

99. Rachel Zoll, "More US Catholics Take Complaints to Church Court," Associated Press, January 16, 2012.

100. O'Malley, "Cleveland Catholics Abuzz."

101. Michael O'Malley, "Vatican Extends Deadline for Review of Cleveland Diocese Church Closings," *Cleveland Plain Dealer*, September 23, 2011.

CHAPTER 9

1. Jay Lindsay, "Lawyer: Vatican Overrules 13 Cleveland Closings," Associated Press, March 7, 2012. It later emerged that just twelve appeals had been upheld. See Michael O'Malley, "Bishop to Reopen 12 Closed Cleveland Parishes," Religion News Service, April 17, 2012. One of these—St. Mary Lorain—did not involve reopening the church but reinstated the parish's original name.

2. Colette Jenkins, "Lawyer: Vatican Overrules 13 Cleveland Closings," *Akron Beacon Journal*, March 8, 2012.

3. Tom Roberts, "Parish Groups Seek Mediation on Church Closings," *National Catholic Reporter*, April 8, 2009.

4. As noted in the previous chapter, Borré is not a lawyer, but the Associated Press mistakenly identified him as one.

5. Michael O'Malley, "Vatican Orders Cleveland Bishop to Reverse Church Closures," *Washington Post*, Religion News Service, March 8, 2012.

6. Lindsay, "Lawyer: Vatican Overrules 13 Cleveland Closings."

7. Lindsay, "Lawyer: Vatican Overrules 13 Cleveland Closings."

8. Jenkins, "Lawyer: Vatican Overrules 13 Cleveland Closings."

9. Colette M. Jenkins, "Vatican's Ruling About Closed Parishes Reaches Cleveland Bishop," *Akron Beacon Journal*, March 14, 2012.

10. Brian Roewe, "Cleveland Parishes Await Lennon's Response," *National Catholic Reporter*, March 12, 2012.

11. Roewe, "Cleveland Parishes Await Lennon's Response."

12. Lindsay, "Lawyer: Vatican Overrules 13 Cleveland Closings."

13. Michael O'Malley, "Catholics Eye Cleveland Closures for National Precedent," *Washington Post*, Religion News Service, March 20, 2012.

14. Michael O'Malley, "Catholics Eye Cleveland Closures."

15. Viktoria Somogyi and Jeff MacIntyre, *Foreclosing on Faith: America's Church Closing Crisis*, documentary, 2017, 42:06.

16. Kuenstler email to Kloos, March 29, 2012. Unless otherwise indicated, all email communications are archived with the Kuenstler Collection.

17. Kuenstler email to Schenk, March 14, 2012, 9:24 p.m.

18. Kuenstler email to Kloos, March 29, 2012.

19. Kuenstler email to Schenk—copy of email sent to Bob Kloos, Wednesday, March 28, 2012, 4:14 p.m.

20. Kuenstler email to Schenk—copy of email.

21. Schenk email to Kuenstler, March 29, 5:44 a.m.

22. The Presbyteral Council is elected by the priests in a diocese to represent them and to advise the bishop.

23. Michael O'Malley, "Parishioners Ask Vatican to Order Bishop Richard Lennon to Reopen 3 Closed Cleveland-Area Churches Now," *Cleveland Plain Dealer*, March 30, 2012, 7:10 p.m.

24. The Associated Press mistakenly cited thirteen reversals, but when the diocese reviewed the Vatican decrees, there were just twelve. As previously noted, Catholics from two other parishes—St. Margaret Mary in South Euclid and St. Martha in Akron—apparently also sent appeals to Rome although these could not later be verified. See Michael O'Malley, "Bishop Richard Lennon Clears the Way for Reopening 12 Catholic Churches, Timeline Unclear," *Cleveland Plain Dealer*, April 18, 2012.

25. Schenk email to Kuenstler summarizing report relayed from priest member of the Presbyteral Council, March 31, 2012, 4:49 p.m.

26. Schenk email to Kuenstler, March 31, 2012.

27. Kloos email to Kuenstler, March 31, 2012.

28. Kloos email to Kuenstler, March 31, 2012; Schenk email to Kuenstler, March 31, 2012, 4:49 p.m.

29. Kuenstler email to Kloos, April 1, 2012.

30. Kate Kuenstler, *Commentary on Vatican Decrees Upholding Cleveland Parishioner Appeals*, March 29, 2012, FutureChurch website and Kuenstler Collection.

31. Congregation for the Clergy, "Procedural Guidelines for the Modification of Parishes, the Closure or Relegation of Churches to Profane but Not Sordid Use, and the Alienation of the Same," Vatican City, April 30, 2013.

32. Congregation for the Clergy, "Instruction, 'The Pastoral Conversion of the Parish Community in the Service of the Evangelizing Mission of the Church,'" Vatican City, July 20, 2020.

33. Kuenstler email to "Lori," "Re Message from oratory at St. Adalbert Basilica," January 22, 2012.

34. Kuenstler email to Kloos, March 29, 2012.

35. Dennis Sadowski, "Canon Law Sets Specific Steps to Follow Before a Parish Can Be Closed," *Catholic News Service*, February 21, 2013.

36. Congregation for the Clergy, "Procedural Guidelines."

37. Congregation for the Clergy, "Instruction"; Mark Nacinovich, "Vatican Instructions Give Parishioners More Hope in Face of Closings," *National Catholic Reporter*, August 6, 2020. See also Christine Schenk, "Let's Use the Title 'Coworker' for Lay People Who Exercise Parish Leadership," *National Catholic Reporter*, August 15, 2020.

38. Blythe Bernhard, "Vatican Court Reverses Decision to Close St. Richard Parish Near Creve Coeur," *St. Louis Post-Dispatch*, February 8, 2024.

39. Canon 50: "Before issuing a singular decree, an authority is to seek out the necessary information and proofs and, insofar as possible, to hear those whose rights can be injured."

40. Kuenstler, *Commentary on Vatican Decrees Upholding Cleveland Parishioner Appeals*, 7.

41. Kuenstler, *Commentary on Vatican Decrees*, 12.

42. Kuenstler, *Commentary on Vatican Decrees*, 18.

43. Kuenstler, *Commentary on Vatican Decrees*, 18.

44. Kuenstler, *Commentary on Vatican Decrees*, 22.

45. Kuenstler, *Commentary on Vatican Decrees*, 14.

46. Kuenstler, *Commentary on Vatican Decrees*, 23.

47. Kuenstler, *Commentary on Vatican Decrees*, 23.

48. Kuenstler email to Schenk, March 14, 2012.

49. Kuenstler, *Commentary on Vatican Decrees*, 10–11.

50. Kuenstler, *Commentary on Vatican Decrees*, 10–11.

51. Kuenstler, *Commentary on Vatican Decrees*, 11.

52. Kuenstler, *Commentary on Vatican Decrees*, 20.

53. Kuenstler, *Commentary on Vatican Decrees*, 21.

54. Kuenstler, *Commentary on Vatican Decrees*, 21.

55. Kuenstler, *Commentary on Vatican Decrees*, 22.

56. Michael O'Malley, "Bishop to Reopen 12 Closed Cleveland Parishes," Religion News Service, April 17, 2012.

57. Colette M. Jenkins, "Bishop Decides to Reopen 12 Catholic Churches; 2 in Akron," *Akron Beacon Journal*, April 18, 2012.

58. Michael O'Malley, "Cleveland Catholic Diocese Parishioners Still Waiting for Bishop Richard Lennon to Reopen Churches," *Cleveland Plain Dealer*, May 12, 2012.

59. Begin email to Michael O'Malley and copied to Schenk, April 30, 2012.

60. Begin email to O'Malley, April 30, 2012.

61. Krivanka, author interview, October 1, 2021.

62. Krivanka, author interview, October 1, 2021.

63. Brian Roewe, "Cleveland Priests Doubt Lennon's Leadership, Call for Removal," *National Catholic Reporter*, May 25, 2012. NCR had received copies of "letters from three priests—whose names and respective parishes were blacked out" which called on the Vatican to remove Lennon.

64. Roewe, "Cleveland Priests Doubt Lennon's Leadership."

65. Minutes of Presbyteral Council Meeting, April 27, 2012, and Roewe, "Cleveland Priests Doubt Lennon's Leadership."

66. Michael O'Malley, "Cleveland Catholic Dioceses Bishop Richard Lennon Sends Conciliatory Letter to Priests, Seeking to Repair Relationship," *Cleveland Plain Dealer*, June 7, 2012; Tom Roberts, "Priest Heading Controversial Cleveland Community Threatened with Suspension," *National Catholic Reporter*, May 31, 2012.

67. Rick Krivanka, email to author, August 29, 2022.

68. Pat Galbincea, "Overflow Crowd Fills St. James Catholic Church in Lakewood to Celebrate Reopening," *Cleveland Plain Dealer*, July 6, 2012.

69. Michel Martin, "Parishioner Takes Church Case Straight to Vatican," National Public Radio, April 20, 2012.

70. Martin, "Parishioner Takes Church Case."

71. Kuenstler email to Schenk, June 27, 2012.

72. Kuenstler email to Schenk, June 27, 2012.

73. Tyler Carey, "Former Roman Catholic Bishop of Cleveland Richard Lennon Dies at 72," WKYC, October 29, 2019.

CHAPTER 10

1. Video of Kate Kuenstler receiving the Louis J. Trivison Award from Future-Church, September 30, 2012, Vimeo.

2. Video of Kuenstler.

3. Video of Kuenstler.

4. Video of Kuenstler.

5. At a public presentation at the Call To Action conference on November 2, 2013, Kate revealed that it was the Peoria diocese that had restructured into clusters after being influenced by her Commentary. Kuenstler Collection.

6. Kuenstler acceptance speech upon receiving the Louis J. Trivison Award.

7. Kuenstler acceptance speech.

8. Kuenstler acceptance speech.

9. Kuenstler acceptance speech.

10. Kuenstler acceptance speech.

11. Kuenstler acceptance speech.

12. Kuenstler acceptance speech.

13. Kate Kuenstler email to Colleen LaTray, August 12, 2012. Unless otherwise noted, all email documentation is available in the Kuenstler Collection.

14. Kuenstler email to Schenk, July 5, 2012.

15. Kuenstler email to Schenk, June 26, 2012.

16. Today the *Canonical Appeals for Dummies* resource has been renamed *Canonical Appeals Resource Process*. Along with the Commentary it is available as a free download from FutureChurch; "Parish Initiative Catalyzes Change in Vatican Policy: Landmark Cleveland Victories Set Precedent," *Focus on FutureChurch*, Summer 2012.

17. "Parish Initiative Catalyzes Change."

18. Kuenstler email to LaTray, August 12, 2012.

19. Kuenstler email to Schenk, August 12, 2012.

20. Kuenstler email to Schenk, August 12, 2012.

21. "St. Philip Neri Church Re-Opens in Miami Gardens," Archdiocese of Miami website.

22. Kate Kuenstler email to Christine Schenk, November 15, 2013.

23. Kuenstler email to Schenk, November 15, 2013.

24. Kate Kuenstler summary of Indianapolis appeals, Kuenstler Collection; Jeff MacIntyre, interview for *Foreclosing on Faith* documentary, December 4, 2015, Kuenstler Collection.

25. MacIntyre, interview for *Foreclosing on Faith*, December 4, 2015; All Saints remains a thriving parish. See its website.

26. MacIntyre, interview for *Foreclosing on Faith*, December 4, 2015.

27. Lisa Gray, "St. Stephen Faithful Protest to Have Church Reopened," *Houston Chronicle*, January 13, 2019.

28. Juan A. Lozano, "All Parishioners Want for Christmas Is Reopening of Church," Associated Press, December 25, 2018.

29. Gray, "St. Stephen Faithful Protest."

30. Lozano, "All Parishioners Want."

31. Kuenstler, telephone call to Schenk, May 22, 2018.

32. Gray, "St. Stephen Faithful Protest."

33. Kuenstler, call to Schenk, May 22, 2018.

34. Lisa Gray, "After Taking Their Fight to the Vatican, Immigrants Reopen St. Stephen," *Houston Chronicle*, September 27, 2019.

35. Gray, "After Taking Their Fight."

36. Gray, "After Taking Their Fight."

37. Blythe Bernhard, "Vatican Court Reverses Decision to Close St. Richard Parish," *St. Louis Today*, February 8, 2024.

38. Kuenstler email to Schenk, July 17, 2014.

39. Kuenstler email to Schenk, July 17, 2014.

40. John C. Seitz, *No Closure: Catholic Practice and Boston's Parish Shutdowns* (Cambridge, MA: Harvard University Press, 2011), 12.

41. FutureChurch tabulation by diocese and parish is available at Kuenstler Collection.

CHAPTER 11

1. Chris Sheridan, "Making All Things New," *Catholic New York*, February 10, 2011; Kalman Chany, author interview, July 7, 2022; Rick Hapson, "Our Lady of Revenue: NYC Churches on the Market," *USA Today*, March 1, 2015.

2. Cardinal Timothy Dolan, "A Letter on Pastoral Planning to the Catholics of the Archdiocese of New York," *Catholic New York*, November 3, 2010.

3. See The Reid Group: https://thereidgroup.org.

4. Jamie Manson, "Preparing for Parish Closures and Mergers in New York City," *National Catholic Reporter*, January 29, 2014.

5. Manson, "Preparing for Parish Closures."

6. Cardinal Timothy Dolan, "Pastoral Letter on 'Making All Things New,'" October 1, 2013; Peter Feurherd, "Opponents Challenge Parish Closings, Mergers in NY Archdiocese," *National Catholic Reporter*, September 23, 2015; Cardinal Timothy Dolan, "Mission, Not Maintenance, Should Be Our Focus," *Catholic New York*, January 8, 2015.

7. Sharon Otterman, "Heartache for New York's Catholics as Church Closings Are Announced," *New York Times*, November 2, 2014; Otterman, "New York Diocese Appears Likely to Shutter More Churches," *New York Times*, December 14, 2014.

8. Otterman, "Heartache for New York's Catholics"; Otterman, "New York Diocese Appears Likely."

9. *Foreclosing on Faith* documentary 26:44 and Chany, author interview, July 7, 2022.

10. Peggy Noonan, "Cardinal Please Spare This Church," *Wall Street Journal*, December 26, 2014; Joan Frawley Desmond, "Should Peggy Noonan's New York Catholic Church Be Closed," *National Catholic Register*, January 5, 2015.

11. Kuenstler email to Schenk, January 25, 2015. Unless otherwise noted, email correspondence is found at the Kuenstler Collection.

12. Kuenstler email to Schenk, February 2, 2015.

13. Feuerherd, "Opponents Challenge Parish Closings."

14. Melanie Grayce West, "Churches Resisting Mergers Appeal to Higher Powers," *Wall Street Journal*, December 23, 2014.

15. Kuenstler email to Schenk, January 5, 2015.

16. West, "Churches Resisting Mergers Appeal."

17. Sharon Otterman, "New York Archdiocese Parishioners See System of Secrets as They Fight Church Closings," *New York Times*, February 12, 2015.

18. Otterman, "New York Archdiocese Parishioners See."

19. Kuenstler email to Schenk, January 10, 2020.

20. Otterman, "New York Archdiocese Parishioners See."

21. Otterman, "New York Archdiocese Parishioners See."

22. Archdiocese of New York website, Decrees, November 2, 2014, https://tinyurl.com/mw66ekxe/.

23. Kuenstler, group email sent by FutureChurch to clients in the Archdiocese of New York, February 14, 2015.

24. Kuenstler email to Deborah Rose-Milavec with copy to Schenk, May 13, 2014.

25. Jeff MacIntyre interview with Kuenstler for the *Foreclosing on Faith* documentary, December 4, 2015. Unless otherwise noted, all interview transcripts are located in the Kuenstler Collection.

26. Tatiana Schlossberg, "Catholic Church Closings in New York Bring Sadness and Anger," *New York Times*, July 31, 2015.

27. Schlossberg, "Catholic Church Closings in New York."

28. Kuenstler, "New Merger Decrees," email to Rose-Milavec and Schenk, April 29, 2016.

29. Kuenstler email response to Mary Lou Sanginari, May 29, 2015.

30. Kuenstler email to Sanginari, May 29, 2015.

31. Kuenstler email to Sanginari, May 29, 2015.

32. Kuenstler email to Sanginari, May 29, 2015.

33. Kuenstler email to Sanginari, May 29, 2015.

34. Kuenstler email to Sanginari, May 29, 2015.

35. Kuenstler email to Sanginari, May 29, 2015.

36. Kuenstler email to Schenk, March 15, 2016.

37. MacIntyre interview with Kuenstler, December 4, 2015.

38. MacIntyre interview with Kuenstler, December 4, 2015.

39. MacIntyre interview with Kuenstler, December 4, 2015.

40. Michael Herzenberg, "Parishioners, Unsettled by Recent Upheaval, Prepare to Host Pope Francis," *New York 1 Spectrum News*, September 14, 2015.

41. Chany, author interview, July 7, 2022.

42. Sharon Otterman, "On the Upper East Side, Silent Prayers to Save a Sanctuary for the Deaf," *New York Times*, November 28, 2014.

43. Otterman, "On the Upper East Side."

44. Otterman, "On the Upper East Side."

45. Chany, author interview, July 7, 2022.

46. Chany, author interview, July 7, 2022.

47. Chany, author interview, July 7, 2022; Archdiocese of New York, "Changing Our World," available on its website.

48. Chany, author interview, July 7, 2022.

49. Chany, author interview, July 7, 2022.

50. Chany, author interview, July 7, 2022.

51. Chany, author interview, July 7, 2022.

52. Chany, author interview, July 7, 2022.

53. Chany, author interview, July 7, 2022.

54. Melanie Grayce West, "Vatican to Review Order to Close Two New York City Parishes," *Wall Street Journal*, March 19, 2015.

55. Chany, author interview, July 7, 2022.

56. Chany, author interview, July 7, 2022.

57. Kate Kuenstler email sent by FutureChurch to parish groups advising them against further appeal to the Apostolic Signatura, March 15, 2016.

58. Kuenstler email, March 15, 2016. Capitalization, bolded, and underlined words in original.

59. Kate Kuenstler email to FutureChurch Staff, "New Merger Decrees," April 29, 2016.

60. Chany, author interview, July 7, 2022.

61. Chany, author interview, July 7, 2022.

62. Chany, author interview, July 7, 2022.

63. Chany, author interview, July 7, 2022.

64. Chany, author interview, July 7, 2022.

65. Chany, author interview, July 7, 2022.

66. Chany, author interview, July 7, 2022.

67. Chany, author interview, July 7, 2022.

68. Chany, author interview, July 7, 2022.

69. Chany, author interview, July 7, 2022.

70. John Reid and Maureen Gallagher, *The Art of Change: Faith, Vision, and Prophetic Planning* (Liguori, MO: Liguori Publications, 2009).

71. Reid and Gallagher, *Art of Change.*

72. David Ramey and Marti Jewell, "Emerging Models and Practices of Parish Leadership, National Ministry Summit," April 21, 2008.

73. Kate Kuenstler, "Diocesan Planning Framework: Companies and Organizations," Presentation at National Call To Action conference, November 2, 2013, Kuenstler Collection.

74. Kuenstler, "Diocesan Planning Framework."

75. Kuenstler, "Diocesan Planning Framework."

76. Archdiocese of New York Office of Strategic Parish Planning, letter to *Making All Things New* Parish Core Team Update, November 27, 2013, Kuenstler Collection.

77. Pope Francis, *Evangelii Gaudium* (in English *The Joy of the Gospel*), November 24, 2013.

78. *Focus on FutureChurch*, Summer-Fall 2017.

79. Kuenstler email to Schenk, April 29, 2016.

CHAPTER 12

1. Kuenstler email to Schenk, February 17, 2015. Unless otherwise indicated, all emails and interviews in this chapter may be found at the Kuenstler Collection.

2. Kate Kuenstler, interview with Jeff MacIntyre for *Foreclosing on Faith* documentary, December 4, 2015.

3. Kuenstler interview with MacIntyre, December 4, 2015.

4. Kuenstler interview with MacIntyre, December 4, 2015.

5. Kuenstler interview with MacIntyre, December 4, 2015.

6. Kuenstler, author interview, August 3, 2019.

7. Kuenstler, author interview, August 3, 2019.

8. Kuenstler interview with MacIntyre, December 4, 2015.

9. Kuenstler interview with MacIntyre, December 4, 2015.

10. Kuenstler interview with MacIntyre, December 4, 2015.

11. Kuenstler interview with MacIntyre, December 4, 2015.

12. Kuenstler interview with MacIntyre, December 4, 2015.

13. Kuenstler interview with MacIntyre, December 4, 2015.

14. John P. Beal, James A. Coriden, Thomas J. Green, eds., *New Commentary on the Code of Canon Law* (Mahwah, NJ: Paulist Press, 2000).

15. Can. 383 §1; Can. 387.

16. Kuenstler, author interview, July 20, 2019.

17. Kuenstler interview with MacIntyre, December 4, 2015.

18. Kuenstler interview with MacIntyre, December 4, 2015.

19. Kuenstler, author interview, October 14, 2019.

20. Kuenstler, author interview, October 14, 2019.

21. Kuenstler, author interview, October 14, 2019.

22. *Code of Canon Law*, Book II, The People of God.

23. Can. 207 §1, §2.

24. Kuenstler, author interview, October 14, 2019.

25. Kuenstler, author interview, August 3, 2019.

26. Cathy Schwemer PHJC, author interview, September 28, 2020.

27. Schwemer, author interview, September 28, 2020.

28. Schwemer, author interview, September 28, 2020.

29. Schwemer, author interview, September 28, 2020.

30. Carole Langhauser PHJC, author interview, September 21, 2020.

31. Judith Diltz PHJC, author interview, September 24, 2022.

32. Diltz, author interview, September 24, 2022.

33. Schwemer, author interview, September 28, 2020.

34. Schwemer, author interview, September 28, 2020.

35. Diltz, author interview, September 24, 2022.

36. Diltz, author interview, September 24, 2022.

37. Diltz, author interview, September 24, 2022.

38. Diltz, author interview, September 24, 2022.

39. Schwemer, author interview, September 28, 2020.

40. Schwemer, author interview, September 28, 2020.

41. Schwemer, author interview, September 28, 2020.

42. Schwemer, author interview, September 28, 2020.

43. Sr. Pat Peters, author interview, September 28, 2020.

44. Peters, author interview, September 28, 2020.

45. Linda Rozycki, author interview, October 6, 2020.

46. Langhauser, author interview, September 21, 2020.

47. Divina Melotti, author interview, December 16, 2020.

48. Melotti, author interview, December 16, 2020.

49. Melotti, author interview, December 16, 2020.

50. Federika Boldini, author interview, June 16, 2021.

51. Boldini, author interview, June 16, 2021.

52. Boldini, author interview, June 16, 2021.

53. Boldini, author interview, June 16, 2021.

54. Boldini, author interview, June 16, 2021.

55. Boldini, author interview, June 16, 2021. For non-Catholic readers, note that Catholic sisters are indeed lay, not ordained.

56. Diltz, author interview, September 24, 2022.

57. Michelle Dermody PHJC, author interview, September 23, 2020.

58. Langhauser, author interview, September 21, 2020.

59. Langhauser, author interview, September 21, 2020.

60. Langhauser, author interview, September 21, 2020.

61. Langhauser, author interview, September 21, 2020.

62. Diltz, author interview, September 24, 2022.

63. Lena Woltering, author interview, October 12, 2020.

64. Melotti, author interview, December 16, 2020.

65. Rozycki, author interview, October 6, 2020.

66. Schwemer, author interview, September 28, 2020.

67. Christine Schenk, "In Appreciation: Sr. Kate Kuenstler, Canon Lawyer for the People of God," *National Catholic Reporter*, November 5, 2019.

EPILOGUE

1. Mary Ann Ahern, "Major Overhaul Will Leave Chicago with 123 Fewer Parishes by July," nbcchicago.com, February 8, 2022. Decrees at: https://www.renewmychurch.org/decisions/decrees-letters.

2. Jonah McKeown, "Cincinnati Archdiocese Announces Parish 'Family' Groups Amid Massive Consolidation Effort," Catholic News Agency, December 6, 2021. Decrees at: https://catholicaoc.org/beacons-of-light/parish-families.

3. Peter Gill, "Columbus Diocese to Close 15 Catholic Churches Amid Declining Attendance. Here's the List," *Columbus Dispatch*, June 6, 2023. Decrees at: https://columbuscatholic.org/search?search=decrees&scope=platform.

4. "Joliet Bishop Announces Merging, Closure of 9 Catholic Parishes," *Our Sunday Visitor News*, January 30, 2024. Decrees at: https://www.diojoliet.org/search?q=decrees.

5. Blythe Bernhard, "St. Louis Archdiocese's Reorganization Will Close More Than 30 Parishes," *St. Louis Post Dispatch*, May 28, 2023. Decrees at: https://allthingsnew.archstl.org/Decrees-and-Letters.

6. Jennifer Brinker, "Archbishop Rozanski Suspends Effects of Decrees for Seven Parishes," *St. Louis Review*, July 31, 2023.

7. Richard Solomon, "Black Catholic Parishioners Asking Bishop Not to Close Church," WBNS TV, September 5, 2024; John Ferak, "St. Joseph's Parish Fights to Exist, Vatican City Will Decide," Patch.com, February 23, 2024.

8. Ahern, "Major Overhaul Will Leave Chicago."

9. Justin Kerr, "Parishioners Appeal St. Maurice Church Deconsecration and Sale," *McKinley Park News*, September 24, 2020.

10. Adam Drapcho, "Lawyer Who Saved 15 Churches Says Libasci Should Reconsider," *Laconia* (NH) *Daily Sun*, July 8, 2019.

11. McKeown, "Cincinnati Archdiocese Announces Parish 'Family' Groups."

12. See https://saveourparishes.org/news.

13. Dan Monk and Paula Christian, "Beacons of Light Cincinnati: If You're Worried About Your Catholic Parish Fading Away, Here's How to Fight It," WCPO *9 News*, February 20, 2024.

14. Monk and Christian, "Beacons of Light Cincinnati."

15. Bernhard, "St. Louis Archdiocese's Reorganization."

16. Blythe Bernhard and Jesse Bogan, "A Mix of Relief, Sorrow and Confusion as St. Louis Catholic Parish Cuts Are Smaller Than Expected," *St. Louis Post-Dispatch*, May 30, 2023.

17. Gina Christian, "Several St. Louis Parish Mergers on Hold as Parishioners Appeal to Vatican," *OSV News*, August 3, 2023; Joseph Young, author interview,

February 19, 2024. Unless otherwise noted, all author interviews and emails are available in the Kuenstler Collection.

18. Jonah McKeown, "St. Louis Catholics Petition Archbishop to Halt Diocese-Wide Parish Merger Plan," Catholic News Agency, April 9, 2023.

19. Christian, "Several St. Louis Parish Mergers On Hold."

20. Blythe Bernhard, "More Catholic Parishes in the St. Louis Area Seek to Stay Open During Appeals Process," *St. Louis Post-Dispatch*, August 4, 2023; Robert Flummerfelt, email to author, March 1, 2024.

21. Blythe Bernhard, "Vatican Court Reverses Decision to Close St. Richard Parish Near Creve Coeur," *St. Louis Post-Dispatch*, February 8, 2024.

22. Jonah McKeown, "Vatican Halts Some Parish Closures in St. Louis Following Appeals," Catholic News Agency, May 15, 2024.

23. Flummerfelt, email to author, March 1, 2024 (capitalization in original).

Bibliography

Beal, John P. "The Protection of the Rights of Persons in the Church." Washington, DC: Canon Law Society of America, 1991.

———. "Toward a Democratic Church: The Canonical Heritage." In *A Democratic Catholic Church*, Eugene C. Bianchi and Rosemary R. Reuther, eds. New York: Crossroad, 1992.

Beal, John P., James A. Coriden, and Thomas J. Green, eds. *New Commentary on the Code of Canon Law*. Mahwah, NJ: Paulist Press, 2000.

Berry, Jason. *Render Unto Rome: The Secret Life of Money in the Catholic Church*. New York: Crown Publishers, 2011.

Clark, William A. *A Voice of Their Own: The Authority of the Local Parish*. Collegeville, MN: Liturgical Press, 2005.

Conference for Pastoral Planning and Council Development. "2003 National Study of Parish Reorganization." Archdiocese of Dubuque: Loras College Press, 2004. https://tinyurl.com/4u3pu4p3.

Congregation for the Clergy. "Instruction, 'The Pastoral Conversion of the Parish Community in the Service of the Evangelizing Mission of the Church.'" Vatican City: 2020. http://tinyurl.com/frenfjc7.

Congregation for the Clergy. "Procedural Guidelines for the Modification of Parishes, the Closure or Relegation of Churches to Profane but Not Sordid Use, and the Alienation of the Same." Vatican City: 2013.

Coriden, James A. *The Parish in Catholic Tradition, History, Theology and Canon Law*. New York: Paulist Press, 1997.

Cozzens, Donald B. *The Changing Face of the Priesthood*. Collegeville, MN: The Liturgical Press, 2000.

General Secretary for The Synod of Bishops. "A Synodal Church in Mission: Synthesis Report." Vatican City: 2023. http://tinyurl.com/sjjansns.

Gibson, David. *The Coming Catholic Church: How the Faithful Are Shaping a New American Catholicism*. San Francisco: Harper One, 2011.

Guthrie, Julian. *The Grace of Everyday Saints: How a Band of Believers Lost Their Church and Found Their Faith*. Boston: Houghton Mifflin Harcourt, 2011.

Kuenstler, Mary Kathleen. *Commentary on Vatican Decrees Upholding Cleveland Parishioner Appeals*. Cleveland: FutureChurch, 2013. http://tinyurl.com/y8a79jx9.

———. "Post-Conciliar Renewal of the Legislative Texts for the Order of the Discalced Carmelite Nuns of the Blessed Virgin Mary of Mount Carmel." *Dissertatio ad Lauream in Facultate Iuris Canonici apud Pontifiam Universitatem S. Thomae in Urbe*. Rome: 1995.

———. "The Fractured Face of Carmel." *The Way Supplement*, 1997.

Martel, Frédéric. *In the Closet of the Vatican: Power, Homosexuality, Hypocrisy*. London: Bloomsbury Continuum, 2019.

Meagher, George T. *With Attentive Ear and Courageous Heart: A Biography of Mother Mary Kasper, Foundress of the Poor Handmaids of Jesus Christ*. Milwaukee: Catholic Life Publications, Bruce Press, 1957.

O'Malley, John W. *What Happened at Vatican II*. Cambridge, MA: Harvard University Press, 2010.

Provost, James H. *The Code of Canon Law*. New York: Paulist Press, 1985.

———, ed. *Due Process in the Dioceses of the United States 1970–1985*. Washington, DC: Canon Law Society of America, 1987.

Ramey, David, and Marti Jewell. "Emerging Models and Practices of Parish Leadership, National Ministry Summit." Washington, DC: National Association of Lay Ministry, 2008. http://tinyurl.com/2946apzu.

Reid, John, and Maureen Gallagher. *The Art of Change: Faith, Vision, and Prophetic Planning*. Liguori, MO: Liguori Publications, 2009.

Seitz, John C. *No Closure: Catholic Practice and Boston's Parish Shutdowns*. Cambridge, MA: Harvard University Press, 2011.

Somogyi, Viktoria, and Jeff MacIntyre. *Foreclosing on Faith: America's Church Closing Crisis*. Hungary, 2017. https://www.foreclosingonfaith.org/about-the-doc/.

Vatican, 1983 *Code of Canon Law*. https://tinyurl.com/xr8jmebk.

Ward, Daniel J. "The Rights of Christians within the Code of Canon Law." In *Readings, Cases, Materials in Canon Law*. Collegeville, MN: Liturgical Press, 1990.

Zech, Charles E., Mary L. Gautier, Mark M. Gray, Jonathon L. Wiggins, and Thomas P. Gaunt. *Catholic Parishes of the 21st Century*. Oxford, UK: Oxford University Press, 2017.

Index

administrative act, 79, 83–85, 91, 108
administrative recourse: parishes
    in Archdiocese of New York,
    167, 169–74, 176–79, 184–85;
    parishes in Diocese of Cleveland,
    108, 111, 115, 125, 129, 143–45;
    procedures and process, 36–41;
    recent recourses in Arch/Dioceses
    of Chicago, Cincinnati, Columbus,
    Joliet, St. Louis, 203–6; recourses
    in other dioceses, 158–63; St. Mary
    Jamesville, 50–57; St. Vincent
    Pallotti, Camden, 78–91
Advocate for the Laity, 43, 45–63
African-American churches:
    Archdiocese of Miami, 158;
    Cleveland diocese, 119–121; cultural
    elements, 120
Akers, Sister Louise, 182
Akron, Ohio, 109–10, 116–17, 149;
    Beacon Journal, 137–38
All Saints Parish, 159
Allentown, PA, diocese, 56–57, 92, 110,
    154, 157, 163
Amendolia, Sister Annette SND, 115
Ancilla Domini High School, 11
Angelicum, 16, 20, 27, 50
Anglo-American jurisprudence, 33–34
Apostolic nuncio, 43, 86, 89, 112

Apostolic Signatura: Boldini, Frederika,
    196–97; Congregation for the Clergy,
    158–159; decision/response, 56–58,
    91, 92; decrees, 57, 61; parishes in
    Archdiocese of New York, 178–80;
    parishes in Diocese of Cleveland,
    137–38, 142, 144; pending, 162;
    Robert Flummerfelt cases, 207;
    St. Mary Jamesville, 45–46, 48,
    54–59, 61, 62, 63, 157; St. Stephen,
    Houston, 160–61; St. Vincent
    Pallotti, Camden, 65, 89–92
Apostolic Visitation: Lennon, Cleveland
    Bishop Richard, 119, 134; women
    religious, 111
appeals, 46–47; active, 207, Allentown,
    92; Boston, 116; mergers, 205;
    parishes in Archdiocese of New
    York, 177–78; parishes in Diocese of
    Cleveland, 111–13, 115–16, 121–22,
    124, 134–35, 137–39, 143–44;
    parishes in Diocese of Indianapolis,
    159; process, 49, 55, 60, 63, 89,
    138; recent appeals in Arch/Dioceses
    of Chicago, Cincinnati, Columbus,
    Joliet, St. Louis, 205–7; sample, 167;
    St. Mary, Jamesville, 50–51, 54–59;
    St. Stephen, Houston, 160–61; St.
    Vincent Pallotti, Camden, 78–79,

81, 83–84, 89–93; successful, 65, 156–57, 16
Arnold, Margaret, 173
Australia, 155, 157, 162–63

Baird, Gabriel, 232
Baranski, Andrew E., 51
Beacons of Light (Cincinnati), 203–5
Beal, John, 33, 34, 138
Begin, Father Bob, 102, 124, 134, 149
Belleville, Illinois, diocese, 13, 29–31, 42; clergy sex abuse scandal, 30; laity, 30; priests, 43
Benedict XVI, Pope, 40, 175, 55
Bernie, Phillip, 127
Berry, Jason 76
BishopAccountability.org, 101
Blake, Clair, 93
Boldini, Federika, 196–97
Borré, Peter, 4–5, 56, 116–17, 137, 138
Boston, archdiocese, 2, 4–6, 41–42,100–101, 103, 116, 145, 206
Braxton, Bishop Edward K., 30, 43
Buechlein, Archbishop Daniel M., 159
Buffalo, diocese, 2, 46, 49–50, 79, 92, 154, 157, 163
Burke, Cardinal Raymond L., 48, 54, 59–60, 63, 65, 90–92

Cacioppi, Theodore, FBI, 76
Cafardi, Nicholas P., 46, 167, 134
Calabrese, Leonard, ix, 102–3, 120
Calgary, 162–63
Camden Courier-Post, 73, 75, 81, 93
Camden, diocese, ix, 2, 46–47, 65, 67–68, 72, 74–77, 79, 81, 87–92, 110–11; lay organizing, 87; merger process and manual, 83, 93; parishes, 68, 70, 74, 82; planning process, 68; presbyteral council, 74
Canada, 25, 157, 162
canon and civil law, 61, 85, 97
canon law, 1–4; defends parishes, 188; educating the laity, 31–33, 108;

Kuenstler finds spiritual guidance in, 190–93; Kuenstler's "huge symbolic impact" on, 196–97; Kuenstler studies in, 14–20, 22, 24–25; parish appeals in Cleveland diocese, 110–12, 142–47; parish rights and obligations, 35–36; reopening churches, 48; rights and obligations of laity, 38–42; St. Mary Jamesville, 50–51; St. Vincent Pallotti, Camden, 79, 82–83, 88–89
Canon Law Ministries, 43
Canon Law Professionals, 43, 80
Canon Law Society of America (CLSA), 33, 141, 195
canon lawyer, ix, 205, 206
Canonical Appeals Resource Process, 112, 157
Canonical Commentary (Kuenstler Cleveland), 139–47, 153, 154, 156
canonical recourse, 45–47, 70, 78, 79, 82–83, 88, 95, 115–16, 167, 204
canonical rights of Catholics, 1, 35, 41, 45, 49, 80–81, 94–95, 108, 162, 203, 205. *See also* rights and obligations
Canuso, John, 72–73, 77, 78
Carmelite nuns, discalced, 21, 24–27; flawed renewal process, 21, 24, 27
Carrù, Monsignor Giovanni, 76–77, 84–85
Casaroli, Cardinal Agostino, 24
Center for Applied Research in the Apostolate (CARA), 6
Center for Pastoral Leadership (Cleveland), 98
Chalker, Rev. Kenneth, 97, 134
Chany, Kalman, 166, 172–80
Chicago, Archdiocese of, 124, 138, 203–5; church closure appeals, 205
Cimperman, Joseph, 109
Cincinnati, archdiocese, 205
Clare House, 25, 191, 194
Clark, Father William A., 107
Clergy sex abuse, 3, 5–7, 29, 33–34, 45, 76, 98, 103; cover-ups, 101–2; crisis,

5, 31; lawsuits, 101; policy, 30; scandal, 7, 54, 9; settlements, 3, 5, 6; victim/survivors, 6, 7, 30, 101, 153
clerical subculture, corrupt, 22
Cleveland, city of, poverty, 96
Cleveland diocese, 2, 4, 6, 42, 95–117, 120–23, 125, 126, 133–34, 138, 142–47, 150–51, 153–57, 161; appeals, 108, 116, 137, 139, 142; decisions, 139, 153; decrees, 153–54, 157; parishes, 42, 46, 88, 98, 103, 105, 108, 115–17, 148; pastoral planning office, 99; presbyteral council, 95, 140, 141 146–47; Rome upholds appeals, 139–51; rulings, 95, 145; victories, 137, 142, 146
Clinton, Regina, 59
Clipps, Phillip and Phillis, ix, 121–22
Clohessy, David, 101
closures. *See* parish closures
CLSA. *See* Canon Law Society of America
clusters. *See* parish clusters
Code of Canon Law, 1, 20, 22, 24, 32, 37–38, 41, 156
Columbus, diocese, 203–5
Communio, 32–33, 36–37
community. *See* parish community
Community of St. Peter (CSP), 129–34. *See also* St. Peter Parish and Historic St. Peter Church
Cooke, Cardinal Terence, 173
Cooperman, Alan, 29
Coriden, James A., 33, 35–36
Cornell, John, 177
Cunningham, Bishop Robert J., 2, 55 56, 58 59, 61–63

Daley, Father John, 53
Daneels, Archbishop Frans, 54, 59, 91
deacons, 29, 38, 69, 98–99, 103–4
deaf Catholics, 173; St. Elizabeth of Hungary Parish, 175–76, 180
DeBottis, Tony, 58
defending parish rights, 41, 108, 161

DeLambo, David, 149
demographics, 99, 107, 111, 114, 143; changing, 76, 166, 181
demonstrative tactics, 116
Denver, archdiocese, 163
Dermody, Sister Michelle, 198
Detroit, city of, poverty, 96
Detroit, archdiocese, 163, 203; Archbishop Vigneron, 168–69
Dilego, Regina, 112
Diltz, Sister Judith, 192–94, 197–99; provincial leader, 193
DiMaria, Carmela, 71
DiMarzio, Bishop Nicholas, 78
DiNardo, Cardinal Daniel, 160–61
diocesan canon lawyers, 185
"Do Not Stifle the Spirit," 42
Dolan, Cardinal Timothy, 165–69, 172, 175–79, 184; archdiocesan churches, 183; decrees, 167
donor intent, 74, 81, 90–91; restricted funds, 90; violation of, 73, 85
Dragonetti, Sister Lucy, 104
Dunnigan Michael, 112, 138, 139

Emerging Models of Pastoral Leadership Project, 181, 183
Endangered Catholics, 116–17, 121, 135, 138–40
English, Sister Carol, 104
Epiphany Parish, 119–21
Errera, Andrea, 196
Estok, Father Edward, 98, 127
Excellent Catholic Parishes: The Guide to Best Places and Practices, 126

Favalora, Archbishop Joseph, 158
Fellowship of Southern Illinois Laity (FOSIL), 30–31, 40, 189
Fernandez-Vine, Faustine, Superior Court Judge, 90
Feuerherd, Joseph, 76
financial scandals, 98, 100; accountability 105
Fitch, Esperanza, 160

FitzGerald, Sister Constance, 27

Flummerfelt, Robert, ix, 206–7

Follieri, Raffaello 75–76; Follieri-
Sodano scheme, 76

Foreclosing on Faith (documentary),
172, 176, 185, 194

Fort Wayne-South Bend, diocese, 15

FOSIL. *See* Fellowship of Southern
Illinois Laity

FOSVP. *See* Friends of St. Vincent
Pallotti

Francis, Pope, 1, 23, 33, 35, 54, 151,
176, 183

Frey, Lisa, 98

Friends of St. Vincent Pallotti, 77–79,
81–82, 85, 87, 91, 93

FutureChurch, ix–x, 40–42, 107–8, 110–
12, 115–16, 139–40, 156–57, 162,
181–82, 184; mission and vision,
153; priest cofounder, 153; tabulation
of merger and closing appeals, 163

FutureChurch resources, 35, 42, 106,
110, 121, 147, 167; downloaded,
110, 206; free, 110; proactive,
107

Gaertner, Rita, 110

Galante, Bishop Joseph M., 2, 46, 48,
65, 68–72, 72, 74–75, 77–86, 88–94,
167

Galveston-Houston, archdiocese, 160,
163

Gary, Leah, 129

Gautier, Mary, 6

Gioffre, Patty, 87

Grand Rapids, diocese, 79, 156–57,
163

Gravens, Terry, 114

grave reasons for recourse, 55, 57–58,
91, 141

Gray, Phillip, 205, 206

Gregory, Bishop Wilton, 29–31, 42, 43

Griffin, Michael, ix, 127–32

Guerin Sullivan, Sister Theresa, 124

Gullo, Alessia, 63

Gullo, Carlo, 54–56, 60

Haase Falbo, Kathleen, 98

Hargrave, John and Ginny, 80, 93

Hatala, Josephine, 150

Hatch, Richard, 90

Herrera, Rod, 71

Hispanic Catholics, 120, 160; oppose
Cardinal, 160

Historic Saint Peter Church, 109, 115–
16, 119, 126–29, 132–34; *See also*
St. Peter Parish and Community of
St. Peter

Hokenson Ken, 100–101

Holy Cross Parish, DeWitt, NY, parish
merger, 49, 51–52, 57–62

Holy Maternity Parish, 71

Holy Name Parish, 206

Holy Saviour Parish, 69

Holy Trinity Parish, Diocese of Buffalo,
57

Holy Trinity Parish, Archdiocese of
New York, 184

Hume, Basil Cardinal, 24

Hummes, Cardinal Claudio, 50, 81,
84–85, 90

Hungarian churches: cluster process,
122; language, 123, 125, 126; St.
Emeric, 134;

Hungarian-speaking community,
largest, 122; priest for Sunday Mass,
124

identical decrees, 169

Immaculate Heart Parish, 109

immigrants, 96, 104, 113, 160;
determined blue-collar, 160; low-
income Hispanic, 160

Indianapolis, archdiocese, 2, 159,
163

Indresano, Michael, 101–2

Infant Jesus Parish, 4

inner-city neighborhoods, 4; parishes, 6;
close, 168; people, 97

intent, 65, 72–73, 83–84, 109, 139, 145–
46, 176, 182; bishop's, 87; law's, 39;
original, 106

international recourses, 163

Jamesville, New York, St. Mary Parish, 43, 45–63, 95, 157
John Paul II, Pope, 21, 24–26, 32, 120, 146
John XXIII, Pope, 32
Joliet, diocese, 203–5
Josoma, Father Stephen, 4
juridic persons: independent, 147–48; parish, 168; public, 82, 91, 144
jurisprudence, 2, 183–84, 191; developing, 142; new, 184; precedent-setting, 82
"just cause" requirement, 169

Kampwerth, Sister Annemarie, 24
Kansas City, diocese, 79, 156–57, 163
Kasper, Saint Katharina, 12; canonization, 21, 194–95, 197; Kasper home, 200
Kelly, Eileen, 113
Kloos, Bob, ix, 116, 129, 131, 139–41, 153, 155, 201
Kownacki, Raymond, 29–30
Krivanka, Rick, 97, 103, 106, 129, 149–50
Kropac, Father Robert, 132–33
Kuenstler, Sister Kate, 1–4, 7, 9, 46, 76, 108, 151, 153, 155, 163, 175, 177, 180, 182, 184, 196–97, 207; canonical expertise/acumen, 47, 48 65, 81,159–60, 162, 167, 178, 183, 186, 188, 193; canonical commentary (Cleveland) 139–47; confidentiality, 80, 193; dark night of the soul, 189–91; death 197–201; devotion to Katherine Kasper, 195; doctoral education/dissertation, 15, 18, 24, 25–27; early life, 9–14; educating laity, 34–43; family, 9–11; legacy, 201; Licentiate studies, 15, 16, 19; Pallotti victory, 92–95; pioneering leadership, 181, 203; pro bono canonical help, 112, 153; Rome studies, 15–28; seminarians 16, 18, 21–23; successful recourse cases, 162, 163

La Sagrada Familia, 120
Lagges, Patrick, 138
laity, 3, 14, 31, 33, 111, 170, 184, 185, 191, 203; rights and obligations, 19–21, 36–38, 40–42, 108, 154–56, 158
landmark ruling, 46, 137–51
Lang, Father James, 51
Langhauser, Sister Carole, 192, 195, 197–99
LaSalvia, Christine, 139, 150–51
LaTray, Colleen (Kenney), ix, 46, 49–50, 53–56, 58–60, 62–64, 157
Law, Cardinal Bernard, 3–5, 100–101
lay Christian faithful, 20, 40, 108
Lennon, Bishop Richard G., 4, 41, 42, 88, 96, 100–108, 110–15, 117, 119–25, 127–34, 137–41, 146–50, 161; appeal decision, 111; Boston auxiliary, 100; reopens Cleveland parishes, 148
Lethbridge, Ontario, 162
Liberi, Frank, 93
Little-Harris, Sylvia, 120
Liverpool, UK, 162–63
Lopes, Bishop Steven, 23
Lorain, Ohio, parishes, 4, 106, 110, 115–16
Lumen Gentium, 37

MacIntyre, Jeff, 172
Maimone, John, 98, 103
Mainiero Antonio, 76, 77
Maldonado, Deacon Lou, 115
Mamaroneck, New York, 162, 184
Manhattan, New York, 76, 162, 166, 173–74, 184
Margason, Father James, 29, 30–31
Marion-Sterling School, 126
Marrone, Father Robert J., 126–27, 129–33
Martin, Michel, 151
Marucci, Monsignor Lou, 47, 65–68, 71–75, 77–80, 82–86, 89, 92–94, 140; integrity 78; sacrificial lamb, 94

Mass attendance, 5, 54, 65, 93, 115,
    124; average Sunday,126; declining,
    205; impacted, 54
McCahill, Monsignor Patrick, 173, 175
McCarrick, Archbishop Theodore, 23
McGonegal, Father James R., 114
McGrory, Brian, 100
mediation, 83–84, 11, 137; requested,
    77, 82
Melbourne, Australia 162–63
Melotti, Divina, 20, 195, 196, 200
mergers. *See* parish mergers
Miami, archdiocese, 79, 158, 163
Milavec, Deb Rose, 182
ministers, 6, 69, 98–99, 103; ecclesial,
    98–99, 103–4; outreach, 30; pastoral,
    95, 98, 107; sacramental, 69, 104
Most Holy Trinity Church,
    Mamaroneck, NY, 162
Moynihan, Bishop James M., 49–52,
    54–55, 57
Mullin, Tom, 121
Myers, Archbishop John J., 86

National Catholic Reporter, 76–77, 133,
    138
neighborhoods, 41, 96, 108, 113–14,
    119, 122, 127, 129, 138, 187; city's
    poorest, 126; gentrifying Houston,
    160; inner-city, 110; parishes served
    low-income, 6, 96
Nelson, Francis, 63
New Orleans, archdiocese, 79, 163
New York, archdiocese, 2, 111, 162–63,
    162, 165–85, 203; parishes, 169;
    recourses, 170; *New York Times*,
    168–69, 173, 176
Nieto, Ester, 161
Noonan, Peggy, 166–67, 172
norms, 48, 146, 194; procedural, 45,
    170, 203
North American College (NAC), 16, 23
Northeast Ohio parishes, 96, 109–10,
    115, 126, 149; activists, 110; resist,
    109

O'Hara, Auxiliary Bishop John, 168
O'Malley, Cardinal Sean P., 4–5, 101–2,
    162
O'Malley, Michael, 140
Opus Dei, 25–27
ordinary Catholics, 1, 7, 32, 35, 40–41,
    98, 156, 191, 207; educating, 34
Oriental Churches, 3
Our Lady of Good Council, 175
Our Lady of Peace, merger recourse,
    184

Palmo, Rocco, 95, 96 100
Pank, Sister Jane, 127
parish administrator, 147
parish appeals, 46, 50–51, 112, 114,
    205; upheld, 93, 144, 148, 163;
    viable, 187
parish closures, 41–42, 105–7, 110–11,
    165–66, 175–76; most parishes
    viable, 187; closing Masses, 117,
    120, 124, 129
parish clusters, 105–6, 109–11; a better
    choice, 178; model, 69–70, 148
parish community, 36–37, 41–42,
    103–4, 107–8, 128–34, 173–74,
    183–85, 192–93; disadvantaged,
    110; expanding/growing, 53, 56, 64;
    intentional, 192; multiethnic, 93;
    rural, 183; suburban, 110; vibrant,
    67, 129
parish council, 78, 121, 128–29,
    132
parishes, 1–6; canonical rights of,
    34–36; indebted, 165, 172; inner city
    and inner ring suburb, 4, 6, 108, 168;
    model of a laity-led, 56; most are
    viable, 187; parishes, Archdiocese of
    New York, 165–75, 177–81, 183–90;
    parishes, Diocese of Cleveland,
    95–99, 103–17, 119–31, 137–51,
    159–62; St. Mary, Jamesville, 45–53,
    55–57, 64; St. Vincent Pallotti,
    Camden, 65–66, 68–74, 77–79,
    84–85, 87–88, 90–94

parish life coordinators, 98–99, 107–8, 115, 147

parish mergers: canonical recourse 41; family of faith versus corporate entity, 185–188; financial motivation, 20; merger manual (Camden), 83; models, 69–70; most parishes viable, 187; parishes, Archdiocese of New York, 165–66, 169–71, 172–73, 175, 177, 179–81, 183; parishes, Diocese of Cleveland, 95, 105, 141–43; parishes, Indianapolis and Houston 159–61; process, 93, 168; St. Mary Jamesville, 48, 52, 57, 59; St. Vincent Pallotti, Camden, 70–72, 74, 77, 79, 82, 84, 88; recent mergers, (epilogue), 203–6; tabulation of merger/closure recourse outcomes, 163

parish rights and obligations, 35, 48, 107, 185; limitations on, 35; vindicating, 36

Pastoral Leadership Project, 181, 183

pastoral planning, 104; derailed, 104; office, 97, 148–50; processes, 49, 165

Pastores Dabo Vobis, 21–22

Paul VI, Pope, 74

Pellar, Miklos and Idilko, 122–25, 134

The People of God, 1–3, 32, 34, 38, 181, 185–86, 188, 191, 201, 207

Peoria, diocese, 154, 163

personal/ethnic parishes, 124, 155, 171–73, 177–78; targeted, 122

Peters, Sister Pat, 126, 128, 191–92, 194, 195

Pettus, Mark, 205

Philibert, Father Paul J., 126

PHJC. *See* Poor Handmaids of Jesus Christ

Piacenza, Cardinal Mauro, 88–90, 142, 150

Pierzynski, Ed, 72, 82, 87, 93

Pilla, Bishop Anthony M., 96–100, 102–4, 106, 113, 119, 120, 123, 127, 130, 147, 149; collaborative decision-making, 96, 99; vision for parish reconfiguration, 100

Poor Handmaids of Jesus Christ (PHJC), ix–x, 9–12, 26, 43, 153, 156, 189–95

presbyteral council, Camden, 74; Cleveland, 129, 140–41, 143–44, 146, 150

priest shortage, 7, 42, 45, 48–49, 51, 70, 95, 107, 146–47, 166; international, 30, 40

pro bono canonical help, Kuenstler, 112, 153; St. Joseph Foundation, 47, 112, 123, 139, 206

Prosak, Christopher, 62

Quinn, Bishop A. James, 97

Reese, Father Thomas, 46

The Reid Group, 165, 180–81, 183

Religion News Service, 138–39

Religious communities/orders of women and men, 2, 7, 42–43, 76, 156, 189; apostolic visitation of women religious, 111

reopening churches and parishes: St. Mary Jamesville, 57–59; Cleveland parishes, 148–51

Rice, Julie, 138

rights and obligations, 1, 31–36, 41, 38, 41, 95; in canon and civil law, 61; ordinary Catholics, 32, 4; parish right to perpetual existence, 91, 145; parishioners, 45, 145, 189; public juridic persons, 82; responsibilities, 31, 165; to appeal, 49, 79, 81, 84; to canonical recourse, 155, 203; to petition for damages, 55

Roamin' Catholics, 122

Roberts, Tom, 133

Romansky, Carol, 110

Rome-based canon lawyers, 54, 178

Rosing, Father Paul, 105–6

Rozanski, Archbishop Mitchell, 204, 206
Rozycki, Linda, 195

Sacred Heart Parish, 109, 110, 115
Sambi, Archbishop Pietro, apostolic nuncio, 81, 86, 90, 134
Save Our Parish Community, FutureChurch initiative, 41–42, 157
Save St. Mary's committee, 54
Schenk, Sister Christine, 107, 137, 140, 156, 181
Schulte-Singleton, Patricia, 134–35, 138
Schultz, Agnes, 11
Schwemer, Sr. Cathy, 191–95, 200
Scranton, PA, diocese, parish appeals, 110, 163
Seasons of Faith National Catechetical Series, 14
Seelaus, Sister Velma, 27
Segliuzzo, Louis, 63
Seiter, Father George, 71–72; summary report, 72
Seitz, John C., 5, 106
seminaries, 21–23, 37, 81, 101
settlements, 5, 29, 90; large financial, 6; original, 30; total, 7
sexual orientation, 130
Siklodi, Father Sandor, 123–26
Sisters of St. Joseph, ix
Slavic Village, 110, 115
Slovak church, 176; heritage, 173
Smith, Bishop John M., 134–35
Smith, Joseph A., 97
Sodano, Cardinal Angelo, 76–77
Sodano, Andrea, 76
Springfield, Massachusetts, diocese, 2, 46, 48, 56–57, 79, 92, 154, 157, 163
Springfield, Illinois, diocese, 13, 21
St. Adalbert Parish, 116, 119–22, 184; close, 121
St. Angela Merici Parish, 206
St. Anthony Parish, 87
St. Barbara Parish, 109, 116, 138
St. Casimir Parish, 109, 116–17

St. Cecilia Parish, Cleveland Ohio, 120; closed, 119
St. Cecilia Parish, Boston, one-thousand-family, 13
St. Cecilia Parish, Glen Carbon, Illinois, 195
St. Charles Borromeo Church, 87
St. Colman Parish, 110, 113–15, 124, 149
St. Elizabeth of Hungary Parish, New York City, 162, 166, 173–80, 184; decree merging, 173; decree relegating, 179
St. Elizabeth Parish, Cleveland, Ohio, 122
St. Emeric Parish, 115–17, 119, 122–25, 134, 163; appeal, 124
St. Frances Xavier Cabrini Parish, 4
St. Ignatius of Antioch Parish, Cleveland Ohio, 110, 113–15; appeal, 113
St. Ignatius Parish, New York City, 177
St. James Parish, Lakewood, Ohio, 110, 113, 115–16, 143, 150; decree, 139–40; successful appeal, 138
St. James Parish, Wellesley, Massachusetts, 4
St. Jeanne D'Arc Parish, 5
St. Jerome Parish, 109
St. John Cathedral, 109, 116, 127
St. John the Baptist Parish, Akron, 116–17
St. Joseph Church, Poughkeepsie, NY, 184
St. Joseph Foundation, 47, 112, 123, 139, 206; nonprofit, 205
St. Joseph Parish, Lorain, Ohio, 93, 104, 110; homeless shelter, 115; merge, 115
St. Joseph Parish, New York City, 175
St. Louis, Archdiocese of, 143, 203–6
St. Malachi, 109, 115
St. Margaret Mary, Euclid, Ohio, 115–16
St. Margaret, Orange, ordered to merge, 122
St. Mark Parish, 206

St. Martha Parish, 116

St. Martin Parish, merge, 206

St. Mary Malaga, 87, 93; Save, 88

St. Mary Parish, Akron, Ohio, 149, 157

St. Mary Parish, Jamesville, 2, 43,
45–64, 142; activists, 59–60; appeals
committee, 50, 51,
53, 55, 56, 58–63; Catholics, 49,
53–54, 59, 62; church, 2, 46–48,
51, 55, 57–63, 157; deconstruct,
57 62–63; reopening, 61, 157

St. Mary Parish, Lorain, Ohio, 95, 110,
115–16, 149

St. Mary Star of the Sea, 101

St Monica Parish, 175–80; debts, 179

St. Norbert Parish, 206

St. Peter Parish, 109, 115–16, 119, 126–
129, 132–34; *See also* Community
of St. Peter and Historic St. Peter
Church

St. Procop Parish, 115

St. Richard Parish, 206

St. Roch Church, Staten Island, 184

St. Stanislas Parish, 115

St. Stephen of Hungary Parish, New
York City, 175, 178, 179

St. Stephen Parish, Cleveland, Ohio,
109, 114; recommended closing, 113

St. Stephen Parish, Houston, Texas,
160–61, merged, 160; reopened, 161

St. Susanna Parish, 4

St. Thomas Aquinas Parish, 2, 16

St. Thomas More Parish, 166, 172, 184;
closing, 167; well-heeled, 172

St. Veronica Parish, 184

St. Vincent Pallotti Parish, 2, 46–48,
65–68, 70–74, 77–81, 84, 86,
88–93, 95, 140, 142, 153; and Holy
Maternity, 71; appeal, 48, 80, 89,
91; assets, 73, 75; building fund, 73;
campus and facilities, 71, 74; church,
48, 66, 81, 92; closure plan, 65, 73;
clustering, 74; community, 78; core
team, 93; decision, 72; donors, 73;
intervention, 154; lawsuit, 90, 92;

parish council, 74; parishioners, 47,
66, 68, 70, 72, 74–75, 77–79, 81,
89–90, 93; parish leaders, 69, 70,
72, 75, 80, 82, 84, 88–91; pastor,
65; planning team, 69–71; recourse,
85–88; renamed, 66; victory, 48, 65;
worship sites, 80

St. Wendelin Parish, 110, 115–16

successful US recourses, 163

suppression of parishes 53, 57, 137,
144–46, 178

Survivors Network of Those Abused by
Priests (SNAP), 101

synodality, 1, 3, 35, 207; synthesis
statement, 35; values, 33

Syracuse, diocese, 36, 48–49, 51, 57,
79, 92, 154, 163

Syracuse Post-Standard, 47, 52, 62

Szabo, Eva, 122

Tayek, Robert, 115, 121,138

territorial parishes, 122, 124, 155, 172,
177; indebted, 122, 172; new, 143;
stable, 143

Thea Bowman Center, 120–21

theology: of canon law, 19; of church,
37; of parish, 185

Tobbe, Sister Sheila Marie, ix, 119–21

Tobin, Cardinal Joseph W., 159

Trautman, Bishop Donald W., 126

Trivison, Father Louis J., 107, 153;
Award, 155

Titus, Frank, 132

Turbett, Peggy, 109, 128, 133

unprecedented rulings: St. Mary
Jamesville, 46, 56; Camden, 84;
Cleveland 137–42

Vassallo, Leah, 87

Vatican Council II, 21, 24–26, 30,
32, 37–38, 102, 108, 191–92;
ecclesiology, 25, 185; ideals, 33;
inaugurated, 32; reforms, 25; vision,
191

Vatican Instruction, 142–43
Vibrant Parish Life, 99–100, 104–7
Vigneron, Archbishop Alan H., 168–69

Wales, Nate, 47
Walton, Andrew, 75, 81
Ward, Father Daniel J., x, 33
Wenski, Archbishop Thomas G.,
   158
West, Melanie Grayce, 176
Westbrook, Jay, 114
Westminster, archdiocese, 24
Wiles, Christopher, 61
Wilkes, Paul, 126
Willett, Mary, 149
Williams, Judith A., 78

Wilson Charles, 47, 112
Wilson, John D., 74
Wisniewski, James, 29–30
Woltering, Lena, 31, 189, 199
women religious, apostolic visitation,
   111

Yeazel, Monsignor Robert, 49, 52–55,
   59–62; and Bishop Cunningham, 63;
   fiduciary responsibility, 53
Young, Joseph, ix, 206
Yuhasz, John, 124

Zack, Bob, 131
zero-tolerance policy, 29
Zwilling, Joseph, 168

About the Author

Christine Schenk, CSJ, has worked as a nurse midwife to low-income families, a community organizer, a writer-researcher, and the founding director of an international church reform organization, FutureChurch. Currently she writes an award-winning column for the *National Catholic Reporter*. Schenk's first book, *Crispina and Her Sisters: Women and Authority in Early Christianity* (Fortress Press, 2017), details original research into iconic motifs of female authority found in early Christian art and archaeology. In 2018 *Crispina* received a first place in the history category from the Catholic Press Association.

Her most recent book, *To Speak the Truth in Love: A Biography of Sr. Theresa Kane RSM* (Orbis Press, 2019), won first place in biography from the Association of Catholic Publishers and a first place in biography from the Catholic Press Association.

She is one of three nuns featured in the award-winning documentary *Radical Grace*. The film chronicles the sisters' passion to transform patriarchy and work for justice in both church and society. See https://radicalgracefilm.com.

She is also prominently featured in the 2017 documentary *Foreclosing on Faith: America's Church Closing Crisis*, which documents the pioneering canonical advocacy of the late Sr. Kate Kuenstler, PHJC, which changed Vatican policy around church closings. See https://www.foreclosingonfaith .org/about-the-doc/.

In October 2013, Schenk stepped down from her position as the founding director of FutureChurch, an international coalition of parish-centered Catholics working for full participation of all Catholics in the life of the Church. She led the organization from 1990 to 2013 and worked to transform a diocesan network of twenty-eight parish councils and one hundred parish leaders into an international organization of over thirty-five hundred parish-centered activists reflecting the values of Vatican II.

A Sister of St. Joseph, Sister Schenk formerly worked as a nurse midwife in Cleveland for twenty years. In 1980 she helped to organize a successful statewide coalition to expand Medicaid coverage to include low-income pregnant women and their children. Schenk credits her community organizing expertise to Cesar Chavez and United Farm Workers Union with whom she worked in the early 1970s as an interfaith coordinator.

She graduated *magna cum laude* from Georgetown University and holds two master's degrees, one in science from Boston College, and an MA in theology with distinction from St. Mary's Seminary and Graduate School of Theology in Cleveland.

* 9 7 9 8 8 8 1 8 0 0 4 7 5 *